THE SLAM

THE SLAM

BOBBY JONES
and the PRICE OF GLORY

CURT SAMPSON
Author of *HOGAN* and *THE MASTERS*

RODALE

Printed in the United States of America
Rodale Inc. makes every effort to use acid-free ∞, recycled paper ◉.

Book design by Christopher Rhoads

Library of Congress Cataloging-in-Publication Data

Sampson, Curt.
    The slam : Bobby Jones and the price of glory / Curt Sampson.
      p.   cm.
    Includes bibliographical references and index.
    ISBN-13 978–1–59486–120–8 hardcover
    ISBN-10 1–59486–120–X hardcover
    1. Jones, Bobby, 1902–1971.   2. Golfers—United States—Biography.   I. Title.
  GV964.J6S36   2005
  796.352′092—dc22   2005000271

Distributed to the trade by Holtzbrinck Publishers

2 4 6 8 10 9 7 5 3 1 hardcover

We inspire and enable people to improve their lives and the world around them
For more of our products visit **rodalestore.com** or call 800-848-4735

For Bill Earley and John Strawn,
my smart friends

"Sometimes he tells me it's the regret of his life that he has to be famous just for his proficiency at a sport. . . . He could enjoy all this if they were following him because of some great achievement in some thoughtful line of work, such as writing or healing. . . ."

—O. B. Keeler, to Westbrook Pegler of the *Chicago Tribune*

"A stroller on Broadway, seeing a queue forming outside a theatre where Charlie Chaplin was opening *City Lights*, asked in some concern, 'What's that—a bread-line or a bank?'"

—Frederick Lewis Allen, in *Only Yesterday*

Contents

Acknowledgments

This book would not have achieved liftoff without editor Pete Fornatale, agent Jim Donovan, and publisher Rodale.

The rest by geography:

Atlanta: Jan and Terry Stotts; Catherine Lewis and the staff of the Atlanta History Center; John Campionette; Cathy Kelly of Westminster Schools; Jody Thompson of Georgia Tech; the Special Collections staff at the Woodruff Library at Emory University (Teresa Burk, Susan McDonald, Keith Nash, Naomi Nelson, and Nancy Watkins); Rick Burton and the staff at East Lake Country Club; Randall Couch and the staff at Druid Hills Golf Club

Augusta: Danny and Nicole Fitzgerald; Lori Elizabeth Herrington; Colonel Tim Wright; Mike Rucker; Sam Nicholson; the staff at Forest Hills Golf Club; Henry Marburger, Tommy Brannen, and the staff at Augusta Country Club; the staff at Augusta Archives.com; Sam Tyson

California: Mary Alice Hinman Gifford; Jyl Porch

Canton, Georgia: Kathy Day of the Cherokee County Historical Society; Nelda Fitzgerald of the R. T. Jones Memorial Library

France: Danielle Delange; Nita Wiggins

Harvard: Carrie Baizer

The Jones Family: Foster Clayton; Clayton Reid; Louis L. Jones; Robert T. Jones IV

Liverpool: Dave, Janet, and Tim Griffiths; Chris Moore and Joe

Pinnington of Royal Liverpool Golf Club; Eunice Williamson of the Wallasey Golf Club

Minneapolis: Dan Dvorak, Bill Sherman, Bill Kidd, Jock Olson, and the staff at Interlachen; Doug Nelson; the staff of the Minneapolis Public Library; Kate Ketcham of Inform Research Services

New Jersey: David Kreitler

Ohio: Kathy Dickerson; Bob and Ann Sampson; Bill Case; Dr. Richard Gordin; Sarah Whalen

Philadelphia: Bill and Terry Earley; Skee Riegel; Bud Lewis; Jim Finegan; Bill Greenwood; Bill Iredale; Guy Woullet; Pete Trenham; Joe Juliano; the staff of the Newspaper and Microfilm Department of the Free Library

St. Andrews: Morris Johnston and Dr. David Malcolm of the New Golf Club; Carolyne Nurse

Savannah: Ed Johnston; Bob Moore; Armin Chisolm; Toby Browne and the staff at Savannah Golf Club

Sea Island, Georgia: Kyle Tibbs Jones

South Carolina: Dove Jones

Texas: Jan Dowling; Allan Morris of the Dallas Model A Ford Club; Byron Nelson

True Temper Sports, Inc.: Chad Hall and Bob Bush

United States Golf Association: Rand Jeris and Patty Moran

THE SLAM

Bobby Jones (center) with his right-hand man,
O. B. Keeler (on his left).

Introduction
Bob the Father

This is a book about Bobby Jones and 1930, his big year. Actually, "big" doesn't begin to describe what Robert Tyre Jones accomplished during that season in the sun. The amateur golfer from Atlanta played in six tournaments and won five, and four of those wins were in major championships. Only twice in history has any golfer won even three majors in a calendar year—Ben Hogan in 1953 and Tiger Woods in 2000. But Jones swept the table, winning all four events in the then–Grand Slam.

If you count the *Golf Illustrated* Gold Vase, a thirty-six-hole warmup for the Walker Cup, then Jones won six out of seven. He captained and played in the Walker Cup, his U.S. team taking on the English at Royal St. George's in Sandwich, England, and he didn't lose a match, so that could reasonably be called a win, too. Seven out of eight, when a single win in a big event could make a career.

He was much more than just a successful athlete. "What we're talking about is not the hero as golfer but something America hungered for and found," wrote historian Alistair Cooke. "[Jones was] the best performer in the world who was also a hero as a human being, the gentle, wise, chivalrous, wholly self-sufficient male. Jefferson's lost paragon, the wise innocent."

Throughout the brash 1920s, it was Bobby's fate to tote similar quotes like heavy suitcases. Although he looked like a million, accepting trophy after

3

trophy in his white linen and cotton and his deep brown tan, the pressure of living up to expectations just about killed him. Alcohol, insomnia, and two packs a day aged him ten years in twelve months. Before the morning rounds of his final tournament, the locker room attendant watched in awe as Jones raised a trembling glass of corn whiskey to his lips. That week Bobby downed another blast of Prohibition liquor at lunch with his chicken sandwich on white, and a good deal more at bedtime to help him sleep. Each week he looked more and more like Big Bob, his baggy-eyed and weather-beaten father. For the most part, however, Jones's success and stoicism obscured his torment.

The few reporters who knew how he was suffering and how he was self-medicating wouldn't have dreamed of writing about it—not that their editors wanted stuff like that anyway. This was the age of ballyhoo, when writers portrayed middleweights and halfbacks as gods on loan from heaven. Games were becoming our national mythology—the stories about ourselves that we tell ourselves, as author/educator Joseph Campbell would say. Getting too personal about the heroes ruined the fantasy.

So the media massed behind the appealing figure of Jones, the golfing lawyer in short pants, a conservative hero for a wild time. General-interest magazines wrote feature after feature about him, and the newspaper people never left him alone. Jones didn't leave the newspapers alone either; twice a week he wrote a lucid legal brief of a one-thousand-word column for the Bell Syndicate, presenting a curious public a window into his champion's mind. It was quite a mind.

Most impressive from a visibility standpoint is that in the summer of '30 you could see Bobby nearly every week in the newsreels at the local Bijou. Movies—now suddenly with sound—had become an essential part of the culture, and a lot of people went once a week. You could leave the theatre laughing or in horror: Two of the biggest films in 1930 were *Animal Crackers*, starring the Marx Brothers, and Erich Maria Remarque's *All Quiet on the Western Front*.

For a quarter, ninety million people a week got the feature preceded by a cartoon—Mickey Mouse was huge—and a short news-and-entertainment show. Newsreels were the best time capsules ever made. Tinny march music would leak out of primitive loudspeakers while Graham MacNamee or some other important-sounding voice narrated a ship launch or a beauty contest or the flickering image of Bobby Jones swinging a golf club at fourteen frames per second. Fox Movietone and Paramount Sound News made Bobby's progress to glory look like a twelve-week climb up a dangerous mountain, which, in a way, it was. "Bobby Jones home with more titles," the graphic read in a thousand darkened theatres: "New York greets greatest of all golfers, arriving from new triumphs on British links."

And a smile would spread like sunrise across Jones's handsome face as he accepted the trophy or rode on top of the backseat of a long convertible in a parade. He nodded, he waved, he recognized someone in the crowd and pointed to him, and the part in the center of his dark hair looked as if it had been cut by a laser beam. He looked like a man you'd like to know. His manner bespoke humility, of course, because he was the perfect hero, but within the humility were intriguing shadings of amusement and embarrassment. "Could I do that as well?" people in the movie theatres asked themselves. "Would I be so graceful with the whole world watching?" No—no one could do what Bobby did.

He did a dozen things better than most men and two things better than anyone: golf and getting along with people. Even the pros whose asses he kicked loved him, which was no small thing. Jones was an amateur, wellborn and relatively wealthy, a smooth operator who had gone to Harvard and the Cotillion Ball, and his personality worked with equal charm on both sides of the Mason-Dixon line. He was on every level a Member of the Club. Golf professionals, on the other hand, were invariably grown-up caddies, poorly educated servants at the club. But Bobby did not put himself above these men, and they evinced no envy toward him. Even Norman von Nida liked Jones, and Von didn't like anyone. A jockey-sized Australian professional golfer with a notoriously bad attitude—once he got in a post-round fistfight in front of a scoreboard—von Nida visited the United States for the first time in 1939 and teed it up with the Grand Slam winner. "Jones still had that long, fluent swing," von Nida recalled. "Apart altogether from his golfing ability, he has a kindly personality, a charming and gentlemanly bearing, and a consideration for others that mark him as a person never to be forgotten." Same deal with his closer contemporaries. Archrival Gene Sarazen was as feisty as they come, and a lot his peers despised him, but he and Jones developed a profound friendship that would last for decades.

It's hard to imagine another sports figure who was so deeply and widely respected. Fans and friends tried to press money into Bobby's hand or to set him up in business. The CEO of Coca-Cola, Robert Woodruff, loved him like a son. A group of Atlanta admirers raised $50,000 to buy him a house, and you could buy a hell of a house in Atlanta in 1927 with fifty. Cynical, seen-it-all sportswriters melted in his arms. "What can I say about my hero?" wrote Paul Gallico of Jones. Grantland Rice, another big syndicated columnist—everyone read his "In the Sportlight" the way everyone went to the movies—wrote, "Bobby Jones is not one in a million persons. I should say he is one in ten million—or perhaps one in fifty million." Oscar Bane "O.B." Keeler, a backslapping, whiskey-pouring sportswriter for Bobby's hometown paper, the *Atlanta Journal*, threw in the journalistic towel altogether. Abandoning all pretense of impartiality, he devoted his life and tens of thousands of words to publicizing Bobby. Personally and professionally, the relationship paid off big-time for both men.

How big was Bobby Jones? In what writer Roger Kahn called "the era of wonderful nonsense"—the vulgar, exciting 1920s, when you couldn't buy a Manhattan in Manhattan because of Prohibition, when women lost their bustles and bows and shimmied into simple shifts, and organized crime hovered in the fumes of bathtub booze—the names of five athletes were virtually synonymous with the games they played: Jones equaled golf; Dempsey was boxing; Tilden, the king and symbol of tennis; Ruth, baseball; and Grange, football.

It was no brotherhood. The other men were primitives compared to Jones—except for Tilden, who had his own problems.

Jack Dempsey was the biggest of them all, bigger even than the Babe, especially on fight nights and the run-up to the fight. A silk suit civilized Ruth, but nothing could disguise the essential scariness of the heavyweight champion of the world. The ham hocks on the ends of the Manassa Mauler's arms dwarfed a normal human hand. He wore his hair very close on the sides, which accentuated the thickness of his skull, the thickness of his black eyebrows, and the uniquely pitiless quality in his eyes.

His family had left poor West Virginia when he was a child for even poorer southern Colorado because there was supposed to be money in the copper, silver, and gold mines. There wasn't much. After completing eighth grade, Jack left home and made his own way. "I was the only guy I knew who actually enjoyed going down a shaft and knocking chunks of ore off a wall," he said. "But what I lived for was the fights." Fights, frequently illegal, that took place on saloon floors or in the lot outside the saloon or in a vacant schoolhouse. Fights with grown men who flattened his nose and curled his ears and broke his ribs and were paid off in peanuts. But Dempsey was as snarling and vicious as a cornered badger, and he won sixty times in the first round.

Dempsey was twenty-one and dead broke when he married for the first of four times. His bride, Maxine Cates, played piano in a bar in Salt Lake City's red-light district, smoked pot—they called the drug "hop" back then—and worked in a room upstairs. Dempsey denied it, but plenty of others swore it was true: From time to time he walked the streets to find clients for his wife. But in a makeshift outdoor arena on a hot afternoon in June 1919, Jack, now twenty-four and weighing 187, gave the 245-pound champion, Jess Willard, a ferocious beating. The sight of Jack whacking Big Jess as he tried to rise from the canvas was unforgettable. But that night Dempsey dreamed he had lost. He jumped out of bed at dawn and ran shoeless into the street to buy a newspaper. Only after he read the headlines did he finally know he was the champ.

Doubt about his game never disturbed the dreams of William Tatem Tilden, though other demons may have come calling. The king of tennis was a confident man with a racket in his hand. He often wore a full-length fur coat as he emerged from the locker room onto the court, and sometimes he didn't bother to warm up at all, preferring instead to sit and sip a bit of champagne before play began. He toyed with inferior opponents—to be sure, almost everyone he played—and often purposely lost the first or second set in order to provide the paying customers a slightly longer show. With his rocket serve and catlike court coverage, Big Bill—his nickname sounds improbable now, since he was a wispy six feet one and a half and 155 pounds—won the U.S. Championships, the forerunner to the U.S. Open, every year from 1920 to 1926, then won again in '29. His career match record was an unbelievable 907–62. Like Jones, he came from a country club—his on the Philadelphia Main Line—and made rather a fetish of good sportsmanship and fair play. But history would not be kind to Big Bill. Although Tilden was as good as Pete Sampras or Andre Agassi, you rarely hear about him today. The official tennis histories chastely refer to his "tendency to self-destruct."

Tilden was gay. Worse, much worse, he preferred barely pubescent partners, particularly German boys, and there were snickers about his "harem of ball boys." When Ty Cobb first laid eyes on this standoffish and imperially slim tennis champion, Bobby Jones's friend and fellow Georgian was supposed to have said, "Who *is* this fruit?"

On the other side of the same coin was Ruth, a world-class pig for food and drink and a heterosexual so enthusiastic that, according to legend, one night he serviced or was serviced by every girl in a whorehouse. But the glorifying press of the '20s kept Big Bill's secrets, as well as the Babe's.

The football hero, number 77 for the University of Illinois, was the boy the other boys just could not tackle. Harold "Red" Grange filled the stadium wherever Illinois played, and his performance in the big game with Michigan in 1924 electrified college football: He scored four touchdowns in the first quarter against the top-ranked team in the nation, and by the end of the game had gained 402 yards on twenty-one incredible runs. Illinois won, the newspapers and newsreels covered it like a moon landing, and a legend was born.

Grange graduated and wanted to do more than take back his old job delivering ice in suburban Chicago. So the Wheaton Iceman, also known as the Galloping Ghost, signed a contract to play for the Chicago Bears. And Red was rich. At a time when a new Chevrolet Roadster cost $495, Grange made about $100,000 from endorsements and public appearances and about half the $250,000 gate receipts from a barnstorming tour in 1925. That its greatest star would turn pro outraged the football establishment, however. "Professionalism will *ruin* football," wailed Grange's college coach, Bob Zuppke. "Countenancing rank dishonesty in playing men under assumed names, scores of professional teams have sprung up in the last two or three years," moaned the University of Chicago coach, Amos Alonzo Stagg, in a press release. "There is nothing that a bunch of gamblers will not do for their purpose and quite often they carry along with them the support of a thoughtless group of businessmen and well-meaning citizens."

Professional or amateur, the sports heroes ascended like angels in the popular mind. But packed stadiums and magazine covers were not the ultimate; the top of the publicity and easy-money pyramid was a movie role. All the sports pantheon went to Hollywood, or wanted to. Dempsey was first. Soon after he won the title, Pathé offered him $50,000 and fifty percent of the gross for a fifteen-part serial called *Daredevil Jack*, in which the leading man rescued the heroine or her property with his "daring fists" in every episode. Dempsey would make other movies, such as *Dead or Alive* and *All Good Marines*, the latter with his friend, actor/mogul Douglas Fairbanks Jr. Doug loved athletes.

The Babe made *Headin' Home* in 1920, which was filmed in the Northeast to accommodate his baseball duties with the Boston Red Sox, for whom he pitched and hit to a win in the World Series of 1918. He played a lovable lug of an iceman (before refrigerators, a big chunk of ice in an icebox kept the food cold), who uses a hatchet to carve a chunk of wood into a baseball bat in his spare time. Long story short, Babe's character falls for a blonde, wins the World Series with his homemade cudgel, and then he's headin' home to see Ma and his sister. It seemed like a hell of a deal for the Babe: He didn't have to memorize any lines ("talkies" didn't come in until the end of the decade), and they paid him $50,000. But the movie bombed, the production company went bankrupt, and most of the Babe's checks bounced. Ruth got only $15,000 and a dozen good stories for happy hour. He liked to take one of his big worthless checks out of his wallet and show it around to his mates at the bar.

Grange acted in a film called *One Minute to Play*, in which he portrayed—surprise!—a halfback who wins the big game. Tilden, the one real thespian in the group, intended to make movies after he turned pro late in his playing career, but his off-putting personality prevented him from landing a role. So Big Bill scratched his creative itch by writing a novel and acting in a play.

Hollywood—and Broadway—wanted Jones, too, and for good money. He didn't go. And that $50,000 house fund his Atlanta boosters gave him? He gave it back.

It was a conflicted age. Jazz floated on the night air like hop smoke, while sex and atheism were suddenly fit topics of conversation, and it seemed that a lot of people believed in both. Widespread secret drinking made bootleggers and mobsters rich and turned millions of tipplers into minor criminals. But the 1920s was also a deeply conservative decade. Moral nerds had taken charge in the United States, the "blue-nosed, crack-voiced hypocrites," as writer Frederick Lewis Allen called them, crones who denied Americans a legal drink from 1917 to 1933. Despite its staggering sacrifice of money and lives, the Great War had not been a war to end all wars, as it had been advertised, and it had not made the world safe for democracy. The stock market was a crazy national lottery and everyone was winning—until suddenly, they weren't. Alienation and disillusionment reigned, especially as themes for novelists. Although the United States was too big and complicated to have only one dominant mood, the empty, desperate party people of F. Scott Fitzgerald's *The Great Gatsby* may have defined the time pretty well.

One reaction to the perceived decline in Western civilization was that a lot of people, frequently sportswriters, got all misty over the Amateur Ideal. Here was Ruth holding out for an absurd $80,000 before spring training in 1930—but that golfer from Atlanta wouldn't take a dime. How wonderful that he played only for the love of the game! A prodigy in the public eye since he was fourteen, Bobby had grown up on the sports page, drawn by the pens of Rice and Keeler and Damon Runyon. Youthful problems with his temper seemed charming in light of his accomplishment: runner-up in the U.S. Amateur at age seventeen! The U.S. Open champion at age twenty-one! And on and on until he'd won everything. He never forgot a name, he shook hands with manly firmness, and always remembered to say thank you. Four times in big tournaments he called penalties on himself for the most minor infractions, breaches that brought him no advantage and were visible only to him. In one instance, the penalty stroke might have cost him the 1925 U.S. Open. He was thoroughly admirable, social, and handsome as a movie star. Every year he turned down a lot of money to remain an amateur.

Of all the athletes of the Golden Age, he was the easiest to put on a pedestal—and to keep there.

But fame is fleeting as the wind, as poet James Wilson wrote, and glory fades away. Dempsey lost the title in a memorable fight with Gene Tunney, Grange hurt his knee, and Ruth too quickly got fat and old. In time, the best American writers deconstructed the heroes of the Golden Age. Robert Creamer wrote *Babe*; Roger Kahn gave us *A Flame of Pure Fire*, the dirty low-down on Dempsey; and Frank Deford recounted the sad life of the tennis hero in *Big Bill*. But except for *Triumphant Journey* by Dick Miller, the Jones story has been told only by Jones himself or by writers who admired him so ardently that their words are little more than numbing gusts of PR. They overdo it. When one of these apostles writes that Jones "is still the only person ever to enjoy two (ticker-tape parades)"—despite the fact that Admiral Richard Byrd had three and seven others had two—is this merely thin research or another adoring lie? Whatever, by ascribing to him every Boy

Scout virtue, they've done the impossible: They've made Bobby Jones boring. They hear organ music from a stone cathedral when they summon his memory; I hear the theme from a James Bond film and imagine Jones—at least in 1930—as Bond himself, an international agent doing the impossible with utter aplomb, his hair perfect, his clothes impeccable, his manner suave and ironic. Neither version is all right or all wrong, of course. For Jones was a real man with sweat on his face and at least the average number of demons in his head, and he was no Boy Scout.

"The key to understanding Jones is to understand his priorities," intones one of his current hagiographers. "They were God, family, occupation, and, lastly, golf." Which is bullshit. God? God! In half a million published words and in over four thousand letters in the USGA museum and Emory University archives and in scores of speeches in which he accepted the trophy for first place, Jones never once thanked the Lord for his blessings. Well, a couple of times he invoked the deity. When he hit his ball out-of-bounds on the second-to-last hole in the 1930 Savannah Open, and it hit a car and came back onto the golf course, Jones commented that "the Lord held my hand." In the '30 U.S. Open, when his topped three-wood skimmed off the surface of a pond and finished safely on the opposite shore, Jones said, "The Lord must have had his arms around me." And he wrote "God Bless You" on his Christmas card to his patron, Bob Woodruff, one year. That's it, or mostly it.

He did use the word *God* often, as in "that goddamn lawn mower" or "that goddamn golf ball." He had been the little boy who asked his parents what people who didn't play golf did on Sundays, and he would be the bedridden old man who converted to Catholicism, after resisting for a long time, just to please his wife.

Family? Yes, quite true. His key relationship was the one with his father, to whom he was closer than anyone on earth. Their history bore a superficial but interesting resemblance to two other fathers and their famous sons, Theodorus and Vincent van Gogh and Vernon and Elvis Presley. The van Goghs of Groot-Zundert, the Netherlands, had a baby, Vincent, who died at birth. A year later, in 1853, they had another child, also named Vincent. Most of a century later, on a frigid early morning in northern Mississippi, Gladys Presley gave birth to twin boys. The first child, Jessie Garon, was stillborn. Elvis Aron was delivered thirty-five minutes later. One of the first things both Vincent and Elvis learned was that they had a dead identical brother looking down on them from heaven. Both V and E struggled all their lives to measure up to the legend of their invisible siblings, who had been so close to them in age and name. Both tried to prove themselves in very public ways. But Vincent would be a suicide, and Elvis, well, we all know about his delusions and drugs and peanut butter and 'nanner sandwiches.

Bobby Jones had an older brother, too. His name was William. The first child of Big Bob and the former Clara Merrick Thomas was born only a year or so into their marriage, but the blessed event immediately became heartbreaking. The child had something wrong with his digestive system—pyloric stenosis? esophageal reflux? Whatever, he just couldn't keep any food down. William lived just three months. The Joneses tried again; their second child was born about a year after the death of the first, on March 17, St. Patrick's Day, 1902. Mrs. Jones wanted to name the baby Patrick, according to family lore, but instead they called him Robert Tyre after his paternal grandfather. But it couldn't have been long before Big Bob and Clara discovered to their horror that their second son apparently had the same disorder that had killed poor William.

The sickly baby cried but survived on liquids (until age five) and love. His parents invested all hope in Bobby; Clara had no more children, and Big Bob carried his heir around on a pillow. There's no record that they whispered the name of William, the blameless dead brother, the way Gladys Presley invoked Jessie to Elvis, but something Big Bob and Clara did or said produced a perfectionist child with an insatiable desire to excel. Some view Bobby's core motivation to have been a desire to please others, particularly his father, but the people who hold this theory are not golfers, because golf above the hacker level is seductively, possibly sinfully, self-centered. It's all about you. Achievement in golf exalts the self just as much as winning a boxing match or an election. Bobby's success made Big Bob proud, of course, but he was no Machiavellian stage father blackmailing his boy to win-win-win to flatter his own ego. Theirs was a healthy and successful father-son relationship, with love and respect moving in both directions.

One measure of the depth of Bobby's feeling for his father was the lie he told every time he signed his name. Starting at about age eleven, and for the rest of his life, he added a Jr. or Jun. to the end of his signature. He wasn't a junior; Big Bob's middle name was Purmedus and Bobby's was Tyre. But the suffix saluted his mentor, his best friend, his dad.

As for his own kids, Miller tells us that Bobby the father "had no great love for children," that he was a distant parent who stayed out of the child-rearing fray until Clara, Robert, and Mary Ellen were nearly teenagers.

Occupation was supposed to be Jones's third priority, another dubious claim. Although Bobby eventually settled on a career in law, throughout his twenties in the 1920s he didn't really have an occupation. But he had a lot of jobs: student of mechanical engineering (Georgia School of Technology), student of English literature (a second undergraduate degree, for some reason, from Harvard), author (a memoir at age twenty-five), real estate salesman (at a golf course development in Sarasota, Florida), law student, columnist, executive of the Atlanta Crackers minor-league baseball team, lawyer (with his father's firm, Jones, Evins, Powers, and Jones often in the dullest corner of the profession, real estate conveyance), public figure, and golfer.

Occupation didn't preoccupy him, but money did. Jones plainly felt that he wasn't pulling his weight financially. He didn't have the time or attention to do much legal work in 1930, but there he was with a house in the best neighborhood in Atlanta, a wife who liked hats, two kids, a couple of servants, and several country club memberships. His grandfather, Robert, and Robert Woodruff were his financial angels. Woodruff would get Jones into the bottling business when bottling Coke was like minting money.

"If I have any genius at all, it must be for play," Jones wrote in his autobiography, *Down the Fairway*. "I love to play . . . It seems I love almost any pursuit except work. I even like going to school." Even this sentence seems playful, because Jones actually worked hard—or hard enough—on whatever was in front of him. He was at Emory, studying law, when he wrote that book with O. B. Keeler. Halfway through the second year of the two-year course, he took the bar exam and passed it. Bobby was obviously more a worker than a player.

Whether this skipping around indicates that Jones was an intellectually restless Renaissance Man or a typically indecisive young man is a matter of interpretation. At any rate, he eased the pain of finding himself with a little bourbon and a lot of golf. Schoolwork and study were not high priorities. Despite his reputation for academic brilliance, the Gentleman's C was his stock-in-trade at the Georgia School of Technology and at Harvard. His transcript at Tech was also littered with lots of grades in the 60s; anything below that was an F.

And where did golf rank in Jones's hierarchy? Could it have really been fourth behind God, Mom, and Justice? No way: It's far more truthful to say that golf was Bobby's religion, and his occupation, and the best and happiest part of his life. And yet the challenge and nuance of golf was not enough for his wide-ranging mind. He liked to read and write and think and drink. Golf obsessed him only in bursts.

Much has been made of how little Jones played during his competitive prime, as further proof of his genius and his dedication to amateurism. This line from O. B. Keeler in *The Bobby Jones Story* (1953) has been quoted over and over: "Bobby without any doubt played less formal or competitive golf in the eight years of his championships than any other first-rank golfer, amateur or professional, in the world." Charles Price was apparently inspired by Keeler's comment in his introduction to *Bobby Jones on Golf* (1969): "Jones played less formal golf during his championship years than virtually all of the players he beat, and he beat everybody in the world worth beating." True, when winter turned the Bermuda grass at East Lake to the color and texture of shredded wheat, Jones seldom got the clubs out. Starting in 1928, his first full year with his father's law firm, his routine called for Wednesday afternoon games with Big Bob and his cronies—Bobby was the kind of young man older men like, not all full of himself—and Sunday golf with whomever, possibly even with Mary, Mom, and Dad. He played one or two other times a week, often with Chick Ridley, the 1924 Georgia Amateur champion. But Jones's pace increased before and during the three or four weeklong tournaments he played each summer. And he'd had intervals in which he kept a club in his hand constantly, such as in Florida in 1926, when he played every day for six months with Tommy Armour, one of the greatest of professional golfers. (Armour had to accept a one-up advantage per nine to make their matches competitive because, he said, "Jones was that goddamn good.")

Jones didn't play and practice constantly for the same reason he didn't practice tying his shoes. He'd gotten it, and four rounds a week, nine months a year was plenty for him to keep it. As for frequency of competition, quantity does not equal quality. Ben Hogan proved this succinctly in 1953, when he teed it up in only six serious tournaments and won five. Jones knew how much practice he needed—not a lot—and how many tournaments were best for him—not many. He found a pace that kept him fresh and interested.

His very public secret weapon was his column, "Bobby Jones Says." Jones was not a fast writer, and he tried to make each essay a little masterpiece—so for most of two days a week he did little but ponder technique, strategy, equipment, fans, his competitors, bunker rakes, and tournaments. He recognized that golf is ultimately a mental game, a contest of self-control; committing his deepest thoughts to paper was therefore wonderful practice.

He had a lot to think about. And a very big secret he never revealed to his readers.

As 1929 became 1930, Jones faced a unique prospect. He'd be like a bank robber who plans to go straight—after he knocks off four more banks. Maybe that writer who put God, family, and occupation one-two-three in Bobby's heart had it half right: The key to understanding Jones was to understand his priorities. And his priority, his first job and preoccupation, contained dangerous and delicious irony.

He had been playing in big-time golf tournaments for fourteen years, half his life. How he'd suffered for his art: emotionally, physically, and financially, the cost of keeping a world-class golf game had become too high. Perhaps the heaviest part of the burden was the weight of expectation. "Tournament golf began to pall," he wrote many years later, "when anything less than victory was regarded as a failure by my friends, and by me."

Like most writers and many golfers, he was a brooder, and he had thought long thoughts on those interminable train trips to this tournament or that, and on ponderous ocean liners crossing the Atlantic, or while staring at the wall in his office. He searched the air for a way out and found it. A simple plan, conceived in 1926 and committed to gradually: Get up on the cross one last time. Embrace like a lover this thing he no longer wanted any part of. Play in all four of the big tournaments, win them, and quit. Jones was canny enough to realize the enormity of the challenge and the enormity of the reward that success would bring. If he could do it, he'd create a brand as indelible as Coca-Cola. He'd set himself up for life.

But everything that happened in the summer of '30 almost didn't. He seemed to abandon the plan for a time. There were shocks along the way. And a big shock at the end.

Horton Smith, the best putter in the world,
had the game to beat Bobby Jones.

1

Is Modest as Usual

"If personality is an unbroken series of successful gestures, then there was something gorgeous about him, some heightened sensitivity to the promises of life . . ."

—F. Scott Fitzgerald, The Great Gatsby

Tuesday, February 18, 1930, 8:00 P.M.
Atlanta

Smith and Jones got on the train. They were two young men in tailored suits. Smith had the long, slim physique of a male model and a smile full of straight teeth. Jones was shorter, rounder, and even more handsome than his traveling companion. In the regal solidity of his body and in the calm, composed way he regarded the world, Jones looked like a man who was always about to be recognized and was ready for it.

Smith and Jones wore hats, as fashion demanded for well-dressed men when out of doors. Beneath their fedoras both men were impressively barbered, with center parts and some sort of hairdressing. Was that the vanilla scent of Murray's Super Light, the pomade in the orange tin? Smith's hair was wavy and light brown. The oiled hair on Jones's head adhered to his scalp and would have looked blue-black in the station lights.

Black men in dark uniforms and red hats hustled around the station. "Allow me, sir," they said at the curb out front, loading luggage onto low carts. "What train, sir?" The red caps off-loaded the carts into baggage cars or into the private rooms of fancy travelers, and then they stood by for a tip. They might have noticed when they stowed the golf bags of the two handsome, young men that one set of clubs clinked and the other clattered. Horton Smith had the latest thing, steel shafts. Bobby Jones was sticking with his hickories.

A blue-suited conductor looked at a Hamilton pocket watch and sang out, "B-o-o-ard," just like in the old movies, and the Central of Georgia Railway Passenger Train Number 4 chugged out of Union Station. The Number 4 rolled south from Atlanta and stopped in Griffin, then Macon, where it connected with a train from Columbus. And then it lumbered through the night southeast to the coast, stopping at intervals—in Gordon, McIntyre, Millen, and elsewhere, for coal and water and mail and passengers. It was just about the route General William Sherman followed in 1864 in the War of Northern Aggression, as they called it in Georgia and call it still. A couple of hours before its 8:00 A.M. arrival in Savannah, the train reached the sandy coastal plain, and the dozing passengers felt the land flatten.

Jones must have felt five ways strange, as the steel wheels rolled and the train swayed in rhythm from side to side. What the hell was he doing? He almost never played a golf tournament this early in the year. If the winter weather was raw, he didn't even get the clubs out until March or April. The *Savannah Morning News* got in a dither when it heard there was a possibility he would return for the inaugural Savannah Open. "Bob Likes City; Wants to Come," the headline read the day before he got on the train.

"I've been trying as hard as I could to get in shape for the Savannah tournament, but the weather has been so tricky here and the greens in such bad shape that I haven't made much progress," Bobby told a reporter, even though he'd just shot a nine-under-par 63 at his home club, East Lake, tying his own course record. Apparently, he was thinking of his first round of the year, a week before, when he played in an exhibition match and shot 80. "The most trying time of the year for the golfer is always the time when he comes out of hibernation and begins to tune his game back to a point where he can enjoy it," Jones wrote in his column of February 15. "After a long winter layoff, each club feels like a broom handle and each ball when struck transmits a shock up the shaft which makes the player think he has hit a lump of iron . . . The first failure is in the length of the backswing . . . "

Jones did not mention in his column that he'd been working out for the first and last time in his career and that there was less jiggle under his shirt than usual as a result. His workout consisted of a game of Doug—named for its inventor, actor Douglas Fairbanks Jr.—which was a cross between badminton and tennis played indoors. The court was on the stage of the underutilized Atlanta Theatre; Bobby knew the owner. A set or two in the middle of the day, maybe another couple of sets after work—it was no triathlon, but it was better than eating.

More headlines followed in the next *Morning News:*

"BOBBY JONES ON WAY TO SAVANNAH"

"Fires Opening Gun Here in Strenuous Campaign"

"IS MODEST AS USUAL"

"Says Pros Will Probably Give Him a Licking"

Over another story entitled "Open Champion Is Due at 8 o'clock," the Sunday paper ran a big two-column knees-to-head photograph of Georgia's hero. Behind the image of Bobby, an artist had drawn a circular design that looked a lot like a halo.

"Bobby Jones stayed with us in August 1924, when I was just two," recalls Armin Cay Chisolm. Her daddy, Gene Cay of Palmer and Cay Insurance, had just built a spacious, hurricane-proof red brick house over by the high school. In an exhibition match, Cay and pro Dave Spittal opposed Bobby and Perry Adair, two young hotshots down from Atlanta. The entire large gallery gasped when Jones took a triple-bogey seven on the first hole at the Savannah Golf Club, but he recovered his poise as quickly as he lost it, and his polite charm. Bobby's infrequent visits became a cherished part of Savannah golf history and Cay family lore. His picture went up on a wall in the SGC clubhouse and hasn't been taken down since. He posed again with little Armin and drank and laughed at the house with Mr. Cay and other cocktail-hour visitors. "We always said there were more drinks drunk in my father's pantry than at Toots Shor's in New York," says Mrs. Chisolm. One night during The Week Bobby Stayed, the cat poked a golf ball out of a bag and knocked it down the oak-planked stairs, waking everyone up. The Cays called the cat Bobby Jones from then on.

"Some time later—I don't remember the year—we were going down to Sea Island to play some golf, and Bobby Jones was in the car," recalls Mrs. Chisolm. "Daddy had borrowed a big old phaeton from Dr. Barrow for the occasion. We slowed down almost to a stop for some highway work, which was being done by a chain gang. The top was down in the car, and one of the men looked in and said, 'Lawd God! Look at Miss Jeannie Cay on her way to Flory-da in a Caddy-lac car!'" Little Miss Cay was delighted to be recognized by Tadpole, one of the caddies from Savannah Golf Club, who was obviously down on his luck.

Now Bobby would give Savannah another story to tell and retell—but at some cost to his routine and to his health. He announced that he'd be playing in six tournaments this year—he sometimes played as few as two—and that he'd be teeing up in all four of the then-major tournaments. In fourteen years as a serious competitor, he'd done that only twice before. Various pundits commented on "Bobby's strenuous schedule," but no one brought up the possibility that he might win the four majors. The idea had no currency; no one used the phrase "Grand Slam" unless they were talking about bridge or baseball. According to biographer Dick Miller, only three people knew the real plan: Big Bob, Mary, and Keela.

That was another odd thing, to be on a train going to a golf tournament without O. B. Keeler, which was pronounced "Keela" by himself and by Bobby. Jones's "shadow," as one of the Savannah newspapers referred to him, had taken the somewhat adventurous step of driving down from Atlanta. Adventurous because not all the roads between the two cities were paved—you could get stuck, or stranded, particularly if it rained, and flats were a constant threat with the thin rubber tires that cars had then. O.B. was bringing his wife, Eleanor, a further disruption; Keeler usually shared a room or a suite with Bobby. But at least he'd be there. Since the mid-1910s, O.B. and his typewriter and his bottle of corn had gone wherever Bobby went.

So no Keeler. In his place was this twenty-one-year-old from Springfield, Missouri, who didn't drink and didn't smoke and looked like the best player in the world. Horton Smith, who had won eight tournaments the previous winter on his first real try at the pro tour, had spent the previous two days in Atlanta. "The tall boy showed up at East Lake and we promptly arranged games for the following day," Jones would recall in his column (Horton stood six feet one; Jones, five eight). Bobby loved the rhythm and simplicity of his guest's upright swing, "but the best part of the whole thing comes after the green is reached," he wrote. "He is the best putter in the world . . . he has every attribute of temperament required and a healthy, strong body, of which he takes perfect care."

Jones had recognized a golfer who could beat him in 1930.

During those two rounds on the course that he had played all his life, Bobby observed how Smith locked his wrists by arching them forward when he putted, a stiff style contrary to his own loose-as-a-goose approach to every golf shot. But Horton hinged and unhinged a lot when he chipped and pitched, and he hit these short shots almost as well as he putted. Jones noticed; he'd been having trouble with the mashie niblick (seven-iron), a club he liked to use from about 100 yards in. So Bobby changed his stroke slightly, in imitation of Horton's handsy technique.

Smith shot 68 and 69 at East Lake with his steel-shafted irons and beat his host twice, but there were no hard feelings: The two amiable gentlemen hit it off well enough to decide to travel to Savannah together and to share a suite at the hotel when they got there. What made Jones and Smith such a good match? Bobby liked that Horton quite obviously knew how to win a golf tournament; he'd done so nine times in his very brief career. The few men who could discipline themselves to keep swinging and thinking under the most severe pressure shared what amounted to a fluency in a secret language.

Horton had gone to college, which Bobby was bound to admire. Two years at Missouri State Teachers' wasn't much when held next to Jones's pedigree, of course, but it made him a scholar compared to the other American pros. More important, Smith showed a pleasing smoothness with a golf club and with people, an unfailing politeness that Bobby himself had always had. In a word, Horton and Bobby were always *appropriate*. Smith became famous for getting in the car or on the train to the next tournament and writing thank-you notes to tournament sponsors and volunteers, while the other guys passed around a whiskey bottle. Both Smith and Jones were meticulous, bordering on fussy, regarding proper conduct and dress, as if they were setting examples for their more rustic peers. When Bobby looked across the dining-car table at the young man from Joplin, he saw a lot of himself.

Smith had planned a career in education, but success at golf had interrupted his momentum toward a teaching degree. After he won the Class B championship of the Midwest PGA in 1926, he gave himself to the game full-time. As the nineteen-year-old pro at Jefferson Country Club in Missouri, he qualified for the 1927 U.S. Open at Oakmont in suburban Pittsburgh, which Tommy Armour won and where he met Jones. Smith's second win on the loosely organized pro tour caused quite a splash because of his youth and because of the identity of the runner-up. Walter Hagen birdied the final three holes and shot 29 for the last nine of the 1928 Catalina Island Open but still couldn't overtake the young man from Missouri. As he won more and more tournaments in '29 and '30, and sensing that Smith was here to stay, writers tried out nicknames to replace his plain vanilla surname. The Joplin Ghost stuck; the Missouri Rover and the Joplin Jigger Juggler did not.

Hagen told a writer in his high-pitched foghorn that of all the new young golfers on the scene, this Horton Smith impressed him most. Praise from Caesar: Not only was the high-living Hagen one of the best professional golfers in the world and the most electric figure in the game, he could make you rich. As the undisputed king of exhibition golf, Hagen often took someone new to join him on a tour of the boondocks to show the locals how well the game could be played. Late in '29, he chose the clean-cut Smith to be his foil on such a tour. Sir Walter drank champagne from a ladies shoe, but the Joplin Ghost never touched the stuff. For about one hundred dates, they were golf's odd couple.

Hagen could also enrich a brother professional in a less direct way. As the semi-permanent captain of the United States Ryder Cup team, Sir Walter was so wired in that for the first couple of Ryder Cups, he picked the team. For the '29 match, the second ever and the first on English soil, he selected Smith, his conqueror at Catalina Island. A place in the international all-star game of professional golf meant instant prestige, which might mean a better club job and a higher exhibition fee.

So in May 1929, Horton from Missourah became an International and a teammate to the best American pros, among them cocky Gene Sarazen and charming Johnny Farrell, two New Yorkers; Leo Diegel, from Detroit, who was strung tighter than a cello; gentle, taciturn Ed Dudley, a Carolina country boy; Al Espinosa, who had beaten Smith in the semifinals of the 1928 PGA; and Hagen.

Horton played one match in the '29 Ryder Cup, against Fred Robson, who stated after his defeat that he'd never had an opponent who made him feel so ineffectual. "[Smith's] swing was smooth and slow and beautiful," wrote

Henry Longhurst of the *Manchester Guardian*, "and he putted like a violinist." Bernard Darwin of the *Times of London* was equally impressed. "Smith is a joy to watch," he wrote, "easy, elegant and of a horrid certainty."

Circumstance and high achievement would tie Smith and Jones together again and again in 1930 and thereafter, and in time their lives would attain an eerie similarity. This was the week they became friends—and rivals. Bobby and Horton were about to engage in a polite death match.

Wednesday, February 19
Savannah

With hisses and clouds from the steam engines and a long shriek of brakes, the Number 4 train arrived at the Central of Georgia passenger station in Savannah. The Pullman porters, who never seemed to sleep, helped the passengers gather their belongings and put on their coats. During the night they had brushed your suit, emptied your trash, and shined your shoes, and now they offered you a newspaper. "Thanks, George," you'd say; everybody called his train servant George, partly for shorthand, and partly in honor of George M. Pullman, the inventor of the sleeper car. In the last act in the ritual, the porter briskly brushed a gentleman's hat and handed it back with a smile. Then the gentleman handed over a tip.

Smith and Jones got off the train. They smiled for the cameras and tipped the red caps and got into a waiting car, which took them the six blocks to their hotel.

The city would have been excited about its first annual Open even without him, but with Jones playing, Savannah got a serious case of the vapors. The Junior League, which volunteered to sell tickets, reported brisk sales of three-dollar, three-day passes. Fred Howden, the tournament chairman, reserved for himself and his brother, Mike, the honor of playing a practice round with Bobby, and he hoped the great man would want to play thirty-six holes (he didn't). "Thursday, Friday and Saturday Savannahians will be treated to a spectacle greater than anything it has witnessed since Oglethorpe gave Tomochichi nine strokes and beat him for the Yamacraw open championship," blustered C. F. Holton on February 19 in the evening paper, the *Savannah Press* (the reference was to the English founder of Georgia and the Yamacraw Indian chief who allowed the Europeans to build Savannah). "With Bob in the ring, there will be some action," Holton continued. "Instead of its being anybody's fight now it is the field against Jones."

The professionals arrived in town in dribs and drabs, two or three to a LaSalle or a Model A, and they were stiff and dank from the six-hundred-mile drive from Pensacola. The tour traveled by car, and the Ford Model A was the Camry of its day, the most popular model in the country. Only it was cooler than a Camry; Hollywood royalty Douglas Fairbanks Sr. and his wife, Mary Pickford, picked up the sporty successor to the Model T soon after it debuted in 1928. Passengers in the Model A's narrow front seat were always bumping elbows, and it rode like a bucking bronco on rough roads, but the A had a spacious backseat and could average forty miles an hour and seventeen miles per gallon if the roads were good. Gasoline cost fifteen to twenty-five cents a gallon. The tank held ten gallons. Bigger cars like the Packard could maintain a speed of fifty miles per hour under perfect conditions, but a Packard Eight cost $2,700, far more than the $795 Ford. Radios and air-conditioning didn't grace any make or model in 1930, of course, and the interstate highway system lay far in the future. Although Buick made a coupe in 1930 with a built-in compartment for golf clubs that had its own cute little door just behind the passenger door, not much could be done to ease the pain of cross-country car travel. Trains were the way to go, if you could afford it.

The touring pros stuck stiff legs out of their cars at the golf course or in front of their hotel, straightening ties and tucking in shirttails. A few of them were staying in the DeSoto, the best lodging in town. It had a pool; a rocker-filled, wraparound eight-thousand-square-foot verandah; and a view of the river and of the moss-hung trees in Johnson Square Park. Smith and Jones would share a suite at the popular but less-fancy Savannah Hotel, which cost only $1.50 a night for a single, $2.50 and up with bath, but no additional charge for the radio in each of its three hundred rooms. There wasn't much charm or sense of occasion at the Savannah; you got out of your Hupmobile, walked across eight feet of sidewalk, and you were in. The front desk was on your right, past the cigar stand.

Jones had been competing against professionals several times a year since he was fifteen, so he'd seen them travel three to a car and three to a dingy room, living on hot dogs and beer and leaded gas, and not getting rich from the tiny tournament purses. That was the answer to those who wondered why he didn't turn pro: He didn't want their life.

But it was a good life for Hagen and a few others. Between his golf club manufacturing company, prize money, and exhibitions, Sir Walter was rumored to have made (and spent) as much as $200,000 a year. Sarazen could afford to buy a little dairy farm in Connecticut partly because he padded his income by endorsing anything and everything: U.S. Trap-Shells, Blue Jay corn plasters, Libby's tomato juice, Bromo-Seltzer, Packard automobiles, Palmolive ("the Shave Cream with Olive Oil!"), Pabst Blue Ribbon beer, and at least three brands of smokes. The ad copy made tobacco seem like a health food: "When it comes to the crucial moment and nerves must be under control, I turn to a Lucky Strike," says brilliant golf champion Gene Sarazen. "They leave a soothing effect upon my nerves and throat."

Not everyone could be as marketable as Hagen or Sarazen, of course, but almost every pro could dream of being Johnny Farrell. "Dapper" Johnny Farrell, as the writers invariably referred to him, caught lightning in a bottle when he won the 1928 U.S. Open at Olympia Fields in Chicago, beating Jones by a stroke in a thirty-six-hole playoff. His surprising victory led to a couple of product endorsements, for Lucky Strike cigarettes and Barbasol shaving cream, deals that were good for the ego and for visibility but paid only peanuts. Winning the U.S. Open gave Johnny the gloss to eventually land something really valuable, however—a job at a top club. *That* was the goal and motivation for almost every touring pro of 1930 and 1940, and

1950, and beyond—to play well enough to get noticed by the search committees at the best country clubs. When Farrell got the head professional position at Baltusrol in 1934, he retired from competition and hung on to his post for the next thirty-one years.

Savannah Golf Club

Most tournaments presented a check to only the first fifteen or twenty finishers. To increase their chances for survival until the snow melted up north and their clubs reopened, a lot of pros entered into agreements to split their prize money. Farrell and Sarazen had such an arrangement for a while, until Gene started to do so well that he opted out.

Farrell, a slight man with a big smile and big teeth, was the happiest pro to crawl out of a car in Savannah. He had won the $800 first prize in the previous tournament, in Pensacola, and wasn't sharing it with anyone. "Twenty-Five-Foot Putt on 18th Whips Italian," the *Morning News* headline read—the Italian being Gene Sarazen, né Saraceni. The $3,000 Savannah Open attracted about every top American pro except Hagen and Macdonald Smith. Sarazen et al. were some of the best and most interesting golfers in the world. But they were not as good or as interesting as Bobby.

The golfers drove two miles east of their downtown hotels on the Thunderbolt car line to the Savannah Golf Club.

And here he came up the walk to the white wooden clubhouse, looking composed while reverent fans fell into step beside him. Jones had changed out of the suit and wore, as usual, light-colored plus fours, a crisp white shirt, and a tie tucked into the shirt at the third button down. His hair was perfect.

And now here was Jones on the first tee, shaking hands with his companions for the practice round: Horton Smith, his new bosom buddy, and the two nervous brothers, Fred and Mike Howden, who had never played with players so good or in front of a crowd so large. Bobby had a wonderful knack for putting people at ease, however, and he would have murmured, "Why don't Fred and I take on you and Mike for a dollar or two? Would that be all right, Horton? Fred, I think we can handle them, don't you?" Jones had a pleasing ability to look serious and amused at the same time. His sweet Georgia drawl made it seem as if his molars were stuck together with molasses, but his words reminded you he'd been to Harvard and Tech and Emory.

And now here was Bobby hitting a golf ball. Even nongolfers appreciated the powerful grace of Jones's swing, particularly with his best club, the driver. He looked awkward when he tried to hit a baseball that summer, and he ran, which was seldom, like the last kid picked for the kickball game. But Jones was a great athlete, with golf's best-ever blend of head, hands, and feet. With his long, languid swing, those ballerina feet were vital. At the top of his backswing, he went way up on the left big toe of his two-toned Bass golf shoe and finished his stroke with the tip of his right shoe stuck in the ground. In between there was a great deal of ankle rolling in response to the very full coiling and release of his hips, shoulders, and torso. But the feet never lost their rhythm or balance. He took a good, hard rip at the ball—he didn't like to hit half shots or punches like many other players did—but because of the amazing grace of his footwork, every follow-through looked like a pose for a magazine cover. Anyone who observed that swing knew they'd seen something special.

"We all hope that the posture at the finish will be an expression of ease, grace, and balance," Jones would write with characteristic formality. "The appearance of the player at the end of his effort will betray his inconsistencies or confirm his perfection."

Bobby's little feet were connected to legs and an ass that looked as though they belonged to a bull. Although his baggy plus twos or plus fours (the number referring to the number of inches the pantaloons hung below the knee) obscured the fact, he had the lower body of a football lineman. Like other smooth big hitters through the years—Sam Snead, Fred Couples, Ernie Els—Jones's muscular base could make it appear that he wasn't swinging very hard. But look how far the ball went!

The first hole at Savannah Golf Club doglegged left, and Bobby played a hook, so he gave full expression to his tee shot. Trees around the tee amplified the crack of persimmon on hard rubber and the whistles and gasps of the gallery. While about a thousand watched, Jones parred the first, the amateur brothers predictably bogeyed, and Smith made a birdie three. During a tournament round, Bobby was as silent as a crypt, but he could banter a little bit when it was just practice. "Say, what did you use on that, your curling iron?"

Bobby asked after Horton hit a big, intentional hook around trees and onto the green with his second shot to the par-five seventh.

You wonder if this mere practice round for a minor tournament had a competitive subtext. Did Jones take pains to beat this nice young man who had just beaten him twice at East Lake, a nice young man who looked perfectly capable of screwing up his secret plan to win the four majors of 1930?

Probably—but not that you'd notice. The Grand Illusion of Bobby Jones was that he never seemed to be trying very hard. His swing, his style, the impressive speed with which he played, and his every mannerism and gesture on and off the course gave an impression of ease. An unconcerned attitude was an important component of the Amateur Ideal, of course: Trying too hard was not quite sporting. But Jones's nonchalance was studied, and his relaxation required effort. He'd sublimated his teenage temper—an ordinary step in maturation for which he received lavish praise—but he never lost his fire. Jones was a subtle gamesman and the most competitive son of a bitch golf has ever seen. Without seeming to be.

With a birdie on the eighteenth hole, Bobby tied the course record and beat Horton, 68 to 69.

Thursday, February 20
Savannah Golf Club

The first round of the 1930 Savannah Open would be Jones's first formal competition since his shocking first-round loss in the 1929 U.S. Amateur six months earlier. He looked ready, and his good-luck charm was in place: Keela.

Oscar Bane Keeler wore glasses with round frames and an air of affability that rubbed off on anyone who came close. He looked as though he could sell you insurance or burial plots and make you like it. But he was a newspaperman, employed by the *Atlanta Journal.*

Who was this man who had attached himself like a barnacle to Bobby

Jones? Was he merely an unusually successful suck-up or was there depth behind his big smile and his glad hand? He insinuated himself into so many pictures of Bobby and the trophy that he looked as though he'd won them, too.
In a way, he had.

A talented writer, the snap and accuracy of a lot of Keeler's deadline re-
porting can't be denied. He'd perfected an easy, breezy style that made you
think his typewriter had had one or two. He was fun to read most of the time.
On those other times, however, when he descended into cheerleading for
Jones and inserted himself into the narrative, a modern reader cringes. His
habit of the incomplete sentence with the unnecessary word ("Golf that
would have annihilated any other living opponent.") and the flamboyant
word ("spectacularity") contrasted sharply with the clear, clean, and often too
formal writing in Jones's columns. But Keeler was always at least good
enough, and his adoration of Bobby inspired his prose.

O.B. also adored the limelight and straight liquor. Aided by his photo-
graphic memory of sentimental poetry, popular fiction, and dirty limericks,
he could hold an audience at the bar for hours. He seems easy to mock
from the distance of years, but his importance to Jones should not be un-
derestimated. Big Bob rarely watched Bobby's tournaments because he
thought he jinxed his son—which deepened the relationship between the
golfer and his flack. They were a team, so much so that Paul Runyan and
other pros assumed that Keeler was on the Jones family payroll in a public
relations capacity.

"Amateur golf tournaments were big stuff in Georgia in those days, and
the *Journal* sent Keeler wherever Jones was playing," says Furman Bisher,
whose career in Atlanta sports journalism began in 1950, when Keeler's
ended. "They definitely had a unique relationship. No, I don't believe the
Jones family paid him. But writers and athletes spent a lot of time together back then on trains and in hotels, and they got a lot closer than
nowadays."

When Jones didn't feel like meeting the press after his round—and this
happened more and more each year—Keeler talked to the other writers on

his behalf and told them what Bobby would have said if he had been there. O.B. was such a charmer and was so good at filling up reporters' notebooks that no complaints were heard. But who else in the history of games had his own spokesman? And what other journalist was ever so close to his source? O.B. 'n' Bob wrote a book together, *Down the Fairway* (published in 1927), which Keeler regurgitated in *The Boys' Life of Bobby Jones* (1931). Between the books and a radio show they did together and sharing hotel rooms and sleeper cars for almost two decades, it was easy to see why people thought O.B. worked for Bobby.

Their relationship was no mere series of transactions, however. Jones loved O.B. like a second father, and when he didn't call him Keela, he called him by his nickname, "Pop." In the preface for a third (posthumous) Keeler retelling of his favorite subject, *The Bobby Jones Story*, Jones reflected on their "very real partnership for the better part of twenty years . . . all in the closest and most harmonious collaboration. I doubt if ever such a relationship existed between performer and reporter in sport or elsewhere."

On that warm, clear February morning when Jones teed off in the first round of the first Savannah Open, Keeler was there. If it had been a normal tournament week, they would have drinks that night. But it wasn't a normal week. O.B. had his wife, and Bobby had Smith, with whom he went to the movies several times that week. But one ritual almost never changed: Bobby hit, and O.B. limped along. A bout of inflammatory rheumatism in 1917 had permanently stiffened his left knee, giving him a hobble that humorists on the tour liked to parody.

Short, flat Savannah Golf Club was relatively easy to walk, however, even for Keeler. Its only hills were the remnants of Civil War breastworks, hastily constructed earth barriers that protected the Confederate gunners trying to discourage the Union Army's invasion. The deep moats encircling the mounds—now water hazards—were intended to repel the enemy's horse-drawn equipment. The Yankees came anyway, in December 1864, three months after leaving Atlanta in a haze of blue smoke. But they didn't burn the beautiful city by the sea.

Because it had no long par fours, which might emphasize the weakest part of his game at that moment, the long irons, Jones reflected in print two months later that Savannah Golf Club "is not an unusually difficult course . . . But it is by no means a simple layout . . . all greens were small and closely guarded."

On the first tee with Jones stood the Tall Boy, a crowd-building pairing of the hottest pro and the king of golf, which did not seem accidental. Keela grazed nearby, as usual. Nearly every spectator on the grounds crowded into the narrow space proscribed by oaks and evergreens and one of those huge mounds built with shovels and wheelbarrows. A handful of official-looking men holding megaphones and long reed poles completed the cast. The state of the art in crowd control involved these volunteers shouting, "Fore, please" or "No running!" through their amplifiers and holding their sticks horizontally to create enough space among the crush for a player to swing. Between shots, excited packs of spectators could and did surround Bobby on the walk up the fairway or to the green, as if they were all rush-hour commuters going to the same train.

Those ineffectual poles symbolized what Jones had come to hate about his life on display. People, people crowding in, people expecting a wink, a nod, a win. He harbored this secret: He didn't like people. He liked his friends, or new friends properly introduced, but the gallery adhering to him like an old Band-Aid? No. If yellow nylon ropes had been used to reduce the forced intimacy of a tournament round, Jones might not have been so preoccupied with retirement.

"I considered the gallery well behaved," commented chief marshal G. M. Maclean, "but too much inclined to talk. I hope there won't be so much conversation tomorrow and Saturday." But with Jones in the field and the holiday atmosphere, and two Savannah pros doing well—Jeff Adams and Fairley Clark—there was a lot to talk about.

And Savannah, God knew, was a social town.

Half-smiling like the good sport he was, Jones shot 67, seven under par, a new course record. He led by one. Smith shot 71.

Friday, February 21

After two rounds, Smith led the tournament. He shot 66 in the second round, breaking Bobby's day-old course record. Jones had what he called a "misadventure" on the 240-yard second hole, a triple bogey that cost him a 75 for the round and allowed Keeler to get out the purple ink. After hitting his tee ball under a crepe myrtle and having to get down on his knees to scoot it out with his putter, he fluffed the ball into a shallow bunker, a wretched shot, "from which he took the ball too cleanly, and over the green it sailed while the gallery swooned in windrows and platoons," O.B. wrote. "When he worked it back seven feet from the pin and blew the putt . . . it seemed that this was the correct juncture for Gabriel to blow his horn."

Keeler was in rare form all that day. He and the Mrs. attended a dinner party given that evening that was important enough to attract the gossip columnist for the *Savannah Morning News:* " 'O.B.' was quite the hit of the evening. He is not only a remarkable writer of sports news but he is equally remarkable as a reader and improviser of poetry and demonstrated his skill at the latter accomplishment to the huge delight of the guests."

Saturday, February 22, Morning

After three rounds, Jones tied Smith for the lead, coming from five strokes back. Bobby shot a third-round 65, still another course record.

Saturday, February 22, Afternoon

The shoot-out the tournament organizers hoped for had come to pass, with exactly the right protagonists firing at each other. The Savannah Open had evolved into a duel between Bobby and Horton with the rest of the field in the dust. "We were at all times acutely aware of the other's presence on the golf course," Jones would recall. It was all about Bobby and Horton; Bobby Cruickshank would finish a faraway third, five shots behind the runner-up. The weather had remained perfect all week: clear with temperatures in the midseventies.

Jones might have been leading by a lot instead of tied for the lead if not for that wretched second-round 75, one over par. In addition to his triple bogey, a few shortish putts had lipped out, several not-quite-knowledgeable fans commented aloud on his failures, and Bobby's ears turned red. It was fodder for a column: "About the most maddening sound a golfer can hear is the guffawing laugh of some over-a-hundred expert in the gallery when a 4- or 5-foot putt wheels out of the hole," he wrote. "I've always wished there was some way to impress upon these loud-voiced persons the real difficulty of a short putt on a fast green when anything of importance depends on the effort." That is so true. But Bobby himself was partly to blame; his success and appealing personality lured new golfers and dilettantes to come out to watch. They were the over-a-hundred experts.

No one laughed at Jones on Saturday morning, however. After a chip-in (with a three-iron) for an eagle two on the 248-yard thirteenth hole, he holed from eighteen feet for another two on the 191-yard fourteenth. But his second course record of the week was built more on brilliant striking than on sudden putter heat. He hit most of the par fives in two on the 6,300-yard course and used twenty-nine putts, about the most you can have to shoot 65.

Bobby was invariably hungry at lunch because his stomach had become too nervous for breakfast on game days. So it was an act of will to eat lightly during the lunch break in the middle of Saturday's double round. For years he dined like a long-haul trucker on such occasions, a full meal with pie or ice cream—or both—at the end. But he'd gotten predictably logy in a few post-luncheon rounds (thirty-six-hole days were common then) and put on more weight than he wanted. Now he had only a tiny sandwich and a glass of tea. He found it hard to laugh when Keeler kidded him about his waistline.

Jones started the afternoon round in the company of dapper Johnny Farrell and Lighthorse Harry Cooper, the fastest player on the tour, just as Smith's group finished its first eighteen. Judging by the report he filed, Keeler seems to have watched Bobby on the first nine and Horton on the second. As usual, most of the gallery followed Jones. None of the contemporary accounts estimated the size of the crowd, only that it was "gratifyingly large."

Both combatants started with six cautious pars. Then it got wild. Bobby hit his second shot with a fairway wood to the par-five seventh about twenty yards to the right of the green. Between himself and the hole, a bunker filled with beach sand waited like an open mouth. The ball sat low in the sandy soil, "a treacherous place," wrote Keeler astutely, "where, if you take the ball a bit thick, you fluff it and if you take it a bit too cleanly, you fire it over the green." Bobby chunked it into the bunker. He didn't hit much of a shot from the sand, missed the par putt, and had a six on a hole he expected to birdie. Horton did birdie it a few minutes later, with an eight-foot putt, and he led by two.

But not for long. Smith started hitting his drives into the trees, Jones birdied the ninth and the thirteenth, and they were tied again. The galleries for the two leaders were close enough so that with a few shouts and whispers both players knew how they stood relative to the other throughout the tense final hours. So when Bobby missed a three-footer on sixteen and had to settle for par on this birdie hole, he knew he'd left an opening he had to close.

Gobel Avenue hugged the left side of the seventeenth at Savannah Golf Club, a quiet residential street with houses that were comfortable but not grand. You got golf balls in your yard if you lived on Gobel, but not many, because a row of tall pines veiled with Spanish moss blocked the way. Besides, most people sliced.

Bobby Jones hooked. He felt himself down by one, so he took an aggressive line with his second shot to the 507-yard hole. His fairway wood to the tightly guarded green looked perfect for a moment. But in its last fifty yards in the air, it bent left and flew into the street . . .

Most recaps of the tournament leave it at that, that Jones was done in by his ball off the course on seventeen. But his Spalding didn't stay out of bounds. It clanged into a car on Gobel—it's unclear if the vehicle was parked or in motion—and bounced back onto the Savannah Golf Club. From there Jones made a two-chip, two-putt six and was glad to have it.

Bobby was a vivid figure in white as he walked onto the final green with Harry and Johnny. The crowd hushed as the dark-haired man lined up a thirty-footer, which he plainly intended to make. Jones stood so upright with his putter that he looked as if he might hit his toe instead of the ball, and his stroke was all wrist. He banged it at the hole and made it, as heroes do. His gallery roared; it seemed Bobby still had a chance. A number of energetic persons peeled back to see if Horton could hang on.

"The pressure was condensing beads of perspiration about Horton Smith's blond bean as the tall boy came down the stretch," Keeler wrote. Smith knew he had a one-stroke lead and knew of Bobby's misadventures on seventeen, so he played the hole on the installment plan and way to the right. Even his third shot, a pitch, stayed far to starboard, stopping thirty feet from the hole. But now the best putter in the world was operating in his comfort zone, and he two-putted without incident. After playing the par-four eighteenth with similar caution, including another two-putt from ten yards, Horton Smith had won by one.

"I was glad to win and to finish ahead of Bobby Jones," he said as he accepted his check for $1,000. "I had some good breaks near the finish, which about balanced off some rather tough ones earlier."

Horton's comments were the essence of bland, but his roommate's remarks were a strange brew. "I did much better than I expected," Jones said—a curious sentiment, since at this stage of his brilliant career, Bobby expected to win and was favored to win any stroke-play tournament he entered. "I hesitated to come over because I had been playing so wretchedly"—but he'd shot 63-70-70 his last three rounds at East Lake, a long difficult course—"that I was afraid of making a holy show of myself." This last thought rings true, even though it also makes no sense. A number of friends and observers have pointed out the abject fear Jones had of making a fool of himself. Before closing with thanks and praise for the weather, the condition of the course, and the people of Savannah, Jones said something else that sounded sporting but wasn't exactly accurate: "Horton played much steadier golf than I and certainly deserved to win." Well, no. Horton deserved to win, but he won not from steadiness but from amazingly good putting.

They gave Bobby a trophy and a fancy Parker shotgun, double-barrel, twelve-gauge. After the ceremony, he gave it back; they took his measurements for an even fancier custom-made Parker and sent it to him later. Mr. and Mrs. Fred Howden entertained Mr. Jones with a buffet supper in their home. Later that evening, the Hotel DeSoto hosted a big dinner dance, held in honor of the visiting golfers. It was a "brilliant climax" to the tournament, the *Morning News* reported, and the social highlight of the week. But Jones didn't go; after dinner, he took the train back to Atlanta.

That evening and the next day, the pros rolled south to Orlando for the next tournament. Bobby would meet them again in a month, in Augusta, for the last professional event of the winter tour. After that, the courses would be opening up north. The pros had to get to work. Bobby did, too.

Tuesday, February 25
Savannah

On the editorial page of the *Savannah Press* was the following item:

THANKS TO BOBBY

Mr. Jones's presence added that indefinable something to the cause of our recent success. It takes considerably more than an ordinary tournament to bring more than five thousand Savannahians to the sunny links for three afternoons on a stretch. . . .

With the newly planted crepe myrtle bush out of his way he would have won the tournament hands down. But, as it turned out, one tree with its spreading antlers was enough to make a score of seven points on the second hole of the second day's play. . . .

There is no other golfer on the records of the game whose presence in the finals is at least a regular fixture like that of the rotund little wielder of the niblick from the ranks of the capital's barristers.

Jones in May at the year's first major,
the British Amateur at St. Andrews.

2

Cherokee 3486

"In retrospect, there is an air of foreboding about the . . . late 1920s, a feeling that everyone of consequence is wearing tennis whites, gabbling manically, and emptying magnums of Dom Perignon in a Rolls-Royce racing headlong toward the edge of a towering precipice."

— *William Manchester, The Last Lion*

On a hot June afternoon near New York City, with the 1929 U.S. Open in the pocket of his plus fours, Bobby Jones's concentration and will vanished. After a couple of goofy triple bogeys, he found himself having to hole a twelve-foot putt with a big left-to-right break on the icy eighteenth green at Winged Foot—to break 80 and to tie Al Espinosa for first. Then Jones suddenly remembered who he was. In breathless silence, he caressed the ball into the hole—"the greatest putt ever made," Grantland Rice wrote—and shot 72-69 in the playoff the next day, beating poor Al E. by twenty-three. Equilibrium had been restored. A happy tune played on the newsreel replay of Bobby's ninth major victory.

Three months later, the new U.S. Open champion shot 67, a course record, in a practice round for the U.S. Amateur at Pebble Beach. Then he shot 70-75 in the qualifier, tying the heretofore unknown Eugene V. Homans for medalist. But the next morning, Jones crashed like a bird flying into a window; his first-round loss to Johnny Goodman was the shocker of the year in sports. The peasant who had beaten the king was the fifth of ten children, a short, almost troll-like young man with dense blond hair swept straight back, a high school dropout, and nearly penniless. Completing the contrast to Jones, Goodman had traveled to California from his native Omaha in a slat-sided cattle car. He couldn't even afford that manure-scented transportation; his ticket had been a gift. After beating Jones, Johnny immediately lost his next match.

About this time, England's Chancellor of the Exchequer arrived in northern California. What a shame that Jones and Winston Churchill did not meet. Churchill, then age fifty-five, had for a month been on an east-to-west tour of Canada, delivering speeches, cutting ribbons, and absorbing the awesome beauty of the Canadian Rockies from Charles Schwab's private railroad car. At last, Churchill and his son, Randolph, reached Victoria, British Columbia, their last stop before a worrisome border crossing. "We are now on the ship bound to Seattle, American soil and Prohibition," Randolph wrote in his diary. "But we are well-equipped. My big flask is full of whisky and the little one contains brandy. I have reserves of both in medicine bottles. It is almost certain that we shall have no trouble. If we do, Papa pays the fine and I get the publicity." But Winston was packing, too: He had decanted a case of brandy into an innocent-looking set of stone hot-water bottles.

(American drinkers had long since accommodated themselves to Prohibition, of course. Enforcement of the unpopular law had always been hit-and-miss, and now, a few years before Repeal, it was mostly miss. Georgians had ten more years of practice with prohibition than most of the rest of the country, having passed a severe dry law in 1907. Bobby's constant companion Keeler, who would die of cirrhosis in 1950, didn't leave home without several bottles of corn whiskey sloshing softly in his luggage.)

Jones and Churchill might have discussed great books, although Bobby liked humorous fiction (his favorite author was Henry Fielding, especially his *Joseph Andrews* and *Tom Jones*), and Winston read history when he wasn't writing it or making it. In the field of art, Bobby was getting into opera and harbored a wish to learn to play the piano; Winston painted. As for sport, Winston had been a keen player of another upper-crusty club-and-ball game, polo. Hearing them discuss the failure of the social experiment that prevented them from drinking openly might have been interesting, but they would not have had much common ground politically; the Englishman was far too liberal for the American. Ultimately, they didn't meet because Churchill didn't give a fig about golf or golfers. He had tried to get into the game again and again, but golf gave him no satisfaction. "It's like chasing a quinine pill around a cow pasture," he said. Churchill and Jones remained two very notable ships passing in the California night.

Bobby's ship actually stood quite still. A poorer sport might have departed in a huff after an embarrassing loss to a guy off a cattle car, but Jones stuck around and remained visible. Besides, he'd paid for his room at the Del Monte Hotel for the entire week, and the tedious train trip back to Atlanta was easy to put off. And no one with an ounce of poetry in his soul can quickly turn his back on the Monterey Peninsula. So Bobby played Cypress Point and had dinner with its designer, Dr. Alister MacKenzie, and refereed a couple of matches. On most of the thirty-nine holes of the Francis Ouimet–versus–Lawson Little contest, as Jones walked onto the green to declare which player was away, the gallery gave him a rousing ovation. Bobby's ears got very red at this, Keeler reported, and he ducked back into the gallery as quickly as he could. But there was no relief there. Exposing himself to hundreds of backslappers without the protection of his clubs or his caddie or gallery guards, Jones discovered for the umpteenth time that his presence made people lose their dignity and forget their manners. He turned people into mouth-breathing, well-meaning, over-familiar louts.

"Uncle Rob *hated* that, the autograph seekers," recalls Bobby's much younger cousin, Foster Clayton, now seventy-five. "I remember once at an exhibition, some of my girlfriends were just *begging* me to go up and get him to sign something for them. Finally I went up to him. 'I don't know why you want an autograph now when you can come over any time and get one,' he said. But he said it with a smile, and he did give my girlfriends his autograph."

Churchill also tarried in California. After inspecting the redwoods, he spent four days with William Randolph Hearst in the wretched excess of his castle, San Simeon. In addition to his duties with the English government, Churchill wrote prolifically on politics and history, and the original media mogul wanted Winston's byline to class up his vast chain of mostly trashy newspapers. Hearst offered £40,000 for twenty-two articles. Churchill accepted. He was putting every spare pound and pence in the U.S. stock market. Like thousands of others, he'd gotten used to extremely gratifying gains in his portfolio.

Before the Churchills headed for Chicago and New York City, they met the stars in Hollywood. Charlie Chaplin told Winston at a party that after his next movie, *City Lights*, he intended to make a film in which he'd portray Jesus Christ. After a pause to puff on his cigar, Churchill asked, "Have you cleared the rights?"

By then golf's Christ figure and his main disciple had begun the long journey back to Atlanta. Jones had refereed the final between Harrison "Jimmy" Johnston and George Voigt—Johnston won in thirty-eight holes—and the next morning got on the Del Monte Special. When the train chugged out of the station in Monterey, the winter of Bobby's discontent began. Soothing scenery rolled past for a few minutes as they rumbled north to San Francisco—Fisherman's Wharf, the boats on the bay, Pacific vistas—but then the train turned inland, and Bobby and O.B. had fewer distractions from the failure of the week. His quick loss had made Jones feel foolish, an emotion he feared the way some people fear snakes. And the crowds of people calling him Bobby. How he despised the childish-sounding diminutive of Robert! Anyone who really knew him called him Bob; within his large extended family he was known as Rob or some variation such as Little Rob or Uncle Rob. Here was the perfect illustration that fame was a deal with the devil: You could literally lose your name.

After long days on the rails through the arid and endless Southwest, Jones stepped out of the train in Atlanta. It was raining. At last he hugged his wife and children and slept in his own bed. His beautifully proportioned two-story red brick Georgian on three quiet acres on Northside Drive fit into its setting like a hand in a glove. It had a gray slate roof, a two-bedroom servants wing, three-inch-thick exterior doors, and the brooding serenity of mansion districts everywhere. Magnolias and pines framed the house and grounds. The back porch faced the dark woods and quiet Tuxedo Road—the perfect place for cocktails. Bob Woodruff lived less than half a mile away in a white house bigger than the White House. Despite this house, Jones was not wealthy. But he had access to wealth, which can be just as good.

He resumed his routines, with recreation the key. Wednesdays and weekends meant golf at East Lake, at least until it got cold or Tech had a home football game (he had season tickets in the west stands). The Crackers season had ended; he attended games when he could, more as a fan than as an executive with the minor-league baseball team. Christmas Eve meant a drive up to Canton to sit with his many uncles, aunts, and cousins at his grandfather's mammoth dinner table. During that unusually cold and wet winter of '29 to '30, with the then-unnamed Grand Slam in mind, Bobby played the strange hybrid indoor tennis game on the stage of the Atlanta Theatre.

At work in his office in the Atlanta Trust Company Building at 31 Broad Street, he kibitzed with Samuel Evins, Jerome Moore, Clem Powers, and the other lawyers; wrote his column; and handled what must have been a modest caseload. The newest partner at Jones, Evins, Powers, and Jones often ate lunch with the senior partner, his father, at the nearby downtown branch of the Atlanta Athletic Club. When the office coffeepot was empty, Bobby liked to walk down one floor to the regional sales office of Swift and Company for a cup and a chat. At least once he had his picture taken with the child of one of the Swift employees on his knee.

Jones, Evins was a respected firm but not the best in town. "They were very casual," recalls an attorney from another firm. "The kind of place where you could show up late and play golf once or twice a week."

Two of Jones, Evins's key clients were Atlanta-based Coca-Cola and Canton Textile Mill. Big Bob had been preparing and evaluating contracts since 1907 for what Southerners call Co-Cola, and that relationship looked unlikely to change. Both the company's founding family, the Candlers, and the new regime, led by Robert Woodruff, liked Big Bob and adored the positive attention his son had brought to Atlanta and the South.

The connection to Canton Textile Mill was made of blood. The company's founding father had been Big Bob's frowning father, Robert Tyre Jones, Sr. Bobby Jones's grandfather, R.T., was a towering figure in Cherokee County and in the family; it's not going too far to say he was the patriarch of both. An enormously successful man, he believed in hard work and hellfire and in populating Canton, Georgia, with Joneses. He had nine children with his first wife, Susie Walker, who appears to have died from an overdose of morphine in the aftermath of her final delivery. Two years and a day after Susie Walker's death, when he was fifty-one, R.T. married a twenty-five-year-old widow named Lilly Coggins Cross, with whom he had four more children.

R.T. was the mayor of Canton, a councilman, the founder of the town's biggest businesses, and a deacon in the Baptist church for fifty-six years. They named the public library after him. Canton First Baptist named its Bible study class for him. He owned cotton fields; the gin, which combed the seeds out of the bolls; the mill, where they wove the ginned cotton into thread and dyed it with indigo to make denim; and the houses where his mill workers lived. He cofounded the bank. His company furnished the white marble on the bank, on the new (in 1925) courthouse, and for the accents on the Baptist church. His employees supplied themselves with everything from cornflakes to hardware to hats at Jones Mercantile, the large and amazingly complete general store. R.T. wore a clerical collar almost every day of his life. Although he did not approve of bridge or poker—and of course he did not drink—he played the card game Rook every night except Sunday.

"He was a very austere figure," recalls Foster Clayton. "When I was a little girl, I remember being told so often to *behave* when we went up to Canton for a visit, that when we walked up onto the porch of this marvelous big old Victorian where he and Grandmother lived, I expected him to hit me—and was so amazed when he hugged me."

R.T.'s decision not to give his oldest son his name is hard to explain. That there were eventually three other Robert Tyre Joneses indicates the value the clan placed in the name. There was Bobby, the famous one; Big Bob's little brother, Albert, produced a second; and in a final bizarre twist, in 1907 R.T. named his thirteenth and last child after himself. In other words, Bobby had the same name exactly as his grandfather and a first cousin and an uncle but not as his father, even though he referred to himself as a Junior. "You'll go absolutely crazy with the names in this family," laughs another of Bobby's cousins, Clayton Reid.

All the sons of R.T. but two stuck around Canton to become the presidents and underbosses of the myriad family companies. Bobby's Uncle Louis succeeded R.T. as the president of the mill; Uncle Paul, a genius with numbers, ran Jones Mercantile and, for a time, the bank; Uncle Albert became involved with Georgia Marble Finishing Works; last-born Uncle Robert (who signed his name R. Tyre Jones and was known in the family as Tyre) had a Chevrolet dealership and a gas station. Uncle Rube ran a Ford dealership. "That Rube kind of skipped around in all the businesses," recalls Louis Lindley Jones Jr., ninety-one, another of Bobby's cousins. "Everybody liked him. Kind of a hale-fellow-well-met. Did a lot of huntin' and fishin'. He sold that Ford dealership after a while."

R.T. had a great but contradictory impact on his oldest son, who wanted his name but didn't want his life. Big Bob (who was only about five feet seven) rebelled against the Southern Baptist strictness at home—and, who knows, maybe against his father's height; R.T. was almost a foot taller than his oldest son. Robert Purmedus raised a little hell, drank corn liquor distilled in the hills of Cherokee County with his friends (who called him Colonel, for no particular reason), and spent countless hours playing baseball, a game R.T. thought an utter waste of time. Strong and beautifully coordinated, Not-So-Big Bob played first base and outfield well enough for the University of Georgia that the Brooklyn Superbas of the National League offered him a contract. "I think that was when my grandfather said to him, 'I didn't raise you to be a ball player, I raised you to be a lawyer,' " says cousin Louis. So Robert Purmedus finished his degree at the University of Georgia, Class of 1897; took as his wife the tiny, birdlike Clara; and returned to Canton to be the family's consigliere. But when Bobby's older brother, William, was born and quickly died, Clara blamed the tragedy on Canton's unsophisticated medical facilities. She would never birth another baby in such a backwater. So Clara and Robert P. moved to Atlanta, or, in Louis's telling phrase, "Uncle Rob left Granddad."

Everything in Bobby's upbringing was a reaction to—and the opposite of—how his remote, pious, and controlling grandfather raised his father.

The briefly parallel lives of Churchill and Jones had one final act. As Bobby went about his business in Atlanta, Winston concluded his in New York. One morning in late October, Churchill heard shouts in the street below his apartment in the Savoy-Plaza. He looked out his window and saw that a man had just thrown himself down from fifteen stories and was smashed to pieces. It was the day after Black Tuesday, the day the stock market crashed. Thirty to forty billion dollars had vanished in the blink of an eye.

Churchill was among the thousands who lost everything. But what happened to the wealth of the Jones family? Not that much. "The Jones businesses did very, very well during the Depression," remarks Foster Clayton. In the slowly growing crisis, shrewd R.T. and his equally astute sons made their self-interest coincide with that of their employees. Recognizing that different economies present different opportunities, Jones Mercantile got into barter. For example, farmers who were loaned fertilizer in the spring paid off in cotton in the fall. Amazingly, the mill laid no one off, but paid its workers in scrip, good only at Jones Mercantile, one business subsidizing the other. It all looked and felt like benevolence and maybe it was: R.T. obviously cared about doing right. He often remarked to the family and the family's customers that "we'll all succeed together, or we'll all go down together."

They succeeded together. Although the mill went to one shift and denim inventory grew to nine million yards, people still bought clothes. Denim overalls were the cheap and durable choice, and the Canton Textile Mill was for a time the largest producer of denim in the country and the only supplier to blue-jean manufacturer H. D. Lee. One of the brothers observed that he preferred life during recession, that it was the best economy of all if you had money. Everything was so cheap.

The markets rallied nervously as the new decade began. "The spring of 1930 marks the end of a period of grave concern," said Julius H. Barnes, a spokesman for President Herbert Hoover. "American business is steadily coming back to a normal level of prosperity." Was he whistling past the graveyard? Maybe not—by the end of March, stocks had gained back about half of what they'd lost on that disastrous day in October. The newspapers still were not often using the word *Depression* to describe the new state of the economy. They didn't yet know how permanent and profound the changes were.

There was still time for play.

Saturday, March 22, 1930
Druid Hills Golf Club, Atlanta

The tiny white building smelled of shellac and leather. The door opened and the U.S. Open champion walked in with three golf clubs under his arm.

"Well, hello, Mr. Jones," said a flat-nosed man in a white shirt and dark tie, his accent a unique blend of Somerset, England, and colonial East Africa.

The man's body and flat boxer's nose made him look like Carmen Basillio, a middleweight from the 1950s. All his features were big—ears, mouth, chin, and wide-set eyes.

"Hello, Harry. I'm pleased to see you." Bobby was warm but somewhat formal, even with friends, even in this place where he had a history. As a thirteen-year-old boy, he had walked to the course from the Jones family house on Lullwater Road and won the club championship, his first real tournament victory. And now Little Bob had become Bobby Jones, a wonderful combination of world celebrity and perfect gentleman.

With a practiced eye, Jones examined the racks of wooden-shafted clubs and club components Harry had for sale. He looked particularly at the long irons, a few of which he compared to the clubs from his own set he'd come in with. Five days after his twenty-eighth birthday, he was going to give himself a present.

Henry Robert Stephens, always called Harry, had become Bobby's pro. Jones had long since outgrown Stewart Maiden, the Scot at East Lake whose swing he'd copied as a little boy. Bobby's insight on method and strategy exceeded Maiden's and possibly that of anyone else on earth; he didn't need a lesson and, indeed, he didn't get them. With time and incentive to think about the game—what with his column and the Grand Slam—Jones discerned the one area that could improve his performance most quickly. Equipment, he knew, was the last frontier. And Harry Stephens was the best club maker around.

Stephens had come to Atlanta in January 1922, six months after the stabbing murder of Druid Hills's English professional Douglas Edgar. "There were rumours which always follow the violent death of a 'ladies man,'" Edgar's grandson wrote in 1982 when asked to speculate about the never-solved homicide. "This small, handsome, moody man was popular with both men and women. Perhaps too popular with the women." Naturally, everyone who knew him was grieved, including Jones, who had played a lot of golf with Edgar. Keeler mourned by suspending his column for a week.

Although good Americans were available, many clubs appreciated the prestige of certain accents, so the search committee looked again to England. Into this unsettled situation arrived Charlie Mayo and his assistant, Stephens. Mayo quit after one month. Stephens inherited the job. A worldly, likeable man, Stephens thought as deeply about golf and its equipment as Jones did. He'd left Somerset as a young man to help build the first golf club in Africa, near Nairobi, and was its pro; he served three years with the East Africa Mounted Rifles during World War I; he'd managed an African coffee plantation; he'd had malaria.

A disoriented lady member of the club asked the wife of the new pro where her children had been born.

"Africa."

"Africa? Well, are they Negroes?"

Mrs. Stephens considered the surprising question while giving the lady a long look. "Madam," she said, according to Druid Hills legend, "if a cat has kittens in the oven, they don't come out as biscuits."

The latest thing in the high-tech golf revolution in 1930—not counting steel shafts—was the matched set, an entire ensemble with similar or complementary weights, lengths, lies, and feels. Bobby wasn't ready. "I confess that I have never owned a set of so-called matched clubs," he wrote in a particularly good essay published on May 3. "Like all the rest of the conservatives, I have chosen to place my faith in the few survivors among the many clubs I have bought and tried and thrown away. . . . Old timers, particularly, like to praise and use the motley assembly, accumulated over years of painful choosing. They like the worn look of most of them, regarding it as evidence of long and honorable service to the game." Early-twentieth-century clubs had so much personality that they had names, not numbers: spoon, brassie, blaster, bulger, baffy, jigger, cleek. Some golfers even christened their sticks with affectionate private nicknames, as lovers do. Jones, for example, had a putter he called Jane and a driver named Jeanie. Everything was handmade. Club making was about three parts art to one part science.

Woods were hard to hit because bulge and roll—the slight top-to-bottom and side-to-side bulging of the face, a geometry that straightens off-center hits—was dimly understood, if at all. Most wood faces were as flat as a sheet of plywood. And torque! A driver head could twist as much as a quarter of a turn during a hard swing, so it was very dangerous to swing hard and vital to swing smoothly. Irons could be impossible, too; few makers or players appreciated the elementary value of the flange. The bit of metal on the bottom of an iron in 1930 was often so thin that it was sharp. You could shave with a typical niblick or slice ham with your mashie. Therefore you could hit the ball atrociously fat with any iron. In other words, if you hit the ground before you hit the ball, the club stayed in the earth and your shot went nowhere.

But times were changing. A numbering system tied to lofts was an idea that made too much sense to ignore, and it was working its way into the vernacular. A few aficionados like Jones realized what a good idea it was to weigh their clubs; several real mavens grasped the more elusive concept of swing weight—or swinging weight, as Bobby called it—which is not a measure in ounces or pounds but a ratio of the weight of the grip end to the clubhead. But more than anything a golf club is a stick, and the appeal of a shaft made of steel was obvious. But Bobby wasn't ready for that step either.

"Before the tournament in Augusta, I had in my bag, the following irons, besides my putter," Jones wrote in his column of May 3. "Numbers one, two and four, a mashie iron (also about a four-iron in loft), mashie (five-iron), spade (six-iron), mashie niblick (seven), and niblick (nine). I had no liking for the one, two, and spade, and had been utterly unable to find a three which attracted me even enough to buy it. In the others I had unlimited confidence and always played well with them.

"Before leaving for Augusta I found a good-looking number one head at Harry Stephens's shop at Druid Hills . . . I also unearthed a two and three which almost looked like golf clubs."

Jones listed nine irons, a putter, and four woods totaled fourteen, which is the modern limit. The rules then put no ceiling on quantity, however, so some players, Jones included, went into battle with twenty or more.

Now Bobby looked for a few good shafts. A visual inspection first: Tight grain patterns were good and "ring hickories" were better; the dark lines encircling such a shaft indicated a strong stick with good whip. The sophisticated shaft-shopper would brace one end of the stick into the ground or between the boards on the floor, then twang it like a string on a banjo, looking for frequency and amplitude resembling the vibe on a favorite club. Jones strummed, studied the results, and found three shafts he liked. Stephens re-shafted the two and three and built the one-iron from scratch. He spiraled a strip of leather down each shaft for a grip and tapped a tack into the bottom to hold it on. He sanded the shafts then buffed the heads of the new clubs until the weight was perfect. . . . But you can't help wondering if during this long process Harry thought or said, "Mr. Jones, this is a waste of time. Wooden sticks are on the way out—let's try something new."

In a small irony of golf history, the man who built the flammable clubs of the best player in the world was helping the world turn to steel. One day in the late twenties, the pro with the pugilist's mug had had a eureka moment in his kitchen. He immediately sketched his idea on paper and sent it to the American Fork and Hoe Company of Geneva, Ohio, a manufacturer of implements, fishing rods, and rudimentary steel shafts for golf clubs. The forerunner company to True Temper liked Harry Stephens's design, which was a refinement of step tapering, a recently invented process that gave a steel shaft a bit of engineered flexibility. American Fork and Hoe sent Harry royalty checks for years.

The clubs Harry made for Bobby were about to conquer the world. And they were already obsolete.

Wednesday, March 26
On the Radio

"I remember the first time I saw him," Stewart Maiden said to Grantland Rice, his interviewer on the *Coca-Cola Radio Hour*. "He was a boy about six or seven with a head much too big for his body. I said at the time if he ever grew to his head he'd be some man."

People who knew the old pro at East Lake were delighted to hear him on the air—not only for the heather and haggis in his thick Scottish brogue but for the unusual volume of words. The notoriously reticent Maiden was now living in New York, where he had a golf school.

Rice mentioned something Bobby often talked about, his dislike of and difficulty with eighteen-hole matches. Jones thought eighteen was not enough holes to make a fair test. Random chance and luck too often trumped superior skill in such a short haul, Bobby said.

"He should have no trouble with any man," Maiden said, "whether the match is one hole or three holes or nine holes or eighteen holes, and I hope he's listening in."

He was. After the show, an Atlanta newspaper reporter dialed Cherokee 3486, Jones's home number, to ask for his reaction. "He [Maiden] knew I was listening," Bobby said with a laugh. "He meant to give me a lecture."

Thursday, March 27, Noon
Motoring to Augusta

"Are we ready, Chick?"

"Ready, Bob."

"O.B.?"

"Let's go, Rubber Tyre."

The pre-launch conversation can only be imagined, but how Jones drove the car requires no guesswork. He turned the key, set the spark by manipulating a lever on the right side of the steering column, then moved another lever on the left, which set the throttle. He pushed in and pulled out the choke knob on the dash. Then he stepped on the starter, which was located high on the floorboard above the accelerator pedal. As the engine came to life, he adjusted the spark and throttle again, checked the mirrors, and found first gear. Cars were called motors in 1930, and the act of traveling in one was "motoring." Not for the first or last time, Bobby was motoring from Atlanta to Augusta. Low-key Chick Ridley and the ubiquitous Keela would be his fellow travelers.

Bobby's second tournament of the year would be his last crack at the pros for a while. In about three weeks, he and Mrs. Jones would take a train to New York and rendezvous with USGA officials and the Walker Cup team, of which he was the captain and the number one player. Then Mary, Bobby, and his friends—they were all his friends—would board the *Mauretania,* an ocean liner a bare notch below the late great *Titanic* in terms of size and luxury. After the five-day crossing, if no icebergs intervened, they'd play the U.S.–versus–England amateur team match, a relatively unimportant competition. Then Bobby's undeclared quest for the Slam would begin. The British Amateur was the first recognized major on the calendar, and it was the only one he'd never won. The Amateur was being held this year at the Old Course at St. Andrews, Bobby's favorite piece of golf ground. He'd been thinking about this trip and its implications for months, if not years.

But first, to Augusta. Long roads never traced a straight line in the days before interstates, and the route east from Atlanta meandered like a river to the sea: to Stone Mountain, to Lithonia, down to Conyers, to Covington, up to Social Circle, to Greensboro, then Warrenton, Thomson, and finally into Augusta. A more northern route via Athens ran pretty straight for the first half of the journey, but then you were stuck with what the highway department called "improved" roads versus paved ones. You navigated by looking at the numbers, colors, and logos painted on telephone poles. The Bee Line Highway, for example, was Highway 4, its symbol was a B over an H, like a fraction, and its colors were black on yellow with black bands. Kind of like a yellow jacket. The Old Spanish Trail was O, S, and T stacked vertically; the number 12; and red, white, and yellow paint. There was the Dixie Overland and the Woodpecker Route. The Dixie Highway (U.S. 41), the precursor to I-75, ran north and south through Atlanta.

The drive required exactly 167 miles (Keeler kept a log), five hours, a stop in Madison to eat, and at least one fill-up with Pan-Am or Crown or Gulf gasoline. Conversation and cigarette smoke filled the car's interior. Jones and Ridley took turns driving. Pollen from pines floated invisibly in the air before settling in a pale yellow film on windows and windshields. Flashes of pink, white, and red stood out in the dark green woods by the side of the road. About halfway to Augusta, the earth grew more buxom and interesting. Georgia in the spring was as pretty as a young girl.

Arriving in Augusta late in the chilly overcast, the travelers turned into the hotel grounds at the crest of a hill on Walton Way. They parked the car under the porte cochere and walked into the echoing marble lobby of a huge, white layer cake of a building. Everything about the Bon Air–Vanderbilt Hotel—the marble, the white stucco exterior, its hilltop setting, the pool out front—was designed to catch a breeze and cool its guests. The upper floors had a good view of downtown and the Savannah River.

Jones liked Augusta. He'd visited the city a number of times over the years, often with Big Bob, invariably for winter golf with friends who came down on the train from the Northeast. Augusta was handy geographically both for the New Yorkers and for the group from Atlanta. Moreover, the owner of the Bon Air Hotel liked Bobby—who didn't?—and was warm and welcoming to everyone in his party. The name of Augusta's minor-league baseball team, the Tourists, hinted at one of the underpinnings of the local economy.

After dinner and drinks and a good night's sleep, Bobby and Chick would have three full days to practice for the Southeastern Open. But Bobby didn't rest easily.

Friday, March 28
Augusta

Since his arrival in the United States in January, sportswriters and readers had been fascinated by 285 pounds of pasta named Primo Carnera. The supersized heavyweight boxer from Italy dominated the headlines as he went through the B-list of American contenders like Sherman through the South.

After one month and three quick knockouts, the "Vast Venetian" had won a startling amount, $47,070. Primo likes girls, the papers reported, and heavy girls especially like him, and he likes to eat. After another month, the writers started treating him a little less playfully. Carnera has had it too easy, they wrote after his opponent of March 27, one George Trafton, allowed himself to be "knocked out" so unconvincingly in the first round of a fight in Kansas City that he was suspended by the Missouri Boxing Commission. Who would step up and give the "Immense Italian" a real fight?

Primomania and the calendar kept golf and baseball down the list as sports topics. But some of the writers who were returning to their home bases in the north after covering baseball spring training in Florida got off the train in Augusta and gave this minor tournament major play. The organizers of the first-ever Southeastern Open supplied a good hook, something even better than Bobby Jones versus the pros: Bobby Jones versus one particular pro, Horton Smith. Bobby's conqueror at Savannah had not planned to play in Augusta because he had to be in Boston for an exhibition on April 2 and the Southeastern Open ended on April 1. Smith sent Bobby a telegram expressing his regret that they would not get to renew their acquaintance and their rivalry in Augusta. There simply wasn't time. Unless . . .

The go-getters from Augusta went to see Smith in Asheville, North Carolina, to present him with a crazy but workable solution: first, an appearance fee, and second, an airplane. He could *fly* after his final round in their tournament. Not all the way to Boston—the plan was to drop him off in Washington, D.C., a four-hour flight, and have him take the train the rest of the way. Smith agreed and signed an entry form. People buzzed about the very idea all week. *Flying!* Only three years after Lindbergh's solo from New York to Paris, getting in a plane still seemed more theatrical than practical.

The *Atlanta Constitution* headlined "Bob Jones–Smith Duel Seen in Augusta Meet" above a story by Dillon L. Graham of the Associated Press:

> The second spectacular duel of the season between Bobby Jones, national open golf champion, and young Horton Smith, who now bills

himself from Cragstown, New York, is in prospect for the Southeastern Open tournament at Augusta, Georgia, March 31 and April 1 . . .

The trail that leads to the champions share of the $5000 pot at Augusta consists of 36 holes over the hill course at the Country Club where 72 is par for 6522 yards and 36 holes over the rollicking, difficult Forrest Hills–Ricker golf course. Par for this golfing test, stretched over 6600 yards, is 71.

The spectacular duel suffered a setback when Jones heard a click in his neck when he woke. It hurt. Was it stress or a pull or a bit of bursitis surfacing on the drizzly morning? Perhaps something more insidious was at work. No one would ever guess it, but this athlete with ballet in his swing had a wheelchair in his future.

At any rate, Jones put up an umbrella and played. But only one round at the Augusta Country Club, not two, and with a painful-looking three-quarter swing. He shot 76 in the wet, 47-degree day. Fielding Wallace, the president of Augusta Country Club, and Alfred S. Bourne, its most generous member, joined Jones and Ridley. A doctor massaged and shone a heat lamp on Bobby's sore neck and shoulder afterward.

Saturday, March 29

Jones rested in the morning. If he picked up a paper and read the sports page, there was a good chance he would have seen his own column. "I have never regarded seriously the tendency of some people to endow certain golfers with superhuman powers," he wrote, referring in all likelihood to himself and to his adoring press. "I have heard it said of them that they are able to pull off whatever is necessary to win. Such an idea is absurd, for if these men were capable of playing golf as they willed, they would never place themselves in a position where they had to beat par to win."

In another section of the same installment of "Bobby Jones Says," the

writer seemed to be musing on his narrow loss to Horton Smith in Savannah. "The difference between a winner and the near-winner is the ability
on the part of the successful contestant to be ever on the look out against
himself," Jones wrote. "Never too certain of what the result may be, he never
plays a shot carelessly or with overconfidence." Words Jones would choke
on in two days.

The sun came out. After noon, Bobby played again at the Hill Course at
the Augusta Country Club. ACC occupied a pleasant hillside lined with pines
and dotted here and there with ornamentals like azaleas, which blossomed a
little more each day. After playing the eighth, a downhill ski slope of a par
five, Jones could look across a muddy, rock-strewn creek to the property next
door. There was nothing random about the spring color there. Rows and
rows of flowering trees and shrubs marched up and down the hilly acres of
the Fruitlands Nursery.

At almost 6,600 yards, Augusta Country Club course was long yet subtle,
very good work by a very good designer, Donald Ross. The greens were unbelievable. Not just the mysterious twists and turns—Ross thought greens
could be hazards in themselves—but their condition. They were so hard
and fast that they were shiny. They didn't seem to have absorbed any of the
recent rain.

The pros started to arrive that afternoon from the previous tournament,
the North and South at Pinehurst, North Carolina, most notably Paul
Runyan, the slight, extremely short hitting pro who had won. Several of the
same top guns who did not play in Savannah did not enter in Augusta: Hagen
was showing Australia how to play golf and drink champagne, Leo Diegel
was on an exhibition tour in Mexico, and Wild Bill Mehlhorn simply chose
not to play. But Sarazen pulled into the parking lot, and Horton Smith was
on his way.

Although it still hurt a little to swing, Bobby pronounced himself cured
from what he called a crick in his neck. His stroke regained its usual fullness,
but his putting looked a bit off. He shot 74. The newspapers covered his
practice round hole by hole on the front page and no one else's.

Sunday, March 30

Charlotte Cobb wanted a divorce.

She was a native Augustan, small and pretty, and tireless with the maintenance of the two kids and the family home at 2233 Williams Street, not far from Augusta Country Club. Her husband had been a Tourist but had gone on to much bigger things with the Detroit Tigers. "He plays baseball like it was the goddamn Civil War," one of his contemporaries said, a perfect metaphor because Ty Cobb believed that with a few more cannons and troops, the South and what it stood for would have won. He lived his life like a resentful soldier no one would ever defeat again, a screw-you attitude that made him hard to live with. But it wasn't only that. He drank. The greatest baseball player of all time often refreshed himself with a quart of milk mixed with a quart of scotch. And he was *never* home. Bird dogs and shotguns seemed to mean more to him than his own family. And now, since his retirement in 1928, he had another reason to go away: golf.

No game could have suited him less. Cobb had become infamous for fighting with teammates, fans, and the opposition and for filing the metal spikes on his shoes until he could fillet a fish with them—the better to injure any infielder who got in his way when he was stealing a base or stretching a single into a double. But golf didn't allow you to spike your opponent, and you had to play your foul balls. As great an athlete as he was, Ty just couldn't get the hang of golf. But it was in his character to get in touch with the greatest golfer and study him like a lab rat to divine the reasons for his success. Bobby Jones would never be able to help him much.

Ty and Bobby had lots of the same people in common, of course—Grantland Rice, for instance—but their key mutual friend was Bob Woodruff. "Cobb is now one of the richest retired athletes," read a snippet in *Time* magazine. "His fortune consists mostly of fat Coca-Cola holdings which he bought long ago on advice from his hunting crony, Coca-Cola's president Bob Woodruff." One year when Ty failed to return his form to reelect Woodruff, the Boss wrote to his strange friend "because I note today that your proxy for 4000 shares of stock standing in your name hasn't been received, and I'm getting pretty sensitive about that. You should be ashamed of yourself." Cobb would eventually accumulate 20,000 shares of $85 Coke stock and own the bottling franchise in Twin Falls, Idaho.

But where was he on this Sunday afternoon, Charlotte Cobb wanted to know. Probably watching Bobby Jones. Or playing golf himself. Or drinking with Jones, Keeler, and Rice at the Bon Air. Typical.

Her second and probably her third guesses were correct. Cobb and a partner played a match against Rice and his partner, in amongst the pros and ams warming up at Forrest Hills. Team Ty won.

That morning Jones shot 69, a course record for the new back tees at Forrest Hills, in the company of Sarazen, Ed Dudley, and Espinosa. The pros had found the course's pine-lined fairways and brick-hard greens very hard to handle, shooting 74, 76, and 78, respectively. They led the buzz about Bobby that afternoon and evening. Keeler kept it going in the morning.

Monday, March 31
Augusta Country Club

"Phrase it how you will," Keeler wrote. "It is the Atlanta amateur against the field. They are out to get him, in all courtesy and friendship and perfect sportsmanship. But they are out to get Bobby Jones—the stocky little Atlanta amateur against the world . . . He's in pretty good shape. He had his crick rubbed again last night and baked as well. It didn't bother him in that card of 69."

The organizers gave the people what they wanted. At 10:00 A.M. on the first tee at Augusta Country Club, Smith and Jones shook hands and came out fighting. The third member of their group wasn't really in their class as a golfer, but Alfred S. Bourne was a great guy and richer than God. He was the son of the founder of Singer Sewing Machine Company. He also had a pretty, dark-haired daughter named Barbara who would soon become very interested in Horton Smith.

Jones putts among friends at the Augusta Country Club in the 1930 Southeastern Open. Ty Cobb was one of the spectators studying Bobby's every move.

The Tall Boy had motored into town after exhibitions in Charlotte and Asheville following the tournament in Pinehurst. He hadn't had time for a practice round on this course he'd never seen before. It showed. While Jones hit greens in regulation, Smith missed them. While Bobby kept grazing the hole on ten footers for birdie, Horton made putts of similar length for par. Their match didn't look even, but it was. About two thousand people walked along and waited for the impasse to break. Ty Cobb was among them, watching Jones intently with his unforgettable light blue eyes.

Bobby shot a 72 that looked much better than that, while Horton's 75 could easily have been over 80 if he hadn't putted with his usual brilliance. The wind steadily increased in the afternoon, dehydrating the already arid greens. No one could hold them—except Jones and Johnny Farrell—and no one could putt them except Smith. A lot of very good players blew up in the sunny afternoon, including Sarazen, who shot 82 after his morning 72.

Thirty-six holes is a long enough journey for excellence to assert itself, and Jones's otherworldly striking was finally rewarded. After bogeys on one and two in his P.M. round, he finally made a couple of putts. With three holes to play, he found himself two under par for the day, seven ahead of Smith. After an eagle on fifteen, Bobby looked and felt satisfied as he walked up to the sixteenth tee, an uphill, medium-length par four that would be no more than a drive and a flip the way he was hitting his driver. He felt the wind at his back and may have noticed the wonderful things the slanting six-o'clock sun was doing to the pink dogwood blossoms behind the tee. Who knows what he was thinking? Bobby himself admitted that his mind had gone blank as he hit his tee shot fifty yards out of bounds to the right.

Smith finished par-par-birdie for 148. Jones ended with double bogey-par-par for 144 and the lead by three over Farrell and Tom Kerrigan, and four over Horton.

Cobb was the first one to join the Jones party at the Bon Air for the post-round cocktails. He wanted to know how Bobby hit it so far off the tee on eleven and what the hell happened on sixteen.

Tuesday, April 1
Forrest Hills–Ricker Golf Course, Augusta

Except for Sundays, the *Augusta Chronicle* ran a cartoon on its front page called "Hambone's Meditations." Hambone was drawn with wide white lips, tiny eyes, and a black face. He observed on April 1 that most of the talk about "on employmint been steered up by nachul-bawn loafers!" The next day he recalled that "Policemens had to sorter sub-jue Tom whils' he drunk las' night—he thought they's fixin' to tek him home to the ole 'oman!!"

Hambone may seem inexplicable, but he's not. From 1928 until 1943, for ten minutes, six days a week, a radio play called *Amos 'n' Andy* absolutely gripped the United States. Traffic thinned and dinners went untouched while two white voice actors named Freeman Gosden and Charles Correll parodied country blacks in the city. *Amos 'n' Andy's* lampoon led directly to Hambone. Understanding the murky and complicated provenance of *Amos 'n' Andy*, however, is work for a doctoral thesis.

Those who would accuse Jones of racial insensitivity in future years may have a case, but they should be sensitive to the world he came from.

The committee allowed Smith to start his double round very early so that he could catch his plane—which now, it was announced, would take him all the way to New York. He teed off in sweater weather at 7:45 with Ed Dudley and Billy Burke and played pretty well. He turned in a 73 at about the same time Jones teed off for his first round. After a final 75, which he knew would not be good enough, the Joplin Ghost motored to the airport. The pilot of the cabin plane was persuaded to buzz the golf course. Jones's gallery wasn't hard to find from the air; the pilot dipped a wing, and Horton waved goodbye.

Jones started fast with a 69 that stretched his lead over Smith to eight. Every part of his game was clicking like a new Studebaker. His soaring drives were a thrilling sight, framed as they were between the pines. He could snuff a candle with his mashie niblicks, the club he used from about 90 to 130 yards, having perfected his technique for this shot from watching the Tall Boy. His swing itself was an exciting piece of kinetic art. And his putting was rolled gold. "A masterpiece of machine-like golf," according to *Chronicle* golf writer Ed Danforth. "No need to recount details of that round. One might

Forrest Hills Golf Club

as well count the brush strokes and calculate the grams of paint used by a Whistler."

Did his happy gallery know what it was seeing? Did Bobby know what he was doing? He realized later that the day before and today he had played the best golf *of his life*. It's funny, then, how much attention his weak finish drew.

After Jones shot a four-under-par 32 on the first nine of the last round, his lead lapped the field. "After I had played the first three holes (of the final nine) the question of winning became of no consequence," he wrote with magnificent understatement thirty years later in *Golf Is My Game*. He'd started the final nine 3-3-3, birdie-eagle-birdie. He needed all his fingers and most of his toes to count his lead. At this point he relaxed and allowed a couple of bogeys, but his lead was too big to lose.

Jones came to the tee of the par-three sixteenth still four under par for the round and seventeen ahead of the airborne runner-up, Smith. Two groups were waiting to play the 192-yard hole. Bobby was tired from the mental effort of competition and from having played 105 holes in the last three days. He lay down on the dry green grass and chatted with Rice and Cobb. Rice and Jones were in business together, in a way: The older man edited a magazine called *The American Golfer*, and Bobby wrote for it. They were old friends and always had a lot to talk about. Besides, the tournament was over.

"Every few minutes Ty would urge me to get up, swing a club, do something," Jones recalled, "all of which very good advice I would laugh off and then keep on talking to and listening to Grant." When Bobby got to his feet, he hacked his way to a triple-bogey six—an iron pulled into the trees, a chunk into the bunker, a poor sand shot, three putts.

Cobb went ballistic. "Did you see what that boy did?" Ty had found writer Danforth in the gallery. "He laid down on the ground. Right when he was warm and keyed up. Why do they warm up a horse before they put him over the jumps? Why does a pitcher warm up? . . . The boy should never do that again as long as he lives. If a ball player of mine did something like that in a tight game, I'd fine him."

Even with the groggy triple and a bogey six on the final hole, Jones shot 71. He won by thirteen strokes. Bobby and his posse accepted Cobb's invitation to come to his house for drinks . . .

"Where I got the dressing down of my life," Jones wrote. "It was not Ty's idea just to win, but to win by the most you could. That's what had made him such a great baseball player. He was wrong this time, though. My trouble had not come from a muscular chill, but mental complacency." But after the lecture Cobb told Keeler, "He is the greatest competitive athlete I've ever seen."

A lawyer had beaten most of the best pros in the United States by thirteen, which, without a couple of lapses, might have been twenty. Now he was going to Europe to play a bunch of amateurs no one in Augusta had heard of. Would Jones destroy them with equal facility, or had he peaked too soon?

A little Scottish pro named Robert Cruickshank had an opinion, which he shared with the ubiquitous O.B. "He'll go over to Britain and win the amateur and the open and then he'll come back to America and win the open and the amateur," Wee Bobby said. "There was never another like him and there will never be one again."

Cruickshank put his money where his mouth was. He bet £50 with a bookie in London that Jones would win all four. He got odds of twenty-five to one.

Lanky, amiable Roger Wethered was a brilliant golfer whose only weakness was Jones's main strength.

3

Jones Goes Left

"I tried harder than anyone else and was willing to take more punishment."

—Bobby Jones, *Golf Is My Game*

Bobby Jones began to execute his life plan during his college years, the least examined but most revealing period of his early life. Revealing, that is, of the charming, uncertain, determined man he'd already become.

Jones was just seventeen when he enrolled at the Georgia School of Technology, having finished Technological High School in three years. Despite his youth, he seems to have fit right in on the bigger stage: He joined a fraternity and lived on campus, even though Mom and Dad's house on Lullwater Road in the Druid Hills neighborhood of Atlanta was not far away. He was the best young golfer in the world, which didn't hurt him socially, and he was modest about it. And he had a car. How cool was that in the Class of '22? Extremely.

"Many of us remember him best driving to the campus in his family's old 1919 Dodge sedan," recalled classmate Walter F. Coxe in a story he wrote for a Tech football program. "Reaching West Peachtree and North Avenue he would call out to any walking student, 'Come on, hop on'—until the old Dodge was covered with Tech boys—running boards, back, and even on the hood at times."

Numerous anecdotes reveal a young man as precocious in human interaction as he was with a golf club. For example, a uniformed veteran of World War I watched Jones play in the 1919 Southern Open in Atlanta and met him very briefly after the round. Following his discharge from the army, the young man landed a job with the Associated Press and was assigned to interview the famous Tech student. The reporter walked onto the front porch of the Sigma Alpha Epsilon house, where the interviewee sat on a couch, talking with his fraternity brothers. "I'm Al Laney," the young man began. "You may not remember me . . ." Jones smiled. "Mister Laney," he said, "you're not as forgettable as you may think you are." What a line. The writer and the golfer became friends for life.

Judging by the number of one-, two-, and five-point passes he got in his classes, Jones's pleasing personality must have also helped with his professors. The stark evidence shows that he was not ready for college, at least for this college. He got a 60 in Steam Engine, 61 in Shop Methods, 61 in Machine Drawing, 60 in Gas Engine, 62 in Mechanics of Materials, 61 in Descriptive Geometry Drawing . . . below 60 was an F. The Mechanical Engineering major at Tech was tough, no doubt about it. The course description for ME 69 hints at the difficulty: "Complete analysis of plain slide valve gears, fixed and shifting eccentrics . . . complete blackboard analysis of link motions. Ryder and Gozenbach gears." Jones got a 71 in ME 69.

It's an odd experience to hold a copy of Jones's transcript in one hand and Dick Miller's biography—open to page 132—in the other. "Jones had graduated in the top third of his class at the Georgia School of Technology," Miller wrote in *Triumphant Journey*. "In four years of mathematics he averaged 97; in four years of chemistry, 87 . . . he scored consistently in the high 70s in his major, mechanical engineering." None of which is true.

Except for College Algebra (95) and Plane Analytic Geometry (96), in four years Jones didn't excel in any subject. He got more Ds (nineteen) than Cs (sixteen). His average in all his courses was 74.5, a Gentleman's C. Deduct the points he got for being Bobby Jones, and he might not have managed even that. He was a bright young man, of course, and there are other measures of intellect than college test scores, but nothing is more at odds with the myth of Jones as the pinnacle of brilliance than his actual performance as a student.

Academic rigor, youth, golf, and the fraternity life may explain Jones's grades, but other explanations are possible. For example, he may have gone through the Georgia School of Technology the way he played a tournament round, trying very hard while trying very hard to make it look effortless.

At some point during his four years of Cs, he must have realized that the whole thing was a mistake. He would never be an engineer. About all his degree gave him was the ability to write boringly on the physics of golf. "Spin is produced by that part of the force of impact which is exerted tangential to the surface of the ball," Jones stated in a snorer of a column on May 17, 1930, "as distinguished from that part which penetrates toward the center and propels it on its way."

What force would spin the reluctant young engineer, and where would it spin him? The answer was obvious. From age fourteen, when he played in his first national tournament at Merion near Philadelphia, golf took him again and again to the north and the east. He liked the people he met at Winged Foot and Brae Burn and Oakmont and Baltusrol. They had accents and attitudes he'd never encounter back in Atlanta. They lived on Long Island or the Main Line, and they worked in finance or law or owned steel mills. They belonged to—or ran—the United States Golf Association (USGA). Jones began to comprehend the workings of the Club beyond the country club, an interconnected world of wealth, prestige, and how-does-your-boy-like-Choate? He wanted to get in—who in his situation wouldn't?

Based on the Club's adoration of golf, he was already halfway there. But for full membership, he'd need the pedigree respected by the power elite. So he applied to Harvard.

He graduated from Tech in June 1922. In July, he sent his application to 20 University Hall, Cambridge, Massachusetts.

> 5. *Religious preference:* [Response line left blank except for a dash mark.]
>
> 7. *What change, if any, has been made since birth in your own name or that of your father? (Explain fully.)* None except I am namesake of my grandfather (paternal) and sign my name as Junior.
>
> 24. *Why do you wish to come to Harvard? (It is important that the candidate make full and candid answer to this question.)* Having earned a B.S. degree, I desire now an A.B. My life work will be either in engineering field or the law. In either case I consider an A.B. degree most desirable. I naturally desire the best training possible and believe I can get this at Harvard.

Henry Pennypacker, the Chairman of the Committee on Admission, had undoubtedly read more scintillating applications, and better academic records passed his desk every day. Moreover, Jones "desired"—his overused word—to do an English Literature degree in one year and then start at Harvard Law. No way, Pennypacker wrote on September 21:

> I regret to inform you, however, that [the Committee on Admission] felt that you could not be accepted as a student in the College under any circumstances which would make it possible for you to graduate in one year. Much of the work which you completed at the Georgia School of Technology cannot be counted in any way for a College degree; and in a number of courses your grades were too low to be accepted for credit. . . .

But Harvard and Pennypacker let him in. Bobby lived at red brick Gray's Hall on the southern edge of the Old Yard. Gray's was one of the nicer dorms, with fireplaces and bathrooms in each room and large comfortable common areas. He seems to have been a typical student, probably a little more social than most. He joined or was "punched"—Harvardese for recruited—into the Owl, S.K., Institute of 1770, and the Hasty Pudding Club, which was famous for its theatricals, its annual drag show, and for naming a Man and Woman of the Year. The three-story red brick Owl Club had a pool table and a card room and stuffed owls everywhere; Jones probably ate a lot of his meals there. He could have, and probably did have, Prohibition drinks in any of his clubs. He'd exhausted his eligibility to compete for the Crimson's golf team, so he volunteered to be college golf's most overqualified assistant manager. He did a bit of binge-drinking—most famously in connection with a postround celebration, when he drank most or all of the whiskey he was supposed to be safeguarding.

In several significant ways, of course, Jones was anything but a typical student. His had been a name in the news and a face on the newsreels for years, so he walked among the old brick and stone buildings of Harvard as a celebrity. From time to time, 1914 U.S. Open champion Francis Ouimet, a local man with a strong local accent, pahked his cah neah Hahvid Yahd to pick up his good friend Bahby for a golf game.

It was an education, all right—Jones saw things he would never see in Atlanta. Snowy streets, for example, and snobs, and rowers churning the brown waters of the Charles River in the warm months, and the vivid changes of the leaves on the trees in the fall. Overachievers were everywhere, in his own classes and at the Massachusetts Institute of Technology down the street. Bobby was not one of these, however. He was Mr. Popular, a charming bird from far-off Georgia with the 1923 U.S. Open trophy. Although he never competed for the Crimson, Harvard would put him in its Varsity Club Hall of Fame.

In his third month in Cambridge, he took and failed tests to show his proficiency in elementary French and German, which he later passed, but in all his time in Cambridge he didn't get a single A. He dropped courses frequently and missed classes regularly. In short, Jones was a "pass man," the Harvard term for a C student. He got by, just as he had at Tech.

"I have an idea that the two years Jones spent at Harvard may have been especially valuable for a young man of his marked sensibility," wrote Herbert Warren Wind, expressing the majority opinion in the foreword to Jones's final book, *The Basic Golf Swing.* "The odds are that he would never have developed his splendid talent for writing if he had not been exposed at just the right time to this stimulating new world." Maybe. Engineering was in his past and law lay in his future, and both are poison for a writer; if a degree in English Lit from Harvard didn't vivify his prose style, then the world isn't round. But becoming a better letter writer or columnist was hardly his goal; Jones's much more important mission was preparation for his life after golf. Lord knows he didn't want the constant travel and hullabaloo of Walter Hagen, the only pro who made the kind of money he had in mind. And the exhausting heat of competition just couldn't be endured for long. In a sense, Jones's degree from Harvard represented the first step in his retirement from golf.

He took the second step within weeks of the cap-and-gown ceremony in Harvard Yard. His last few moments as a single man found him in another yard, this one the backyard of Mr. and Mrs. John Norton Malone on Springdale Road in Druid Hills. The humid June evening and his black formal wear—including white gloves—gave Jones's serious face a damp glow. Strings of little electric lights behind pink shades illuminated the musicians, the women's dresses, and the round lenses of O. B. Keeler's glasses. "I never saw so many men at a wedding in my life," one of the lady guests commented.

The music came up, and Mary glided out of the house in lustrous white satin. Her dress was scalloped and appliquéd at the bottom, and the rosy light caught her headdress and her beautiful gap-toothed smile. It was a face Jones could see with his eyes closed; he and Mary had been sweethearts since they were kids. Among the hundreds in the yard were her parents, and Bobby's parents, and Bobby's paternal grandparents, including the righteous R. T. Jones, the business and moral leader of Canton, Georgia.

One of Bobby's cousins from Canton remembers running around in the yard that night, having a ball in the festive atmosphere. Another cousin recalls the evening a bit differently: "She was a Catholic. For a Southern Baptist, that was like marrying a Jew."

After the ceremony, the couple left by motor for their honeymoon in Asheville, North Carolina.

Thursday, May 1, 1930
On Board the *Mauretania*

Jones sometimes froze in front of moving-picture cameras, which were still something of a novelty in 1930. So when a newsreel crew arranged the celebrities in a soft semicircle on the deck of the big ship, Bobby wore an uncertain smile and remained motionless. But there were others in the group who could look right into the lens and say something.

"I know it is the sentiment of everybody in the audience to wish Mr. Jones and his team good luck this spring," enunciated Douglas Fairbanks Jr. crisply, with a winning smile. In the era of the small mustache, Fairbanks may have been the best-looking actor in Hollywood. He appealed to women generally and to bisexual actresses Tallulah Bankhead and Marlene Dietrich specifically—and to some men. So the executives at his movie studio were supposed to have breathed a sigh of relief when he married actress Joan Crawford in 1929. Gay was not good box office.

So Fairbanks liked girls—and athletes. He befriended the stars of the day—Jack Dempsey, Tilden, Jones, and others. "Doug," that tennis/badminton game Bobby had played all winter, was his invention, and he'd supplied his friend in Atlanta with the racquets, balls, and net required to play it.

Fairbanks was so keen about Bobby Jones, he announced on the ship, that after watching him in the Walker Cup and returning to the United States, he intended to sail back to Europe a second time to watch him play in the British Open. "I want to see the greatest artist of them all," Doug said.

Then another entertainer in the group became animated for the camera, in fact, did some shtick. Bald, age fifty-nine, and wearing a kilt and a sporran, the man tapped his cane and said in an Edinburgh brogue that he hadn't played golf in two years, "not since I lost my ball." The cheap Scot joke was the stock-in-trade of Sir Harry Lauder, a tremendously popular singer-songwriter-author-comedian whose most enduring hit would be a song called "Roamin' in the Gloamin'." King George V had knighted Lauder for his fund-raising and troop entertaining during the Great War. He'd played Atlanta in February.

When the media moment concluded, deck hands unwound the thick ropes from the cleats and threw them to the dock. And the mighty *Mauretania* began its five-day voyage to the southern tip of England. Among the passengers on the floating luxury hotel were the two entertainers; a third performer, the debonair French singer-actor, Maurice "Mo" Chevalier, who had two movies out in 1930, including *The Playboy of Paris*; the world's most famous art dealer, Sir Joseph Duveen; the eight golfers of the Walker Cup team (Jones was player-captain); a few men from the top of the USGA hierarchy; the ubiquitous Keela; "quite a party of Atlanta people," as Keeler described them; and Bobby's wife of almost six years, Mary.

Mary Jones's presence was out of the ordinary. Between the need to help the nanny maintain Clara and Robert T. III and the boredom and stress of the golf widow, home and hearth were usually preferable to Britain or Baltusrol. Add the burden of being Mrs. Bobby Jones amidst his adoring public, and going on the road with Bobby looked still less appealing. But things were different at this moment. For one thing, the cost of ship, rail, meals, and hotel for a large part of the journey would be picked up by the USGA. For another, her husband had promised a vacation in France in the intervals between tournaments. Moreover, Mary well knew that they might never pass this way again, whether her husband won or not. There's no question she participated in Bobby's big decision, and there's no doubt about how she voted. She not only wanted him to quit competitive golf, she was adamant about it.

Keeler and his similarly reverential successors hardly mention Mary in their biographies of Jones; wives were irrelevant or out-of-bounds, according to the conventions of some forms of personal history. But based in large part on his conversations with Clara, the Jones's first-born child, now long dead, Dick Miller took pains to paint a mostly unflattering portrait of Mary Rice Malone Jones in *Triumphant Journey.*

She was, according to Miller, an insubstantial society girl with a substantial fear of being rejected by Atlanta's better families because her own family was Catholic. "She overcompensated," Miller writes, "by becoming very exacting and prim in her behavior. To Mary, manners marked the person. Orderliness was next to godliness."

Furthermore, Miller finds that "there was merely a modicum of intellectual compatibility between" Bobby and Mary. "Having only attended Atlanta's Mary Washington Seminary for Girls, Mary was educated and raised to be an ideal woman of leisure."

Miller describes her willfully subservient, possibly passive-aggressive role in the marriage. "Mary was barely five months younger than Bob, but she guarded those months as if they were fifteen years," he writes. "These were childish emotions she enjoyed, but . . . [she] always remained the child of her own dreams." Her relationship to the third party in their union—golf, and by extension, Keeler—seems to have been an uneasy one at best. She "never did try to comprehend the nature of golf." When she went to a tournament, she never watched. And "while she enjoyed her husband's fame, she couldn't accept the price that went with it . . . Privately, she threw stormy fits of jealousy. That day . . . when Jones retired from competitive golf was one of the happiest days of their married life."

But Miss Malone must have had something that Miller didn't quite discern and the other biographers did not address. Because Bobby played great while he was married to Mary, and they had kids and he kept coming home. And he took her along on this long journey.

Saturday, May 3
At Sea

If you've seen the movie *Titanic*, you've seen the *Mauretania*. The largest, fastest, and most opulent ocean liner of the '20s could do twenty-five knots for hours on end, its gigantic steam turbine engines cutting the waves, running on oil, not coal, the dark exhaust smoke billowing through the four back-slanted black stacks on the deck. Its Grand Staircase was grand, indeed, but the two-story dining saloon was still more magnificent. Its steel-ribbed domed glass ceiling displayed the twelve signs of the zodiac.

Outside, the ship was all gleaming hardwood and polished brass and spotless white paint. Inside, gilt was everywhere. But was guilt anywhere? Ticket prices revealed the difference between going in style and just going. To cross the pond in first class on the pride of the British Merchant Marine cost £200; second class cost just £10; and third, £6. On westbound trips, the spartan accommodations below decks were usually filled with immigrants.

Cunard Line, the owner/operator of the ship, gave what it called "very special rates" to the team and accompanying members of the USGA executive committee.

The first-class passengers strolled along the promenade deck and sat on chairs of teak and drank tea and talked. They took real drinks, too, out in the open like civilized people; Prohibition did not reach international waters. Keeler pecked out a few words on his Olympia, renewing his fondness for the phrase "cobalt blue." The golfers amused themselves with a driving net and a little putting track with bumpers, like a miniature-golf hole. Jones hit a putt or two for the cameras, but he found the net and bumper track useless, even for exercise.

Much more worthwhile was the happy renewal of his acquaintance with the men of the United States Golf Association. When Miller described Jones's relationship with the USGA as "a perfect marriage," he was doubly right. It was perfect because this was an organization run by amateur golfers for amateur golfers—the only occasion on which they had to deal with the mercenary former caddies who called themselves professionals was during the U.S. Open—and Bobby, the very image of the gentleman golfer, would never turn pro, despite being the best player in the world. Perfect. And it was a marriage because they did things for each other. Jones exalted the USGA just by being himself while winning five U.S. Amateurs and four U.S. Opens. He even joined the association in a significant way, becoming a committeeman in 1928 and captaining the Walker Cup team twice, including the 1930 squad.

Jones and his friends had last seen each other in January in New York at the annual meeting of the executive committee. "The next order of business is selecting a captain for our Walker Cup team," said USGA president Findlay Douglas, while secretary Prescott Bush took notes. "Move that Robert Tyre Jones Jr. be named captain," someone said. "Second," said someone else. "All those in favor?" There was a chorus of "ayes." Opposed? Silence. "Motion carried." The new captain was asked to recommend players for his team. Jones read eight names for the first string plus two alternates. After a motion, a second, and a unanimous vote, the Walker Cup was done.

The USGA always stood by Bobby, and he by them. During his competitive career, he was allowed to write his golf column without breaching the rules of amateur status (the USGA changed that rule after Jones retired). When Jones asked Harvard to allow him a month off in the spring of '23 to play in the Walker Cup match in Rye, England, the college administration checked on his grades at that moment and found one B+, two of C-, and two "not yet in." Harvard said no and that was that. But USGA secretary Cornelius S. Lee wrote an impassioned letter on Bobby's behalf, and USGA president J. Frederic Byers wrote a polite one. That support was nothing, however, compared to the house deal in 1927.

Jones had just won the U.S. Amateur at Minikahda in Minneapolis, Minnesota, his second major of the year, and his boosters back home were bursting with pride. Bobby had done so much to elevate the city and the region and the game—and he'd done it with such class—but he had nothing material to show for it. He was an amateur. With stints at Georgia Tech, Harvard, and Emory Law, he was more or less a perpetual student. Except for a flirtation with selling real estate for his old friend Mr. Adair, he'd never really had a job. He certainly didn't own any real estate; he and his wife lived with his parents. It just didn't seem right to E. R. Black and his fellow members of the Atlanta Athletic Club (AAC). In September of '27, they circulated a telegram to select men of means around town:

> Atlanta raising fund of Fifty Thousand Dollars to buy home for Bobby Jones as substantial recognition of what he has done for Atlanta stop We will be delighted to have you wire your subscription for One Thousand Dollars

At a dinner at the AAC, Jones was handed a note informing him of the existence of the fund. Someone took a picture, the picture got published, and the newspaper cutlines read, "Champion golfer Bobby Jones of Atlanta accepts a check in the amount of $50,000, a gift from his friends in Atlanta for the purchase of a new home." At his very first executive committee meeting at the USGA headquarters in New York, Jones found himself having to explain his own actions rather than adjudicating someone else's. "He was of the opinion that the gift was perfectly in order and that nothing wrong had been done in violation of the amateur rule," read the meeting's minutes. "He, however, was agreeable to have the matter fully discussed and considered by the Committee and would appreciate the suggestions and point of view of the Committee."

What that point of view was is murky. Jones stated plainly a week later that the USGA approved the extravagant Christmas gift; that is, it declared that accepting a free house did not constitute a breach of its rules for amateurs. The logic required to state that accepting a $50,000 present did not make

Jones a de facto professional can be called twisted or hilarious, but it can't be called logical.

But the deal fell apart, and it seems at least possible that some of his friends in the USGA advised him to back away from this questionable arrangement. Jones was still in New York on January 13, 1928, when he released a letter addressed to the contributors to the Home Fund. "I should not retain the gift," Jones wrote:

> At the time the gift was made to me it appealed to me as the most generous and sincere tribute a man's friends could pay him, and it was accepted by me in the spirit in which I knew it was intended. You and I know that there was nothing connected with the subscription of the fund, or the use to which it was to be put, which was not entirely proper. A portion of the general public is aware of that fact also, but it seems that another and respectable portion entertains some doubts . . . In other words, criticisms from various sources have come to my notice, and it appeared to me in light of them that not only was Amateur Golf in danger of serious injury wholly unjustified by the facts, but both my Atlanta friends and I were apt to be placed in an awkward position . . . It was to avoid any chance of misunderstanding that I decided the best thing to do was to return the home . . .
>
> When the U.S.G.A. approved your action in making the gift, and mine in receiving it, as proper, it seemed to me that the moment had arrived for a final announcement.

At this crisis point—possibly just before it?—the Pope of Cherokee County interceded. Grandfather R.T. loaned his famous grandson the $50,000. Not quite a loan, really, since their contract stated that the mortgagee had to pay back only $1 a year. So Bobby, Mary, Clara, and three-month-old Robert Tyre Jones III moved into that great house on Northside Drive in February, a happy ending for all concerned.

"The USGA approved your action in making the gift, and mine in receiving it." The USGA had gone to bat for him, and before the summer was over, Jones would return the favor. He'd do something for them that was incredible under the circumstances. And the USGA—in the person of Prescott Bush—would help Bobby in a way that was simply shocking.

Tuesday, May 6
Southampton, England

The passengers gathered at the rails in the cool, clear late afternoon as tugs tugged the *Mauretania* toward the dock. As Jones stepped off the ship at about 5:00 P.M., he told a reporter from the *Times of London* that he was very glad to be back in England, where he had so many friends. No, he said, he did not intend to play in the Royal St. George's Champions Grand Challenge Cup on Saturday—"which will be a sad disappointment to many amateurs of golf who have been looking forward to watching him there," read the report the next day. Such things are hard to quantify, but Jones may have been even more popular in England and Scotland than he was in the United States. His appropriateness and reserve were almost British, while his good looks earned him the nickname "Bonnie Bobby."

Mr. and Mrs. Jones motored to the Savoy Hotel in London. The north wind blew. A heavy frost coated England that night.

Wednesday, May 7
Addington Golf Club, Croydon

On their first full day in country, the U.S. Walker Cup team played a round at the 6,200-yard course on Shirley Church Road in the south London suburb of Croydon. The attentive crowds, which normally followed Jones, did not hear about the outing, but the golf writer from the *Times of London* did. When Bernard Darwin skedaddled down to Addington on that cold, windy day, it wasn't to see Don Moe.

"Of the eight men playing seven looked, as of course they are, good golfers, but the eighth not only looked supremely good he played almost perfectly into the bargain," wrote Darwin, the grandson of Charles, the famous naturalist. "I watched Bobby play the first nine holes, which he reeled off without unduly bestirring himself in eight 4's and a 2 . . . He holed one long putt and the rest was like the monotonous shelling of peas."

Doug Fairbanks, a four handicap back in southern California, also played at Addington with Leo Diegel, the very talented and tightly wound American pro who was in England for a few paying events before the big one, the Open Championship at Royal Liverpool (a.k.a. Hoylake) in June.

The Royal and Ancient Golf Club had declared steel shafts legal for tournament play in 1929—some say the day the Prince of Wales showed up fully metallic on the first tee at the Old Course at St. Andrews had been the change agent—so Darwin peeked into every bag to see where the Americans stood on high tech. Like the prince, Francis Ouimet was using all steel. Jones and George von Elm were all wood; Diegel used all wood except in his putter; and the others had steel shafts in the woods and hickory in the irons.

Friday, May 9
Sunningdale Golf Club, London

The headlines in the *Times of London* sum up the preoccupations of the English at this time:

"New Rioting in India—Police Stations Burnt"

"Mob Atrocities"

"Stock Exchange Quiet and Dull"

In addition to a very sluggish economy, the English had to deal with this very serious and very distant threat to the Empire. "That little brown man," as Churchill derided Mohandas Gandhi in private, was causing all sorts of nonviolent trouble. He got his people to boycott salt and new clothing and stop paying taxes. What next? For respite, perhaps, His Royal Highness the Prince of Wales invited Sir Phillip Sassoon and two of the nice young chaps from the U.S. Walker Cup team to go two loops around Sunningdale. You picture the prince pulling rank on the first tee: "I say, Phillip. Why don't you just have a go with Harrison "Jimmy" Johnston. I'll take Bobby Jones."

Their thirty-six-hole match ended all square.

Tuesday, May 13
London

"The Arrest of Mr. Gandhi"

"Amateur Golf Championship"

"The Draw for St. Andrews"

The Walker Cup held general interest because Jones was in it, but its result was a foregone conclusion. The Americans had won each Cup since the event started in '22, usually by a lot. The real deal was taking place in a fortnight: the Amateur. After that came the other big bang on the gong, the Open, in Liverpool. Professional golf could be enchanting, but until Bobby left the scene, the amateur side of the game was just as important.

And popular. Two hundred and seventy-two worthies entered, a new record. I. Sidebottom would play Redmond Simcox in the first round, it was announced; Lieutenant-Colonel J. T. C. Moore-Brabazon would contend with C. M. Grant-Gowan; and S. Roper had drawn R. T. Jones Jr. These first five names were meaningless. Everyone knew that the only ones with a chance to win at St. Andrews were on the two Walker Cup teams.

Thursday, May 15
Royal St. George's Golf Club, Sandwich

The Amateur preoccupied Jones. Later he would refer to it as the "most important tournament of my life" because he had never won it and because he couldn't win the Grand Slam unless he did. But now they were raising flags and playing anthems, and his competitor's mind clicked on and focused like an x-ray. Jones did not vary the level of his effort too much; he knew that the best practice for winning is winning.

He never said or wrote it, but in the warmup rounds for the Walker Cup Jones undoubtedly scouted his opposition for the Amateur. In *Down the Fairway*, which was published in 1927, Jones and Keeler posited that the key to success in tournament golf was ignoring the human opponent and concentrating instead on the golf course, on "Old Man Par." Bobby got a lot of mileage out of this bromide—and a definite psychological advantage—because Keeler and others kept repeating it. His cool, dissociated strategy meant that the other guys would have to break par to beat him! But Jones did not suddenly stop evaluating his foes and gazing into their eyes on the first tee like a boxer before the bell.

Over the years he'd given the long look to two of his teammates and lost—the owlish Ouimet and the Teutonic George von Elm had both beaten him in match play. Who else might beat him? Don Moe? No. Too young. Oscar F. Willing, D.D.S.? No. Too old. Flat-swinging, one-putting George Voigt was a tenacious competitor who was hitting the ball not far but very well; in an eighteen-hole match, he could beat anyone. And Harrison "Jimmy" Johnston had won the previous year's U.S. Amateur, the one at Pebble Beach where Jones had lost embarrassingly in the first round.

And who on the English team could give Jones trouble at St. Andrews eleven days hence? That was easily answered: the defending British Amateur champion Cyril Tolley, a robust-looking gentleman who seemed like he could wrestle a bear, and Roger Wethered, a gangly man who looked as though he might wrestle a chipmunk—and lose.

Wethered and Jones, the two captains, shook hands ceremoniously, and the Walker Cup began. The simple format called for a foursomes (a.k.a. alternate shot) match on the first day and individual combat on day two. In mild weather in which only one American left his mittens on, Jones teed off in the second match with Dr. Willing the dentist, who, Jones wrote many years later, "was the most inclined of all our boys to be a bit unorthodox . . . If there should be any question of any two of our players working well together in double harness, the problem would involve Dr. Willing." The Doc could be a pain in the ass to his partner, in other words, but he and Jones teamed superbly and won the first three holes and combined for a two-under 33 on the first nine.

After Willing drove off the tenth tee, the fashionably late Prince of Wales walked up the sunny fairway and shook Jones's hand. The prince, who had just arrived by plane at Sandwich, was a vision. Bobby had been the sartorial star of the day up to that point in a dusty blue sweater with matching stockings, but the prince easily outdid him: a chocolate-, red-, and white-checked plus-four suit; beige stockings; a brown-and-white-checked cap; and a big red-and-white-checked umbrella. Jolly good. But the crowd continued to notice Jones more than the prince's new clothes. From 160 yards on the fairway on ten, Bobby zinged an iron to fifteen feet, and Doc Willing made the putt. Bobby-Doc won eight and seven.

The English team won only one match. Tolley chipped in three times and holed at least that many long putts as he and Wethered beat Voigt and Von Elm one up on the thirty-sixth green.

Friday, May 16
Royal St. George's Golf Club

It seemed like the right thing to do for the captains to play each other in the singles. It started as a good match—all square after nine holes. Then Bobby began to attack the golf course, while Roger began to attack the gallery. Jones went par-par-birdie-eagle, each one a win on holes ten through thirteen. His chip-in from thirty yards on thirteen put him four up. Meanwhile, Wethered hit spectators on the thirteenth and fourteenth with vicious hooks, and his tee shot on fifteen beaned a third victim, knocking him unconscious. Not surprisingly, the stewards lost control of the crowd of three thousand at that point. With no assurance that the rough was a safe place to stand when the English captain had a driver in his hands, people ran here and there like unbroken retrievers, and some coalesced into little bands, like Old West settlers circling the wagons.

Jones shot 69 on his morning round and finished the job after lunch, winning by nine and eight. The U.S. team won the Cup, ten matches to two.

With France so close and the Amateur still ten days away, Keela went to Paris. Bobby and Mary checked out of the Ramsgate Hotel in Sandwich by the sea and returned to London. Traveling with them were Sherwood Hurt and his wife, and Mrs. James D. Cross, Bobby's cousin. Hurt, a wealthy stockbroker, played golf regularly with Jones at East Lake.

Tuesday, May 20
Sunningdale Golf Club, London

Jones adored Sunningdale, the first great inland course in England. He'd shot 66 and 68 there in the qualifying rounds for the 1926 Open, which he won at Royal Lytham and St. Anne's. Thanks partly to Keeler's pen, that 66—with 33 putts and 33 other shots—became famous as one of the most perfect rounds ever played. "I wish I could take this course home with me," Jones said.

On another mild May day, the wooded course west of London hosted a thirty-six-hole competition for the *Golf Illustrated* Gold Vase. Voigt, von Elm, Willing, and Jones participated, as did the English Walker Cuppers and a smattering of other good local players. But that American foursome looked formidable; a bookie offered four-to-one odds that one of them would win.

"And I do not know that he was temerarious," commented Darwin in the *Times.*

Darwin could have chosen another more familiar modifier to describe the bookie such as "reckless" or "rash," but that wouldn't have been Darwin. And Jones could have shot a couple of 75s in this very informal tournament, but that wouldn't have been Jones. Actually, he did shoot 75 in the first round, finishing 5-6-5 against a par of 4-4-4. But then he had a talk with himself.

"At luncheon I got to thinking that it was a pretty silly thing to play in any sort of a golf tournament without trying hard to win it," Jones wrote in *Golf Is My Game.* "So, not that the amount of money was important, but merely to give me some sort of focus for the recapture of my concentration, I made a bet of one English pound, a 'quid' as he called it, with Dale [Bourne, his playing partner] that I would 'break seventy' in the afternoon round. It worked quite well."

Jones shot 68 and returned to the hotel with the lovely Gold Vase. And a quid, then worth about $4.85.

Saturday, May 24
The Old Course at St. Andrews, Scotland

Jones teed off unannounced for a practice round immediately in front of the Scotland-versus-England and Scotland-versus-Ireland team matches. At least half the gallery changed its plan and followed him.

Sunday, May 25
St. Andrews

Keela and his wife raced up from France. From Le Royal Hotel in Paris, they took a cab, a train, a ferry, another train, then the night train from

London to Edinburgh. When he disembarked, O.B. discovered how thoroughly the capital of Scotland shut down on Sunday morning—no trams, trolleys, or trains operated to get him the final fifty miles to St. Andrews. So with a couple from Boston, the Keelers rented a big Daimler and sped to the coast, where they boarded the 9:00 A.M. ferry that crossed the Firth of Forth to Fife. And then they motored across the smooth, green hills of the shire into the medieval city, weird, wonderful St. Andrews.

St. Andrews town sits on a cliff above the cold, gray sea. Everything is hundreds of years old and made of stone, including the university, which enjoys prestige equal to Oxford or Cambridge. The castle and cathedral ruins and the "GW" in white paint on the road make time feel elastic, like the Reformation was yesterday. GW was George Wishart, the sixteenth-century priest who was burned at the stake above that spot of paint. Down below, in the sandy land that links the land and the sea, lie the golf courses.

No golfers roamed the Old Course the day before the Amateur—as always, it was closed on the Sabbath. A lot of the contestants in the big event tried to stay sharp by playing a round at Gleneagles, which was not too distant and open. Not Bobby. Keeler found him in the old gray town at Mason's Golf Hotel and happy to talk with his public confidant. He wasn't playing at Gleneagles today, he said, because the greens there "are radically different from these. I found that out in 1927."

That was the year love bloomed between Bobby and St. Andrews. Neither had made a good impression on the other his first trip there six years earlier. In the third round of the '21 Open, he shot 46 on the first nine and then double-bogeyed the par-four tenth, often the easiest hole on the course. The atrocious start deteriorated into a nightmare in one of the hellish sandpits by the eleventh green, the one on the left, the Hill Bunker. It was one of only four on the course with revetted sides—that is, sod stacked on sod like bricks—and it made the Hill even nastier. After a good bit of thrashing and rising color on his neck and ears, the nineteen-year-old boy snatched his ball off the green rather than hole out for a triple-bogey six, disqualifying himself. He didn't dramatically tear up his scorecard as legend had it, and he didn't walk off the course. He was even allowed to play the next day—he shot 72—but failing to hole out was beyond the pale. Shocking behavior, observers muttered. Not done.

But in 1927 at the same course in the same tournament, everything had changed. Jones was an older, better golfer and an older, better person. He was also the defending British Open champion, and so popular and accomplished that he and Keeler had written his memoirs, and Minton, Balch & Company of New York had published them. He started fast: On the par-five fifth hole of the first round, Jones got his ball just barely on the biggest green in the world in two and had probably the longest putt he'd ever look at, about 120 feet. He gave it his usual wristy slap . . . and it rolled and rolled and rolled and rolled in.

More important than improved luck, however, were the new eyes with which he regarded the test in front of him. He embraced its quirks, such as the score of bread-box-sized survey stones (*march stones* in Scottish), which run like a spine through the middle of the course. He came to grips with the endlessly complex mounding around the greens that sometimes make pinball-style chipping the way to go. The Old gets intriguingly complicated, almost mathematical, when a player gloms on to the fact that each choice of type or direction of play can lead to three more decisions and three more branching from each of those. While complexity and strategy appeal to golfers like Jones, who like to think, the Old's deepest secret charm lay not in its mystery but in its *solvability*, it's not to be played mechanically, and it's not a random collection of bunkers and bumps. There is a correct way to play its chessboard, and the correct way changes with the wind off the bay.

Thus from, as he put it, "puzzled dislike," Bobby learned to love the Old Course. As for the passion the residents and spectators felt for the young man, St. Andrews historian Dr. David Malcolm asks you to consider what no one in golf talked about or wrote about until Arnold Palmer came along: sex. "Sexual energy was in the air around Jones, definitely," Malcolm says. "These Americans—Jones, Hagen, Sarazen—were like film stars. They wore two-toned shoes, for chrissakes! Who wanted to look at Andra Kirkaldy dressed in brown after that?

"You have to appreciate that it was a big fucking deal just to go to Dundee back then. You had women with *margarine* in their hair. Social life was a soiree at the church, or an occasional entertainment put on by the town council— but mostly, golf. So then Jones comes to St. Andrews in the '20s, an age of hysteria, and he creates a greater hysteria than Arnold Palmer ever did."

At the award ceremony in '27, Jones asked the Royal and Ancient Golf Club to do him the honor of just keeping the Open trophy, the Claret Jug, right there at the R and A. This PR masterstroke sealed the deal. They loved Bobby fiercely, Scottishly, in St. Andrews after that. And now he was back.

But there were whispers that he might never return if he won the Amateur, the only big tournament he'd never won. The rumor sharpened Scotland's desire for its American hero.

Monday, May 26, 3:00 P.M.
The Old Course at St. Andrews

Keeler could not contain himself. "What a wonderful thing it would be if only Bobby Jones could win the British amateur championship at St. Andrews!" he wrote, not for the first or last time giving objectivity a knee in the groin. "Now the only gem lacking in his royal crown is the British amateur. . . . If he can win it here—well, I'll call it a day and a career, and if he elects to hang up his clubs and practice law until he is blue in the face and gray in the hair it will be all right with his Boswell. All I want is the British amateur championship."

Bobby's Amateur did not begin until the middle of the afternoon, a cruel wait for a man with a churning stomach. "Throughout the early morning of every competition," Jones had written, "I have found myself continually on the verge of active nausea." He usually couldn't manage more than tea and toast, if that.

In the hour before the Jones match, men in tweed and ties and women in sensible dresses flocked to the first tee as if the R and A was giving away money. Indistinguishable from the mulling crowd was the opponent, Henry Sidney (sometimes spelled Sydney) Roper of Woolaton Park, Nottinghamshire, which is in the center of England between Birmingham and Manchester. Keeler had scouted Roper for his liege but didn't find out much. It seemed that Sid was a steady five-shots-per-hole man and had been a coal miner once. But he turned out to be an unawed fellow who was about to lay a Johnny Goodman on Bobby's ass—almost.

"I could make a pretty fair appraisal of the worth of an opponent simply by speaking to him on the first tee and taking a good measuring look into his eyes," Jones wrote in *Golf Is My Game*. "I thought I could tell whether or not he would be likely to play his best game under pressure. What I observed of Mr. Roper in this respect was not at all reassuring . . . he had the look not only of a golfer, but of a competitor as well."

Before examining their match, we should remind ourselves of several differences between the game then and the game now. No one at the British Amateur said a hole was a par three, four, or five; holes were instead short, two-shotter, or long. In fact, par wasn't talked of much at all; the player's relationship to fours provided the most used yardstick. Since eighteen fours equals 72 and 72 often equals par, "fours" is still a useful and easy-to-understand tool. Some golfers still keep track of their game with respect to fours or fives, but only relatively aged golfers remember the stymie. This croquetlike corner of match-play rules until 1950 was an offshoot of a bigger rule, the one that said you couldn't touch your ball once you put it in play until you picked it out of the hole. Thus one ball on the green could and often did block the path of the other to the hole (only if the balls were initially within six inches of each other could the closer be picked up so the farther could play). Stymies were a cutthroat game within the game; it was kosher to try to obstruct your opponent's ball if the need arose. Such violence was distasteful to most casual players, however. They asked each other like a mantra on the first tee, "Are we playing stymies today?" But some really interesting and interestingly unfair situations developed because of the stymie. You had to be ready to chip your putt or try a spin shot or attempt to block the blocker. Jones supported the stymie. Later he would write a column about it—and another about Roper.

The match began in overcast sweater weather. In an impressive performance he would never repeat again on such a stage, the Englishman played as if he'd read Jones on forgetting the human opponent. He embraced Old Man Par (or Old Man Four) and would not let him go. The match lasted sixteen holes, and Roper scored fifteen fours and one five.

But Jones demonstrated the elementary and unavoidable weakness of making par after par: Birdies beat it. While Sid opened with 4-4-4-4-4— three pars, a bogey, and a birdie—Bobby showed him 3-4-3-2-4—a par, three birdies, and a hole-out from about 140 from a bunker with a spade mashie (six-iron) on the fourth for an eagle. The ball trickled in as if it had been gently putted; it did not slam into the stick. "It was the best shot I ever hit, whether it went in or not," Jones said.

The match stayed right there, for the most part, until the end. Steady Sid laid Jones a stymie on the short eighth and won the hole. He fought to the finish but finally lost on the sixteenth, three and two. Jones was four under fours for the sixteen holes, probably the best score of the day. Roper may have had the second-best total. Then he went back to Nottinghamshire and anonymity.

The day turned cold and dark with a suggestion of mist in the air, which the Scots call *smirr*, not quite a *haar*, which is a freezing fog that billows in from the firth and really chills the bones. Jones walked off to find food and drink, and rest, and Mary.

In the pubs the buzz built about the match everyone had seen coming. If a couple more Sid Ropers could be disposed of, Jones would have a match on Wednesday afternoon against possibly the toughest player in the field, the defending champion, Cyril Tolley. That would be one to turn out for.

Tuesday, May 27

The wind blew briskly from left to right as you looked down the first fairway, as if it were a long exhalation from the cold stone buildings by the eighteenth fairway out to sea. No *haar* this day, but the breeze dried the greens so much that they began to shine. The high plateau of the eleventh green looked waxed.

Two American Walker Cup players, both from the Northwest, couldn't handle the disorienting wind and the unfamiliar ground. Oscar Willing of Waverly Country Club in Portland, Oregon, lost in the first round to William Spark. "When the wind blows like this over home," said Don Moe of Washington State after his first-round loss to Rex Hartley, "we don't bother about playing golf." Dr. Willing stayed around most of the week to cheer on his teammates, especially his captain.

Jones had the day off.

One hundred twenty-eight players remained, but everyone talked about just two.

Wednesday, May 28

Seagulls' cries wake you in St. Andrews if the conditions are right and your window is open. It's a high, lonely sound at times and a comfort at others, evocative of every beach and harbor in sleepy memory. This was not one of those mornings. All you could hear was the wind.

Jones looked out the window of his room at the Grand Hotel and saw sand pluming on the beach and blowing out to sea. It was the same wind as the day before only more so. If he'd looked out on the course from the hotel roof, he'd have been able to see feathers of black dust flying from the coal sheds by the seventeenth fairway.

At 8:12 he stood on the first tee, feeling slightly ill as usual and looking miserable in the cold. He blew on his hands then shook the hand of his opponent, Cowan Shankland, a Londoner. Keeler and Darwin hovered nearby; not surprisingly, the best-known writers of golf in the United States and England had become battlefield friends and complimentary of one another in print. Darwin's admirers often referred to him as the Shakespeare of golf writers. O.B. was more Mark Twain stuck on the sports page.

Shankland-Jones had none of the thrills of Bobby's previous match or the one to come. Overmatched and playing like it, Cowan made timid fives on the first three holes, and Jones was three up with three standard pars. Then Bobby looked out of sorts for a while and gave back two holes with lackluster bogeys. Shankland hit it close on the short eighth but followed with four nervous putts and lost the hole. Finally Jones prevailed four and three. On the half-mile walk in from the fifteen, the west wind tried to take off his tweed cap. His baggy plus fours blew sideways to his left.

C. Tolley got past W. Fowlis a few minutes later by the same score at the same green as Roper-Jones. Tolley had the same hike back to the R and A clubhouse that Jones had had and the same time to think about what lay ahead. By the time he walked past the Road Hole, he could see the dark mass of people gathering for his match with Bobby.

The first tee at the Old Course felt like a theatre. The ground was as broad as the stage at Radio City Music Hall, and the intimate audience peered down from a path behind and beside and from the windows of the stolid stone clubhouse of the R and A. If Mary Jones looked toward the tee from their hotel window behind the eighteenth green, she would have seen, first, that it was no day to be out and, second, that a mob had gathered to watch this match. Yes, a mob. The St. Andrews shops had closed, and Dundee, the nearest big city, had declared a holiday. The Babe Ruth of golf was playing a big match, and admission was free. About twelve thousand ruddy-faced fans got off the train or out of a car and hustled out to the links.

It was just too many bodies in too small a space. The Old Course is an extremely narrow collection of holes with scant room to hold what Darwin described as "great, unthinking waves of people." Players and caddies in other matches, he wrote, had to get down on all fours to try to guard a ball in play from being trampled or kicked. Contestants not named Tolley or Jones had to wait as long as a half an hour for a hole to clear. And the wind blew so fiercely that it took sand from the bunkers and caused people to shelter themselves behind dunes when not much was happening in the big match.

Darwin uncharitably referred to the crowd as "rabble." At least it was a nicely dressed rabble, most of whom loved golf and Jones in that order. They knew when to cheer and when to be quiet.

The great crowd hushed to Sunday silence as Jones put his square-dimpled Spalding on a wooden peg, which he thrust into the earth. Without fuss he hit a screamer to the left of the first fairway that the wind blew back to the center. A manly cheer rose from the gallery. Now came the mighty Tolley, who had once driven a ball 350 yards. A birdie machine, his handicap had been as incredibly low as *plus six* at his club, Eastbourne Downs, a lovely course on the southern tip of England with a view of the Channel. Twice now the British Amateur champion after last year's win, Tolley stood burly and hatless in the gale. A stockbroker, Tolley was a very good tennis player, age thirty-five, about five feet ten, well over two hundred pounds, gray at the sideburns and temples, as dignified and likeable as Jones, and just as secretly fierce. But more majestic; Cyril James Hastings Tolley did something rather magnificent with his walk and the way he held his head. The great man teed a ball and looked coolly down the broad fairway.

And now Cyril begins his swing, and now he lets it go, and now the air is shattered by the force of Cyril's blow . . . But the ball dribbled along the ground like a squirrel with a sprained ankle, so weakly it barely crossed the road in front of the tee. He had to lay up in front of the burn in front of the green on the 370-yard hole.

Jones went one up with a par. Tolley tied it with a par on two.

It soon became apparent that in addition to the conflict with the course and the weather, this was a cool contest, a battle between two early-twentieth-century Fred Coupleses. Both men played without delay with a studied nonchalance that was part poker and part acting the role of the it's-just-a-game-to-me gentleman golfer. "Neither Jones nor Tolley condescends to reveal by the slightest trace or symptom of eagerness his intense desire and his concentrated will to win," Keeler wrote in his column. "I should say that Tolley is even more casual than Jones, for Bobby cannot by any trick or superior power of the will keep his face from growing gray under the furious strain, or his eyes from sinking deeper in his head."

Jones wrote later that that afternoon he "felt the desperate urgency I should expect to feel in a battle with broadswords or cudgels" but except for a couple of uncharacteristic slices—forgivable in that wind—he didn't say much or show much, and the ballet never left his swing. How did he stay so cool? Because of at least two things: He felt comfortable in the mano a mano of match play, with a here-and-now opponent to react to or who would have to react to him. Stroke competition, on the other hand, felt to Jones like a battle against an invisible army. The second thing that put ice in Bobby's veins was that he liked this crowd.

"[Crowds] numbering 15,000 and more are not uncommon," Jones had written in his column just weeks earlier. That is, they weren't uncommon for him. "A large number of spectators is a distinct advantage . . . They will find his balls . . . define the greens and bunkers, they will make lanes for him to play through, and they will inspire him to do his very best, and sometimes even a little more."

No one should think that everyone was pulling for Bobby, however. Wagering spiced the action for many, and some people, obviously, bet against him. And others wanted to be there on the historic occasion when Jones lost.

Marshals shouted, the wool-wrapped crowd formed corridors through which the golfers hit, and as soon as the ball was in the air, they swarmed like Sioux around Custer at Little Big Horn.

Both men played brilliantly and neither could go two up or even hold a lead of one up. Tolley drove on or over two par-four greens, both his feet facing the target in the aftermath of his violent swing. Jones nervelessly holed putts on slippery slopes. Then in the middle of the match, there was an interval that would have seemed comic if the atmosphere hadn't been so tense. The eleventh in a fresh wind when the green is hard is one of the least-inviting tee shots anywhere. The target 172 yards away is broad but very narrow and defended by bunkers that look like giant empty eye sockets. Tolley had the honor and hit a strong shot that hung interminably at its apogee like a punted football. It hovered high above the green but boomeranged back toward the tee on the way down into an awful, half-buried lie in sand the wind had blown out of the Strath bunker and into the fairway. Jones overcompensated for the headwind and blasted his shot over the green onto the bank of the Eden River. As he watched Cyril get ready to play from his poached-egg lie, Jones thought how easy it would be for his opponent to hit it fat into the Strath. Actually, he hit the ground so far behind the ball that he remained short of the bunker. Then he fluffed it again—there were no decent wedges in 1930—and fell into the nasty Strath. At last Cyril found the green with his fourth. Bobby's turn: Momentarily refusing the invitation to win the hole, he also hit the big ball (planet Earth) before he hit the little ball and remained on the grassy riverbank. But then he stiffed his third, and Tolley conceded. Jones went one up.

The rest of the holes played mostly downwind. Both men drove over the green on the mysteriously bunkered 316-yard twelfth, but the Englishman chipped and putted for a three that squared the game. Jones holed from thirty-six feet on thirteen and went one up. Tolley walloped his second to the long fourteenth to three feet, a real magic trick, for a conceded eagle. Even. Bobby won fifteen, a long two-shotter, with a conceded three. Cyril won sixteen when Bobby hit his tee ball into another bunker with a name, the Principal's Nose. All square with two holes to play.

The Old Course returns to town on the seventeenth. Sheds for drying lumber (including hickory for golf shafts) and storing coal served as outposts and aiming points for the sharp dogleg right. On the nearest shed to the tee was painted D. ANDERSON in letters more than a foot high; conventional wisdom held that the D in "Anderson" should be the target on this blind tee shot, which sounds simple. But nothing was simple on this excruciating hole because no one with an IQ above an after-dinner mint could avoid thinking about the next shot while playing the present shot on the Road Hole.

From the teeing ground 461 yards from the hole, Tolley and Jones thought of the narrow unseen green, its flagstick cut behind a deep, little bunker, and the gravelly maintenance road on the right that gathered the shots of the slicer and the coward. But it was not an easy time or place to mull. Darwin described it as "a nightmare of rushing mob and shouting stewards."

A perfect drive required a risk neither fatigued man wanted to take. On this day the ball needed to be aimed over the *S* or the *O* or even the *N*, which would start it well out-of-bounds so that the quartering wind would—in theory—bring it back into the right side of the fairway. Anything started center or left entailed less risk from the tee but would leave a highly undesirable, if not impossible, shot over the Road Hole bunker. Jones drove over the D, very long but too far left. Tolley hit over the E, even longer than Bobby and just about dead center, with a tantalizing chance to sneak a shot into the skinny opening between the bunker and the road. Ad Tolley.

In a temporal sense, this may have been the longest shot of Jones's life. He normally played quite briskly, but now he walked ahead one hundred yards, halfway to the green from his ball, and stood on a little hill. He stood there for thirty seconds, pondering, while the huge gallery moved to get a better look. His mind made up, Jones trudged back to the ball, pulled a four-iron from the bag, and aimed on an unexpected vector—not on the usual line short of the green and to the right, but left. Murmurs and mumbled comments— where was he going? He was going *left?* No one went left. Keeler was walking with Dr. Alister MacKenzie, the golf course architect. "It is a very bold conception," Mac said. "It will take some clever playing." But Jones was not being temerarious. He had a plan. After another delay, he swung his mashie iron, remembering during the stroke to give it a little extra goose; if he didn't get his ball past the sandpit, he'd be in real trouble.

The shot came off just about as he'd planned. It landed even with the ball-gobbling Road Hole bunker and took one giant bounce. Ordinarily there would be nothing to stop it from bounding down toward the eighteenth tee or onto the road, but today a thousand Scots ringed the green. Jones had already hit at least three of them that afternoon, and now he hit one more. The ricochet off a Scottish torso or noggin gave someone a story for the pub that night and left the ball on smooth grass just a couple of steps off the edge of the kidney-bean-shaped green. Ad Jones.

Bobby explained later that with his angle and the adamantine ground, he feared that the usually safe play was actually the most dangerous. He decided he couldn't aim right. The ball could too easily roll onto the road. The road was death.

As for the accusation then and later that he'd purposely used the immobile crowd as a backstop, Jones vigorously denied. "This was definitely not the case," he wrote in *Golf Is My Game*. "I should never be so heedless of the possibility of inflicting injury upon a spectator. I made completely audible requests to the stewards to move the crowd back on the left side, and even mounted a high piece of ground to motion them back myself. I played only after several minutes, and after it had become apparent that the crowd could be moved no farther."

After Tolley observed how well Jones's shot had turned out, his path was clear. He'd have to go for the green. But thoughts of the road on the right and the bottomless sandpit on the left caused him to chicken out midstroke, at least in Jones's reading. His mishit iron landed way short and curled left at the end on the unpredictably sculptured ground, leaving a nasty shot over the Road Hole bunker.

The thousands advanced to the green. They were golfers; they saw that Tolley would go first and that he had no safe way to play. He'd have to loft something soft as a kiss over the pit while trying not to recall botching a similar shot—twice—on eleven. But he clipped the ball perfectly and landed it mere inches over the bunker on just the right patch of rock-hard green. The ball finally expired two feet from the hole. Tolley would consider this to be the best shot he ever hit, but his opponent did not give him the putt.

Jones putted poorly from the fringe to eight feet. He had a handful of reasons to miss the next putt: the whipping wind, the worn-out grass around the hole, the speed, the break, the pressure. But he hit the thing with such perfect pace and direction that the ball didn't touch the sides of the hole, just its bottom. Tolley tapped in and the match was even. To eighteen, and the thrilling paradelike march into town.

The ancient stained stone buildings to the right of the fairway—Rusack's Hotel, the New Golf Club, Tom Morris's place—concentrated the gallery and its excitement. Both players reared back and fired long drives on the wide-open two-shotter. Jones played the second shot first, from about forty yards from the hole. Andrew Kirkaldy, the first honorary professional of the Royal and Ancient Golf Club, tended the flag. With a shallow-faced club, Bobby chipped through the Valley of Sin, the deep depression in front of the green, but too strong, about twenty-five feet past. Tolley maneuvered his ball to about ten feet below the hole. Jones missed and Tolley took the stage. While he dithered, Jones went through what he called "the most agonizing moments of that entire year."

Tolley may have milked the moment a little. Jones had always thought that his friend had a little of the thespian in him, a certain "grandeur," as he put it, a showmanship similar to that of Walter Hagen. The late-afternoon sun shone brightly as Cyril examined the blades of grass on his putt for glory. He could beat Bobby Jones with this one. He paced around, he lined it up, he took his stance. He missed.

The golfers walked, and the gallery ran to the first hole for sudden death. The exhausting drama turned on Tolley's hooked second shot, which missed the green to the left. He chipped adequately—to four feet in Darwin's account, and seven feet in Jones's reminiscence. But Bobby had a putt for a three on the same line, which turned out to be crucial. He hit the ten-footer with a feather touch not quite hard enough for it to go in, but since his little Spalding now blocked the hole, it was as good as a make. Gravely, Tolley considered his plight. Bravely, he tried to spin his ball around the stymie with an iron. He couldn't do it. The great match was over.

Four bobbies surrounded Bobby for the walk back through the happy crowd. At times, it looked like the policemen, who had hooked their arms in his, were carrying him. Back in town Jones said he felt like he'd aged six years. Keeler wrote that his man had been "half-killed" by the match with Tolley.

Thursday, May 29

Keeler's comments in the *Atlanta Journal* about the decline of Jones's health resumed the next day—"Bobby was gray and worried and his face was sunken"—and continued for the rest of the year. It wasn't just O.B. being the mother hen; Darwin, a more neutral observer (though still a tremendous fan of Jones) also noticed how this tournament was apparently draining the life from Bonnie Bobby.

As Jones stood on the first tee in the morning, no wild west wind threw sand in his eyes or attempted to tear off his clothes. Today's breeze from the east could barely blow the steam off a cup of tea. Four other members of the eight-man U.S. Walker Cup team would also play on this pleasant day. Still alive in Jones's bracket were Harrison "Jimmy" Johnston and George Voigt, while Ouimet and von Elm still drew breath in the other half of the draw. If Jones won his morning match, he'd likely face Johnston in the afternoon. Which was precisely what happened. With a machine-gun burst of threes— four of them in six holes, beginning at the sixth—Bobby took out G. O. Watt by seven and six. Meanwhile, Johnston, who looked like a young Henry Fonda, defeated D. C. Murray, five and three.

Jones-Johnston started calmly enough, with crowds smaller and less frantic than those for Jones-Tolley. Bobby played the front nine in even fours and stood one up, then he drove the green on ten, got a three, and went two up. Then he stymied his opponent with a great, long approach putt on twelve and was three up. Harrison "Jimmy" Johnston stumbled a little with a poorly hit iron into a bunker on thirteen to go four down. But then he abruptly stopped stumbling. Against the wind from one hundred yards on the long fourteenth, he hit it to four feet, made the putt, and won the hole. Jones was three up. On fifteen, Bobby three-putted and was now just two up. Sixteen was halved with par fours, Johnston holing a twelve-footer. On seventeen, Jones took care not to flirt with the road or the Road Hole bunker, but John- ston played the hole aggressively, and perfectly, chipping dead for a four. He walked to the eighteenth tee with the honor, the momentum, and only a one-hole deficit. This was the point at which Keeler saw the death mask on Bobby's face.

"It was said that with a comfortable lead I had 'faltered unaccountably,' " Jones would write a few days later in one of his most heartfelt columns. "Let us see how unfair such an estimate was to me and particularly to Jimmy, who had made a really great finishing fight . . .

"I have for this very reason an unspeakable aversion to the word 'guts' as it is so often used as an attribute of a golfer. Not only has the ability to finish well or to play golf at all for that matter, nothing in the world to do with physical courage but it will be found that sensational recoveries and tragic failures are almost always accomplished by the co-operation of the two sides."

Both men drove well on the home hole, and both hit pitches too strong into the upper-left-hand corner of the green. Johnston putted first, to about three feet from the cup. Jones looked at the hole, looked quickly down and put the putter head in front of the ball, looked briefly at the target again, moved the putter back to the starting position, then gave it a wristy tap. But he tapped it way short, leaving an eight-foot downhill, breaking putt to win the match, with the world watching. It was the same damn thing as the Tolley match. He lined it up and repeated his routine. His very erect, just-standing-there stance made him look quite relaxed, even casual. He wasn't. "That was the longest eight-foot putt I ever saw," Bobby said a few minutes later. "Lord, what a tournament!" Keeler wrote that night.

Jones had made it, of course, dead center. He had guts.

Friday, May 30

So many friends and enemies have come and gone that the late stages of a match-play tournament have a spooky feel. Battles fought, which were for a while the most tangible thing on earth, have decayed to a few lines of ink in a newspaper, or to nothing. A few of the defeated sometimes remain on the scene, forlorn figures tending to strong drink and rueful stories. "If I hadn't hit it in that divot there," they say, or "If he hadn't laid me the luckiest stymie there . . ." Those still in the hunt sometimes feel a bit of survivor's guilt; they know they've been good, and they know they've been lucky, but do they deserve it? And can they keep it up? Eight men remained in the 1930 British Amateur. At the end of the day, there would be only two—the finalists.

Two more U.S. Walker Cup players had lost—von Elm, who was really dangerous, and Ouimet, who wasn't. One besides Jones was left: George Voigt, he of the short, flat swing and the magic aluminum putter. He'd be Bobby's opponent if both won their next match.

A pattern had developed in the Jones matches—a relatively one-sided contest in the morning followed by a nail-biter in the afternoon. The trend seemed to stop against Eric Fiddian in the quarterfinals, when Jones blew his drive from the first tee way, way right, into a part of the burn that did not often come into play. But the pinch-faced former English Boys Champion from Birmingham, whose hair was even more severely parted and pomaded than Jones's, could not keep the one-hole lead for even one hole. Bobby birdied six, parred seven and eight, and he was four up. The match ended at fifteen. Jones walked in, feeling exhausted.

Voigt, the steady man from Long Island, led in his match but was still on the course. There was time to kill. Lunch filled midday for most people, of course, but Jones felt too keyed up to eat. At his suggestion, he and Mary went up to the second-floor sitting room that had a view of the eighteenth green. Jones ordered a glass of sherry. "I felt that it might steady my nerves, quiet the butterflies, or rid me of some of that tired feeling," Jones would recall. "I could not have made a greater mistake." By the time his glass was empty, Jones was drunk.

Voigt was anything but. A slight man with prominent ears and foxy eyes, he played golf like a metronome. "I never saw anyone whose ball is so unnecessary to follow with the eye," wrote Darwin, who watched Voigt win his morning match. "It is straight down the middle every time with the tee shot, right on the middle of the green with the approach and right into the middle of the hole with the putt every time." And he played that way against Jones, who endured a frustrating two hours, his unfocused eyes causing him to miss short putts at the fifth and the seventh. On eleven, he hit over the green and almost into the estuary, and on thirteen he fluffed a pitch like a ninety-shooter. "Some of the nameless music had gone out of his stroke," wrote Darwin of Jones—he, of course, did not know the music had been stolen by a glass of high-proof Spanish wine.

The match turned on fourteen, when the alcoholic flush left Bobby's face and George lost his mojo. The intent crowd huddled close to the tee of the fierce Long Hole with the annoying Beardie bunkers on the left and a low stone wall with a round top signifying out-of-bounds on the right. Perhaps Voigt didn't feel how briskly left to right the wind was blowing at that moment because the gallery shielded him from it. Maybe the line he took indicated overconfidence or sudden nervousness; after all, he stood on the brink of doing the best thing he'd ever done in golf, beat the great Jones in the semifinals of the British Amateur. He knew he'd win the final over whomever if he could just get past Bobby. At any rate, he hit a high drive over the corner of the thigh-high wall, the wind caught it, and it flew out-of-bounds onto the bordering Eden course. Jones won the gift-wrapped hole and had new life—only one down now with four to play.

Voigt followed his double bogey with a bogey and another bogey, and the match was even. Both drove well on the Road Hole. Jones played conservatively to about five steps short of the surface. Voigt went for it a little harder, and his ball rolled well up onto the green, paused, and rolled slowly back to the front edge. Bad luck. Jones chipped twelve feet short. Then Voigt hit his last and only really good shot of the final five holes, a perfect lag putt with his Mills mallet putter. Jones needed to drain from four yards to tie.

Suddenly, the angels sang. In a warm rush similar to that a quick glass of sherry brings, confidence filled Bobby like the Holy Spirit. He'd never had a feeling quite like it. When he surveyed his putt, he saw the line as if it had been painted on the green. He knew he could not miss, and he didn't. Again, the manly roar from the Scottish crowd—American galleries by comparison sound as if their voices haven't changed—and the stampede to the eighteenth.

Voigt must have known his big chance had passed. His second to the final hole replayed his second to seventeen: It rolled halfway up the green, then slowly rolled back down into the bottom of the Valley of Sin. Bad luck. Jones hit a beautiful high niblick—to six feet the way he remembered it and to ten feet in Darwin's account.

But both historians agreed on what happened next. George putted to a spot just inside Bobby's. Jones missed for the win. Voigt missed for the half. Handshakes and deep-throated cheers.

It would be Jones versus Roger Wethered, the English Walker Cup captain, in the final.

Saturday, May 31

"Sock Him, Roger; Sock Him, Roger; Sock Him, Roger; Sock Him, Roger . . ." The London *Daily Express* supported its countryman while advertising itself in posters it had printed and hung around the first tee. But could he? Wethered's willingness to sock had been in doubt since an incident at the Old Course in 1921.

He had just finished a most incredible British Open. The English Bobby Jones was a student at Oxford, exceedingly pleasant, and a wonder with a golf stick. The son of well-off parents from Devon, Roger and his sister, Joyce, learned golf as children at the family's summer home in Scotland, which echoes the way Bobby was introduced to the greatest game. But Wethered wasn't like Jones at all in other respects. Bobby would never get all absent-minded and incur a stroke penalty for stepping on his own golf ball while lining up a putt—which Wethered did on the fourteenth green in the third round. And Jones could never be blasé about winning and losing, which Roger was after he shot 71 in the final round, a record for an amateur in the Open, which tied him for first. There'd be a playoff the next day. Or would there? No, sorry, chaps, Wethered told an amazed group by the eighteenth green—a group that included Jones—he had promised the chaps back home he'd be there to bat and bowl in a cricket match the next day. You're going to concede the Open championship, his friends asked, in favor of a neighborhood cricket match? Although Roger stayed and played, his limited supply of fight seemed to be gone. Jock Hutchison won their two-round playoff 150 to 159.

"Wethered is one of those easy-going, impersonal British sportsmen who consider it bad form to show their desire to win," reported *Time* magazine. Jones did not have to peer into his eyes to take his measure on the first tee. They'd played each other just two weeks before in the Walker Cup, and after an interval of competitive play at the beginning, Bobby had won six holes in a row and crushed him. In the midst of the crushing, Roger frequently bent his skinny six-foot-two-inch frame down to chat into the ear of the five-foot-eight American; everything in his body language indicated he was more a fan of Bobby than a reasonably optimistic and determined opponent of Bobby. He was beat before they started at Royal St. George's, and he was beat today before a single ball had been struck. Both men knew it both times.

But before dismissing Wethered as an underachiever, let's recall what a golf monster Jones had become. If not for a slip of the grip in Savannah, he would have defeated every man in every tournament he'd played this year: the Southeastern Open, the Walker Cup, the *Golf Illustrated* Gold Vase, and, this week, Roper, Shankland, Tolley, Watt, Johnston, Fiddian, and Voigt. Jones had been a great player for years, but now he was exceeding himself. More than ever, it seemed, his handsome face closed like a door on the first tee. When play began, he opened his mouth only to smoke a cigarette. Yet despite the pressure he must have felt, his swing stayed as rhythmic and pretty as a waterfall. If Wethered weighed the evidence and concluded he couldn't win, well, he wasn't crazy.

About two thousand people waited on the first tee on the cool, clear morning. Jones, in a cap, light colors, and a checked tie, won the toss and hit a bullet. Wethered—hatless, long-legged, with a cardigan over his pullover—followed with something twenty-five yards short of his opponent, and the tweed army advanced. Repeating the pattern of their singles match at the Walker Cup,

Roger hung close to Bobby for the first nine. But Jones did not look or feel burned-out; knowing that his friend didn't possess the game or ultimately the desire to beat him made this the one game all week that he enjoyed. And this was a thirty-six-hole match, the long form that Bobby preferred.

Despite his supposed preoccupation with Old Man Par, Jones studied the opposition during competition. And on the tenth green, he saw Roger crack. Bobby had holed from six feet for a par four. From a foot closer, Roger missed for a half and fell to one down in the match. "I read in his face his belief that he could not keep this up much longer," Jones recalled. As they stood on the seventeenth tee about an hour later, Jones was five up.

The crowd swelled. Men hoisted their children onto their shoulders and had the wee ones describe the shots they could not see.

Someone who noticed that Bobby had done every hole in three or four thus far mentioned to him that no one had ever played the Old without at least one five on his card. So with this interim goal in mind, he began to play his third shot quickly and confidently from the Road Hole bunker—which put the stewards in a panic. Perhaps they'd gotten hell for not moving the gallery from around this green in the Tolley match, when Bobby hit the shot that hit a Scot. So with comic speed and shouted whispers, the marshals tried to clear the humanity so if the bunker shot was hit too hard, the ball would roll into the road. Jones paused, chuckling, and soon hundreds of others got the joke and joined in the laughter. The punch line: He feathered the ball to four feet but missed the putt. Wethered had hit the green with a badly hooked driver and a brassie and won the hole with a four.

On eighteen, with the narrow old Swilcan Bridge crowded with pedestrians, lots of men and women in ties and tweed jumped the ditch. Not everyone made it.

At the lunch break, Jones found that he could eat. He had a glass of milk and a fruit salad.

Trains and buses full of fans had unloaded all morning until the crowd reached fifteen thousand, a staggering number to follow one match. The latecomers got a party, but they didn't get to see much golf. Aided by a stymie he laid Bobby on the first hole in the afternoon, Wethered kept hope alive for a while, but birdies by Jones at the long fifth and the tenth increased his lead to six. Roger ran out of rope two holes later. He missed a three-foot putt, shook his opponent's hand, and the fifteen thousand emitted a hair-raising roar. What could be better? They'd seen Bonnie Bobby, and they'd watched him win with grace and guts on a sunny afternoon at the Old Course. "There goes a real champion of golf," Wethered said as Jones and his thousands of fervent friends began the long walk from the twelfth green. Someone wrote that his admirers "engulfed Bobby like wild tribesmen."

They wanted to touch him. As the bobbies escorted him through the throng on the long walk back to the clubhouse, many reached out to put a worshipful hand on the dazed-looking man.

Jones, victorious.

Mary and Robert Jones, the handsome couple from Atlanta, on their European tour.

4

Concavity

"Such another victory and we are ruined."

—King Pyrrhus of Epirus (319–272 B.C.)

When an athlete wins the big one, reality dissolves into disbelief. One minute he's trying to step on an opponent's neck, and the next he's listening quietly to speeches so dull that clocks stop. Relief, fatigue, and surreal boredom blend uneasily in the new champion's head, and then some genius with a notebook or a microphone asks, "How do you feel?" There is only one reply: "It hasn't sunk in yet."

So it was for Bobby Jones as the sun slowly set on May 31, 1930. Victory numbed him. "They tell me I won the British Amateur championship," he wrote in the long Scottish twilight—somehow he found the time and energy to crank out about eight hundred words for his syndicated column. Or did he? It's harder to imagine that he and Keeler *didn't* collaborate on this chore from time to time than that they did; after all, getting words on paper was Keeler's job, and helping Bobby was his fondest wish. In fact, the compound sentence that began this day's report sounded more O.B. than Bobby: "I can't realize it yet, but I have made a speech and thanked everybody for a bunch of cablegrams and telegrams which came with congratulations and suppose it must be a fact."

A moment after the match ended, the happy St. Andrews mob had carried him along from the distant twelfth green back into town, as if he were a leaf and they were a stream. A good deal of unseemly bumping and jockeying took place on the one-mile journey as people tried to get close enough to touch or to look into the eyes of the hero. More than one worshipper fell or was pushed into a bunker. Near the seventeenth green, Jones—surrounded by four uniformed constables who looked as if they meant business—disengaged from the largest golf gallery most people had ever seen and walked the rest of the way in the road. He drew close to the hotel—it's nice to imagine Mary in a window, hands clasped, beaming at the wondrous sight below—and went right up to his room. Keeler followed; the writer noticed that Bobby's eyes looked an inch deep in his face. "I'm awfully, awfully tired," he said.

Keeler, on deadline, got out a pencil and a pad and asked a few questions. Were you satisfied with the way you played? "Perfectly satisfied," Bobby said, except for missing a few short putts.

Will winning this tournament increase your ardor for the Open—the British Open—in two weeks? "On the contrary," Jones replied. "The way I feel right now, nothing else matters much."

You mean this was the biggest tournament of the year for you? "Of course, I'll do my best at Hoylake [Royal Liverpool] and in the American competitions, but this was the big shot. I've always wanted to win it and some way I never felt I should." Jones often sounded precious, such as when he used an auxiliary meaning of "should" when "would" would have been clearer. Blame Harvard and Emory Law.

At about this time, some three thousand miles away, an Associated Press reporter telephoned Stewart Maiden to inform him that Jones had won. The normally unemotional old Scottish pro, Bobby's first and only instructor, choked up. "I suffered with him during the week," said Maiden in his brogue.

"One who has never been through a championship like this cannot realize what it takes out of the players. Bob, it seems to me, suffers more than most. I'll bet he hasn't eaten a real meal all week nor had a full night's sleep."

Jones looked in the mirror and brushed his hair and straightened his tie, then put on a jacket and walked the one hundred yards or so from the Grand Hotel to the top step of the R and A clubhouse. He listened to speeches, then accepted applause, a chorus of baritone hurrahs, and the trophy. Public speaking terrified him, but he usually acquitted himself pretty well. His standard approach was to say that this wouldn't really be a speech at all, since words could not express how thankful he was for the courtesy shown him by everyone all week. But today he began his oration with a sly joke that caused a brief wave of hilarity. "Ladies and gentlemen," he said. "I always enjoy being where people eat well and sleep well. Thank God, that's the way people at St. Andrews do. That's why I love you and this grand old course."

Why that was clever and funny requires a bit of explanation. The "eat well" part referred to the St. Andrews club tradition of holding a dinner the night before every golf event, whether it was the toe of a footnote like the Autumn Mixed Stableford Four Ball or a historic occasion like the Amateur. At these dinners the warm fellow feeling of kindred spirits eating and drinking together was increased by a sweepstakes—betting, in other words, on the outcomes of various matches and the tournament. The phrase "sleep well" had to do with, of all things, religion. The Scottish Reformation had started in St. Andrews in the sixteenth century, and the city remained the home of an important branch of John Calvin's religion, Presbyterianism. Thus, in this virtual Vatican City for Protestants, sleeping well meant living well, that is, with a clear conscience. Jones's joke sounds vague here and now, but everyone got it there and then.

The crowd quieted, and the handsome American turned serious, inviting them to share his gratitude. "I honestly feel fortunate winning," he said. Remembering, perhaps, how difficult his Georgia accent was to understand in Scotland, he spoke slowly, with full stops after key words. "I have never worked harder. Or suffered more. Than in trying to get it." That suffering theme again: Later Bobby admitted that from the moment it began, he couldn't wait for the match with Wethered to be over. Much later he wrote about how enjoyable the match had been, but the earlier reaction seems more credible.

After that it was all packing and bustle for the Jones party. Mary had presumably tired of doing not much in Scotland. For a nongolfer, the enchantment of St. Andrews wears off after a few days, and Mrs. Jones had been there for a solid week. The Jones party boarded a very fancy Pullman car that night, on a special 8:30 train to London. And thence to France.

Sunday, June 1
Paris, France

"Apres quelques victoires difficiles lors des premieres rondes, Jones a facilement dispose d'un denomme Roger Wethered par 7 & 6 en finale."
—*brief coverage of the British Amateur in France*

Mr. and Mrs. Keeler participated in the toasts on the victory train, but then they broke off from the main group to visit Italy. O.B. made it a working vacation by cabling travel stories back to the *Atlanta Journal* from Rome, Naples, and on board Italian trains. He trotted out his beloved "cobalt blue" to describe Lake Como, and he told of being among the sixty thousand blessed in the square by Pope Pius XI. But Keeler's absence and the relative apathy of the French press mean that there's little record of the Jones's week in Paris. There'd been some discussion about a side trip to Berlin, but there's no evidence that happened. Probably Bobby and Mary and friends drank in the beauty of the City of Lights from the top of *la Tour Eiffel.* Perhaps they strolled to a café and watched the sun set on the Seine with a bottle or two of good wine, ordered in French with a Georgia accent. "Board-o, seal voo play."

Jones said when leaving St. Andrews that he had two goals in Paris: to sleep late in the morning and to eat. He never commented on the quality of his mattress, but the food did not satisfy. "I remember thinking on the boat coming back across the Channel," he recalled, "how good it would be after all that rich French cooking to get back to some cold mutton and boiled potatoes."

Monday, June 2
Golf de Saint-Germain, Saint-Germain-en-Laye

Jones played publicly once during the week in France, in an exhibition match with Harrison "Jimmy" Johnston as his teammate against the French Amateur champion, Andre Vagliano, and Marcel Dallemagne, a pro who would win the French Open three times in succession later in the decade.

Under lowering skies, Johnston and Jones met at the course on Route de Poissy in the forest of Saint-Germain, ten miles west of the heart of Paris. A large crowd gathered despite the threatening weather to see the Amateur champions of the United States, Britain, and France, and most of the gallery stayed when it began to pour and kept pouring.

The Americans beat the French, one up.

Jones didn't hit another ball all week.

Wednesday, June 4
Paris

Nothing much happened in Paris this day or this week, but the news from overseas made you grip your newspaper a little tighter. In Chicago, more mob hits. In Germany, they'd caught the Dusseldorf Vampire, the murderer—by penknife—of seven women. In Berlin, an intense little man with shiny eyes and a strange mustache testified in the treason trial of two of his followers. Herr Hitler spoke bombastically and in a loud voice from the witness stand about the injustice of the world. In India, two hundred people were killed and two thousand injured in riots in every part of the country, from Peshawar to Rangoon to Bombay. In addition to the unrest in its largest colony, England was dealing with unemployment that now had reached two million. And the House of Commons announced its opposition to the construction of a tunnel under the English Channel to France.

The sports pages in Paris, London, and New York ran the usual news of horse racing, tennis, cricket, polo, baseball, cycling, boat and auto racing, boxing, and golf. Except for an oblique reference in a Keeler column in Atlanta, no account of Jones's win by any writer or press association on either side of the Atlantic mentioned the possibility that he had won the first leg in a possible Grand Slam. The name didn't exist, and except in the back of Jones's mind, the idea didn't exist.

In Great Britain, however, a great deal of excitement attached to Bonnie Bobby's shot at winning the (British) Amateur and the Open in the same year. It had been done once before, in 1890, by the immortal John Ball Jr. of Royal Liverpool. This was a feat with a very well-known name: "Over here, we didn't give a toss about the Grand Slam," says St. Andrews historian Dr. David Malcolm. "All we cared about was the Double."

Monday, June 9
Calais

The party was over, and the Jones group retraced its steps of a week before. They traveled by train to the coast, through towns and terrain north of Paris that were not memorable, and boarded the ferry at Calais. As the ferry sailed north, a white line on the horizon slowly grew the way seconds grow into a minute. Watching the water and the distant white Cliffs of Dover can force the mind to think.

Dark-haired, dark-eyed Mary had had enough. She'd likely never been away from her kids or from Atlanta for so long in her life, and she missed all three terribly. Meanwhile, her husband had not been fully available to her either, what with the enervating stress of competition and his adoring crowds and the press and his own writing. When their ship docked in New York in three weeks, Mary and her father would get on a southbound train. Bobby would immediately travel west, to Minneapolis and the U.S. Open, as his exhausting summer continued.

Two things, maybe three things, can be stated about Jones's frame of mind as the ferry crossed the Strait of Dover. We know that he was happy to leave the béarnaise and hollandaise behind. We also know that his considerable mental energy had begun to focus on the next challenge, the Open at Royal Liverpool, because it was always thus. When Keeler questioned his enthusiasm for the Open, Bobby was slightly offended. "I have never taken a golf tournament casually," he wrote. "It did not make sense to me to travel three thousand miles for a lark."

The satisfied feeling he'd expressed moments after winning the Amateur obviously did not last. Jones described the progression of his emotion in *Golf Is My Game*. "During the few days in Paris," he wrote:

> I had realized that this championship had taken a big load off my chest, or back. Now, even if I should fail to win the British Open, I felt I should be entitled to consider the expedition to Britain had been a complete success . . . With it I had now won, at one time or another, all four major championships. I should, therefore, henceforth feel no obligation to myself, or even to Keeler, which was about the same thing, to continue playing in competition unless I felt like it. Finally, the inescapable fact was that I could not win all four without the first one.

And he couldn't win all four unless he won the second, a prospect that seemed in serious doubt when Jones discovered, postvacation, that he'd lost his game. Not all of it, to be sure, but the carefree perfect striking he'd had in Savannah and especially in Augusta and when he needed it at St. Andrews—that had fled. Disuse could have caused the wildness he found when he began practicing for the Open, but his return to earth may have been inevitable. Brilliance has a shelf life.

As the first round of qualifying for the Open approached, stress and pressure, deep and dark, descended on Jones.

Wednesday, June 11
Royal Líverpool Golf Club, Hoylake, England

Visitors on the perimeter of the 1930 British Open walked from the train station through a pleasant residential neighborhood with modern, turn-of-the-century construction, a sharp contrast to the Middle Ages feel of St. Andrews. But the friendly face on the large prosperous dwellings on Meols (pronounced "mells") Drive hid a triangular-shaped two-hundred-acre monster. "They say Hoylake is a good course for dentists," commented Chris Moore, the club secretary, in 2004. "You can expect four hours of pain."

The pain came first from length—6,750 yards—then from wind that tried to blow your hat off, and finally from a peculiarly mesmerizing quality of light that made distances hard to judge. "The fiercest test of ground we possess," wrote Darwin in his preview, "we" meaning England. "It's an odd-looking place—a flat expanse intersected by a number of turf walls—locally known as cops. It looks very plain sailing but it is not. There's trouble on both sides not [just on] one as at St. Andrews.

"I know no course in the world that has a more severe finish. The seventeenth has got a road as perilous as that at St. Andrews. No man is safe until he is past that hole."

Hoylake's subtlest threat was the simplest and most unusual hazard in championship golf: a field of grass. The rounded rectangle of fescue that served as the practice ground impinged like an ingrown toenail on the first and sixteenth holes. Out-of-bounds yet maddeningly in play, its borders were vaguely defined by a ditch in one section and everywhere else by a lightly raised grass border, like a three-foot-high piecrust. It was a dramatically undramatic hazard. Bunkers, burns, and lakes throw out cautionary vibes, but that field of grass at Hoylake gave you nothing—until the first time you hit into it, and then you couldn't get it out of your mind.

Although its terrain stretched into the distance without much change in elevation, Royal Liverpool enjoyed two glorious views—four, if you counted the portraits in the stairwell. John Ball Jr. and Harold Hilton, the dominant amateur golfers of a generation past, remained at their home club in oil paint on canvas. At the top of those stairs, a great, airy room provided inti-mate views of practice-green putters and first-tee hitters; in the middle dis-tance were the first and sixteenth greens; most of the rest of the course could be seen with a longer lens. At the farthest point from the clubhouse was Hoylake's other great vista. From the high greens and tees on holes eight through thirteen, you stood above the estuary of the River Dee, whose vast mirrored surface changed in the sun like a kaleidoscope. A purple and pink summer sunset on the wet sand at low tide could take your breath away. That was Hilbre ("hill bray") Island in the middle of the river, a few acres inhabited only by hundreds of birds and surrounded by millions of unseen oysters and mussels. The quiet hills in the distance were in Wales.

Jones didn't like Hoylake. Although he was far too politic to criticize then, he thought the course, with its length and its tenacious rough, put too much pressure on the driver. "Singularly lacking in subtleties," he said of it much later, perhaps comparing it to the amusing and endless complexities of the Old Course. He shot 71 in his first practice round but had to putt brilliantly to do so. He was hitting a big pull hook off the tee.

Thursday, June 12
Beeston Fields Golf Club, Nottingham

While Jones had rested in France, others got ready for the Open by com-peting in relatively minor events. Early in the month, George von Elm won the French Amateur at La Boulie near Versailles, while many of the top Eu-ropean pros played in the Irish Open at Royal Portrush. The professionals with the most marketable names sharpened their games in exhibition matches. Since 1930 was not a Ryder Cup year, only a handful of American pros had sailed to England. Without the PGA of America paying their expenses, these men proved by their mere presence that they were serious contenders; the trip from the States took too long and cost too much for a dilettante. But two of these cold-eyed experts, Macdonald Smith and Leo Diegel, were not mere mercenaries hungry for a check. Golf drove them both so crazy that seventy-five years later they seem not only understandable but lovable.

Smith, a Scottish émigré to the United States, warmed up in his old home-town and home club of Carnoustie and joined in the annual match of fifty golfers from Carnoustie versus fifty from the links at Leven. An amateur named McRuvie made a name for himself and a headline in the *Times of London* when he beat Mac two and one. But no worries: Smith had lost before in his colorful life, and he would lose again. Every golfer lost. But a couple of Mac's defeats were so vivid that people forgot all the times he'd won.

He'd been born in Carnoustie in 1892, the youngest child in one of the greatest golf families in history. Willie, Alex, George, Jimmy, and Macdonald all became U.S.-based golf pros, and three of them rose to the heights as competitors. Willie won the U.S. Open in 1899. Alex won it in 1906 and tied for first with his baby brother in 1910. Alex won the three-way playoff—Johnny McDermott was also involved—but Macdonald's march to golf glory seemed inevitable, which he proved when he was the first, or among the first, to break 280 for a seventy-two-hole event. Then World War I interrupted his and millions of other lives. The roar of the cannons in the French bat-tlefield cost him a lot of his hearing—or maybe it had been the sound of the machinery in the shipyards where he worked. At any rate, by war's end he'd lost a lot of his ability to perceive sound. He began to drink heavily. "He was such a drunkard that his wife picked him up out of the gutter and I mean the gutter in the street," recalled Wild Bill Mehlhorn, one of the top American pros in the '20s. "She taught him a little Christian Science, got him not to drink, and got him back to playing golf. Out in San Francisco he hit 1,000 balls a day for a whole year and never played a round of golf for that whole year." Mac returned to tournament play in 1923, after he wed his savior, Mrs. Louise Harvey. Because of his poor hearing, he didn't talk much. They called him the Silent Scot.

With his big, smooth Carnoustie School swing that resembled none so much as the stroke of Jones, Mac Smith rose to a level just below that of Hagen, Sarazen, and Bobby. He could get no further, however, because he could not win either of the two biggest events, the British or American Opens. But Lord, he was so close, and so often—he finished within three shots of the top a staggering twelve times. The most heartbreaking of his many narrow defeats had to be the '25 Open at Prestwick, when he needed only a 78 in the final round to win. For the last time, the R and A didn't charge admission, and it seemed like half the country turned out to have a few pints and to give the native son a beery cheer to victory. But the holiday atmosphere of a county soccer match distracted and worried Mac into an 82. He blamed the crowd and the tournament administration that didn't control it. He boycotted the Open for the next three years.

Mac had a sad, rubbery face and a taciturn disposition; Diegel, from Detroit, Smith's opposite, had a hard look and was as nervous as a cup of coffee. Leo "Eagle" Diegel could always get exhibition work because his golf was so good and his style was so entertaining. He perched his tee ball on top of a two-and-a-half-inch tee—everyone else liked to start a lot closer to the ground—and gave it a rip on an unusually upright plane. Like others with his metabolism, he was a lousy putter, so he invented a hunchbacked, arms-akimbo putting method that everyone called "diegeling." Between tournament rounds he molded and sculpted the head of his putter continually, as if it was a work of art.

If his odd rigor mortis with a putter didn't make you laugh, his general comportment just might. After he or a fellow competitor hit a tee ball, little Leo would often jump up and down as if he'd mounted an invisible pogo stick, the better to see exactly where and how each ball lay. He found it practically impossible to walk slowly up the fairway like the other guys; his urgent need to evaluate his next challenge made him break into a race walk or even to run. Then he found it practically impossible to play a conservative shot rather than the perfect shot, a high-risk impulse that added to his entertainment value and led to really startling bursts of low scoring.

And to heartache. Shades of Mac Smith: Seven times during his career he would finish fourth or better in the two big Opens.

It was not for lack of trying. "In all my years in golf, I have never seen anyone whose devotion to the game could match Leo's. It was his religion," recalled his frequent partner, Sarazen. "Between courses at the table, Leo used to get up and take practice swings . . . At the 1925 (U.S.) Open in Worcester, he would lie in bed chain-smoking, fretting about the large tree that stood on the edge of the fairway on the twelfth hole." Diegel blew smoke at the ceiling, muttering that that tree shouldn't be there, that someone should chop it down, that he was going to hit it before the tournament was through. In the fourth round he did hit it, the first in a series of errors that cost him another Open.

Diegel's preparation for Royal Liverpool in '30 involved three exhibition matches with English professional Abe Mitchell and an interesting contest in Nottingham with Horton Smith and two other upper-tier English pros, Charles Whitcombe and Archie Compston. The Americans won the morning four-ball. In individual play that afternoon, Horton, Jones's conqueror at Savannah, squeaked out a one-up win over Whitcombe.

But there was nothing squeaky about the way Compston demolished Diegel. He won by seven and six, played out the bye holes, and scored a 67. Compston was startlingly unlike his contemporaries: With a build so slim and a face so geometric, he could have been a model for Ralph Lauren; so tall—six feet two—that he was often referred to as the Giant; and so extroverted, informal, and loud that he seemed more American than British. He threw clubs. He gambled. He was very popular. "A lonely and lovable man," wrote Henry Longhurst of the blond athletic Giant. "Ever searching for something he never quite found."

Compston had made his name around the world two years before, due to the astounding result of his seventy-two-hole challenge match with Walter

Hagen. That is, it was supposed to be seventy-two holes or something close to that, but Archie threw so many birdies at Sir Walter at two English courses that only one hole of the final round had to be played. Archie won eighteen and seventeen and collected £500. Hagen would never forget the confidence with which his opponent played or that Compston had his caddie carry around a big stuffed animal, a gay affectation if ever there was one. The toy black cat was Archie's symbol for himself and his good-luck charm.

Although Hagen, the defending champion, didn't show up, the field for the Open at Hoylake was the strongest at any tournament all year. Outstanding in this outstanding group were the two Smiths, Diegel, and Compston. With the right breaks, any of them could beat Jones.

Saturday, June 14
Royal Líverpool Golf Club

Since the course would be closed on Sunday, many of the entrants got in one final practice round. As ever on the day before the Open, golfers worried, fans studied, and writers hyped. "Nearly 300 golfers from a half a dozen countries will tee off tomorrow," wrote Frank King for the Associated Press, "but the tournament seems to revolve around Jones." Francis Powers of the Consolidated Press made the same point more grandly: "Jones is the glamorous figure of the sports arena and brings a breath of romance back to a world that has been greatly commercialized. His square shoulders that have carried the weight of ten national championships will be the target for some of the greatest amateur and professional shot makers in the game."

When two of those greatest shot makers got together before the Open, Horton Smith would surely have looked in Bobby Jones's brown leather golf bag. And he would have seen the crazy-looking club he'd given his friend, a twenty-five-ounce sand wedge with a concave face. It looked like a very large soupspoon with a shaft and a grip and felt like an anvil on a stick. In theory, the thick flange and protruding leading edge of the scooped-out face got under the ball and bounced it straight up from any lie; then the top of the spoon propelled it forward. You hit the ball twice with this thing, in other words. A club designed for a double-hit? That was a problem, because hitting the ball twice on the same swing cost a one-stroke penalty.

But no one, including the user, could say for sure what was happening underneath the exploding sand when this club hit a ball. The R and A and the USGA were testing what they referred to as "the sand wedge"—always surrounding this new term with quotation marks—but had drawn no conclusions (the invention of the modern sand wedge, the one with bounce in its sole, remained about one year in the future; Gene Sarazen was its Thomas Edison). Hagen had been manufacturing concave-faced wedges for two years, and while they hadn't caught on, they hadn't been discredited. Smith became so interested when he saw a version made by a man in Houston that he bought the rights and contracted with a company in Detroit to manufacture. He'd showed Jones the extra-heavy, oddly shaped niblick when they were roommates in Savannah. Horton gave him one, and Bobby agreed to try it out. The British Open would be the first time he used it in competition.

He would hit the most important shot of the tournament with it.

A year later, the USGA would declare the club illegal.

Sunday, June 15
The Adelphi Hotel and Wallasey Golf Club, Liverpool

Coal smoke stained the stone buildings of Liverpool, but regular cleaning kept the limestone on the Adelphi gleaming softly white. The best hotel in town sat like a seven-story wedding cake on a hill above the turgid Mersey River. Good views were available from the upper floors, but the Joneses always stayed close to the ground because Mr. Jones did not like heights.

The interior of the grand hotel in the grimy city echoed a luxurious ocean liner, which made sense because many of its guests had just sailed overseas or were about to; the Adelphi's posh Sefton Suite was a replica of the first-class smoking lounge on the late lamented and Liverpool-based *Titanic*. The inappropriately sexy mirrored reception area led to a magnificent ballroom with a thirty-foot-high ceiling. The restaurants were good, though a bit overpriced, and there was an indoor heated swimming pool, a sauna, and central heat in every room. In ten years, the Adelphi would be a place from which to watch Hitler's Luftwaffe rain bombs on the Liverpool shipyards. In thirty years, in a grubby club two blocks from the hotel, the Beatles would start to become famous.

Jones left the Adelphi on this fair Sunday morning and motored a few minutes to Wallasey Golf Club, one of the two qualifying sites for the Open. He had an unusual task to perform before his final practice round: to sit without moving for half an hour on a chair in the clubhouse. Jones had sat for very few portraits over the years, never for one in Britain, so they regarded his assent as a coup at Wallasey. The project required the effort and cooperation of four people: the extremely competent artist, John A. A. Berrie, a member of the club, whose 1931 portrait of King George V was valued at over £250,000 when it was stolen in 1999; Sir Ernest Royden, a well-off Liverpool businessman and a former captain at Wallasey, who commissioned the portrait and donated it to the club; a third member, Jock Liddell, a man about Jones's size who had already posed for the torso part of the painting; and Jones, who earlier in the week had loaned his body double a great-looking dusty blue cashmere pullover he'd worn a couple of times on this trip.

While the artist sat at his easel with his brushes and oils and a headless figure on his canvas, Jones gripped a glass of whiskey and soda—the first record of his morning drinking in 1930. "Mr. Berrie kept me occupied for not more than thirty minutes and during that time pleasantly refreshed," Jones would recall. "As an object lesson in painless portraiture, this was the best I have ever seen." Although the artist could only rough in the shadows and lines and shape of Jones's face in half an hour, Bobby liked the result so much that he made the unusual gesture of signing and dating the portrait himself, in a fine, firm hand in black oil paint on the bottom right of the canvas. And when

Berrie tried to give the sweater back, Jones told him to keep it as a souvenir. "This is how I try to teach my models to hold themselves," commented fashion producer Jan Strimple, as she examined a copy of Berrie's extraordinary painting in 2004. "Winning obviously did not surprise this man. Did he pluck his eyebrows? It looks like he did."

Jones posed with his right eyebrow arched slightly, a counterpoint to the part in his hair, which was on the left and not down the center as it usually was. His look expressed confidence, composure, and perhaps a bit of irony. Some who know his backstory will look in his face for a sign of weariness, even of dread for the week ahead, and they will find it.

Monday, June 16
Royal Liverpool Golf Club

Where was Walter? Although the fashionably late and nick-of-time arrival were Hagen trademarks, the qualifying rounds started at Wallasey and Royal Liverpool, and the defending champion didn't disembark from a Rolls-Royce limousine and stroll to the first tee. Hagen had thought seriously about a return to England over the winter, but then the building blocks for an exhibition tour to the East had suddenly and unexpectedly fallen in place. New Zealand was in for $5,000, Australia for $10,000, and Japan for $6,000, plus there'd be moneymaking stops along the way in Honolulu, Pago Pago, and Manila. Although Hagen loved the prestige of winning the Open—he'd done it four times, including once at Royal Liverpool—prestige didn't pay his liquor bill. The fans flocked to him in England and called him High-gen! which flattered his monumental ego, but there were other fans to see and new friends to make. So he and Australian trick-shot artist Joe Kirkwood had sailed on February 1 for Hawaii.

There were other considerations. Jones's apple-polishers cited Hagen's lack of success in recent years against his amateur nemesis as evidence that Sir Walter was merely avoiding another whipping. No way. Hagen feared no one. But he was afraid that time and lifestyle had robbed him of the ability to play in and win the British Open, sail home, get himself to the U.S. Open site immediately, and win there, too. Jones had done this very thing in '26 and was plainly planning to do it again now. Hagen, at age thirty-eight and with high mileage, was ten years older than Bobby. He did not like to rush.

Where was Walter? As the 296 teed off for the qualifying rounds at Wallasey and Hoylake, Hagen's ship approached the west coast of the United States. From there he'd train straight to Minneapolis and his rental house at Interlachen in suburban Minneapolis. He'd be giving his best effort to win the U.S. Open, mostly because he felt it would boost the money he could charge for exhibitions. And with dollars in mind, he followed the progress of the British Open avidly. If one of his brother pros could win—say, Sarazen or Armour—there'd certainly be opportunities for a big-bucks exhibition between himself, the four-time Open champ, and the new holder of the Claret Jug. But a win by Bobby would be bad for business. A "world championship" match had been proposed just the year before, in which Hagen, the holder of the British Open trophy, would play Jones, the U.S. Open champ. "All attendance records would have been broken," Walter recalled sadly—"sadly" because it didn't happen. The USGA spat on the idea. Such a contest was too overtly commercial for an amateur, it said. Probably Jones wasn't all that keen about the match anyway. Why would he want to bother? As an amateur, he could not accept payment, and no real status would attach to winning. Thus to Sir Walter and the other pros in the Open, it was Anybody but Bobby.

Qualifying began in uncharacteristically sultry, humid weather that popped an unexpected color at Hoylake—green. Most years, the unwatered fairways were already turning to tan as the summer began, but late-spring rain after an extended drought had made the course almost lush and the rough, in spots, terrifying.

Jones teed off at 12:36 at Hoylake, having already disposed of two of his sternest competitors. That is, with late scratches by Tommy Armour and Gene Sarazen, they had disposed of themselves. Bobby had played in scores of these thirty-six-hole qualifying tournaments before the main event, and he'd almost never had a problem. The best one hundred finishers qualified; he could make the low one hundred and ties with his tie tied around his eyes. He therefore rarely showed all his cards in the serious but usually low-tension preliminary rounds. But in precisely five days he would be observed wandering around the Hoylake clubhouse holding a drink with two hands and with such a used-up, burned-out look that his friends became worried. Therefore, even his pre-tournament golf was worth examining.

Again, he didn't hit the ball well, by his standards, and began the day by driving into the ditch bordering the fearsome field. Jones missed green after green, but deadly chipping and putting allowed him to "boil three shots down to two," as Darwin put it. He hit an atrocious second into a bunker on the twelfth hole, a long two-shotter that doglegged left around the mother of all grass-covered sand dunes. It cost him a six, which he followed with a wobbly four on the thirteenth, a little downhill par three with a great view of the Dee from the tee. But he steadied himself and finished with a 73.

"Are you satisfied that these scores are correct?" his marker asked when it was over.

"Well, I'm not exactly satisfied with it," Jones said. "But there's nothing I can do about it now."

Keeler's reminiscences don't make it clear when he said it, but on this day or the day before, Bobby moaned about the state of his game. "I simply don't know where the darn ball is going," he said (although it's doubtful he said "darn"). "I guess I'm trying to steer it, and of course that's the worst thing in the world to do. But what can I do? This is a tight course. You can't get up there and [just] slam away. . . ."

The leaders at Royal Liverpool were Diegel—driving with a brassie all day—and Compston, both with 70. Mac Smith joined them at the top with a 71. At Wallasey, which was about two shots easier than Hoylake and a little bit more fun, the 68 by English professional William Thomas Twine tied up first place in the strange race whose only goal was to be in the top one hundred.

Six time zones to the west, rain poured down on the Town and Country Club in Minneapolis, but still the local U.S. Open qualifying tournament went on. Among the hopefuls who had paid the $5 entry fee was Willie Kidd, the Scottish pro at Interlachen, the club that would host the Open in less than a month. Kidd must have felt good about his chances after a 70 in the morning round, but then the heavens opened after lunch, and he was un-prepared. With no jacket or umbrella, Kidd slipped to a drenched 80. Others had trouble, too, however, so his 150 total was among the low eight. He qualified.

"The field at Interlachen will be the greatest that ever has been assembled for a golf tournament," wrote a local sportswriter. Three weeks before it began, Minneapolis was already getting giddy about the big event. Jones and Hagen would be there on July 10, the first meeting of the year between un-doubtedly the best amateur and possibly the best professional in the world.

Tuesday, June 17
Wallasey

Almost all of Wallasey was visible from the tower at St. Nicholas Church, a solid-looking kirk on the other side of Bayswater Road. Some spectators spent the day up there—likely they were members of one insti-tution or the other or both—and had a merry time watching Wallasey's debut on the main stage of big-time golf. They peered through binoculars, chatted, ate, drank, smoked. The blessedly brief heat wave was over. Sweaters were comfortable.

In addition to its view, St. Nicholas enjoyed another claim to fame: the golfer's window. The stained-glass image of a man with a club and a caddie made a remarkable juxtaposition with the usual Christian images of Jesus and apostles. Visiting dignitaries were always taken to see it. Jones fit the bill, of course, so after his round he allowed himself to be brought into the nave and up to the altar. He looked to his left at the rectangle of glass, metal, and oxide. The window was not all that impressive, but surely he said something admiring to his escorts, and then he was gone, back to the Adelphi, to write his column and to rest for the first round of the Open.

He had qualified easily. A police sergeant in blue had met Jones on the first tee and, with baton in hand, walked close to him all day. Although the armed security prevented invasion of his personal space by the three to four thousand fans, golf needs a lot of room and there were a lot of people. As Jones was about to attempt a twenty-foot putt for a bogey on the eighth, a couple of blinkered observers blithely walked across the green to get a better look. Bobby had to stop his stroke just as he was about to start it. "Please do not walk across the green," he said, then missed the putt.

"My round is a thing I would rather not think about," Jones wrote later that day, plainly in a bad mood. "It was entirely unsatisfactory from start to finish . . . It would be putting it mildly to say that I was absolutely rotten."

Although the hooked tee balls and missed putts in his 77 seemed to have disappointed his walking mob, a London newspaperman named Bob Howard wrote a few words that afternoon that Jones liked so much, he put them in his own book thirty years later. This, obviously, was how Bobby saw himself and liked to be seen: "Although he said he was very dissatisfied with his golf, I am quite sure he could have done considerably better if the need had existed. Jones on a highly important occasion somehow creates the impression that he is trying about twice as hard as anybody else, and it is precisely this element that seems to produce his world-beating golf."

Darwin filed no report on Jones's day because he stayed at Hoylake to follow Horton Smith. "He looked like he could not possibly make a mistake," Darwin wrote, clearly fascinated by the Joplin Ghost. "[Smith made] the game look ridiculously easy." The golf correspondents from the *Times of London* and the *Atlanta Journal* predicted a win by Smith if not by Jones.

No one with a well-known name failed to get under the magic number, 158. Walker Cuppers Don Moe, George von Elm, and Cyril Tolley made the field without incident, as did the four most noteworthy American professionals: Diegel, both Smiths, and Long Jim Barnes. In the nearly meaning-less contest to be low qualifier, Compston won, with 141. Englishmen Henry Cotton and William Thomas Twine finished second and third.

One last bright incident occurred as night fell. When Jones had finished his round, he shook the hand of his caddie—who wore a tie—and signed a golf ball for his marker, the daughter of Joseph Boardman, the captain of the club. Then, as mentioned, Bobby and Captain Boardman went to see the golfer's window. If anyone there smelled smoke, they must have assumed it was incense from a censer. It wasn't. One of the spectators in the tower had flicked his cigarette toward the ground five stories below, but it had landed in a bird's nest in the eaves of the lady chapel—a part of the church dedicated to the Virgin Mary. After smoldering for hours, the roof burst into flames and lit the night sky. But the fire brigade arrived in time to save the church and its famous piece of glass.

Wednesday, June 18
Royal Liverpool Golf Club

The Open began in a breathless hush, punctuated by cheers. Then the main sound was the drumbeat of rain on the roof or on the brim of your hat.

Anyone who knew the tournament favorite and that limping man who was always whispering in his ear knew that Jones would not be competing just against Tolley, Smith, Smith, Diegel, and Compston for the next three days. Bobby played against history now, and history had a face and a name at Royal Liverpool, and a portrait in the clubhouse.

Wiry, silent, and always wearing a yellow tea rose in his buttonhole, John Ball Jr. still stalked the unforgiving ground at Hoylake—at least his memory did. In 1890, the year he won the second of his *eight* British Amateurs, Ball's supporters inveigled him to go up to Scotland in the fall, as he rarely did, to play in the Open at Prestwick. It was a thirty-six-hole, one-day tournament then, which no amateur had ever won. A fierce west wind blew bunker sand into the air the day of the event, but Ball never lost his balance. Conditions could never be too tough for him; he disparaged raked bunkers, calling them "geranium beds." With his head-high cleek shots penetrating the Prestwick gale, he shot four nine-hole scores of 41. For severe conditions in the dead-ball era, that was pretty damn good. His 164 beat the pros, interrupted the Scottish monopoly in the Open, and won the Double. He was an amateur and a gentleman, and a member at Royal Liverpool. He was a hero.

His father owned and operated the Royal Hotel near the seventeenth green at Hoylake. Locals talked of Johnnie Ball's Gap and pointed out the monument in the ground on the long sixteenth, commemorating a gutsy shot he'd hit over the dangerous nothingness of the field. Ball was everywhere—and not there at all. Aged sixty-eight now, he lived not far away, across the Dee, in a little cottage on his little farm just over the Welsh border. But he did not attend the start of the tournament to watch Jones try to do what he had done. John Ball was an exceedingly modest man—he gave away all his golf medals—and probably did not wish to cause a stir. When he visited Hoylake the day before the Amateur more than a decade before, he'd hid himself from view as far as possible, talked to a few friends he hadn't seen for a while, then disappeared like a mist. Now, if he thought of another return to his home club, he might have been discouraged by the gray, rain-laden sky.

Jones had an about-to-burst look himself that morning. The starter announced his name on the first tee, he took his stance, and two thousand spectators went quiet. One of them moved—Jones backed off. Visibly nervous—which was *extremely* unusual—Bobby paced back and forth for a few moments, then tried again. The tight landing area, with out-of-bounds right—the field—and left, made this the toughest first swing of any of the Open courses. Jones hit an awful drive that headed for the field but stopped in the dry ditch at its border. He missed the green with his next two irons and needed a good chip to save a bogey five on the 415-yard hole.

At that point, Bobby knitted his possibly plucked eyebrows together and played without a word but very well. The game proceeded briskly, which Jones liked, because of the brisk, brusque Liverpool fishermen who handled the gallery ropes. "When not catching shrimp," wrote Keeler on Tuesday, "[they] handle a golf gallery better than I have ever seen one handled before. . . . the average time of a [practice] round was two hours and thirty minutes instead of the three hours usually consumed largely in standing around and losing tempers." Jones holed from twenty-five feet on ten but otherwise had poor putting luck until the very end, as several times his ball lipped out or hung on the edge. He and von Elm saw each other when Bobby was on the fifteenth green and George stood by the nearby thirteenth. Von Elm asked with his hands "how are you doing?" and Jones responded by pretending to break his putter over his knee. For von Elm, the only appropriate pantomime was to hold up both hands and stick out each finger but one—or perhaps to extend only one finger. In a nightmare that proved how tough were the rough and the Hoylake bunkers—and how fast the greens had become—George made a nine on the par-four fifth. He would shoot 81.

Jones finished strong on the vicious final three—holes named Dun, Royal, and Stand. His birdie-par-birdie gave him a two-under-par 70 and the lead. The wind freshened, and sprinkles fell as he walked back to the clubhouse, past the first tee where Mac Smith and Long Jim Barnes were about to tee off. Jones had the clubhouse roof over his head and a glass of whiskey in his hand when the storm broke.

The hard rain caught Horton Smith on sixteen; he finished with a 72. His new friend Henry Cotton came along a while later, trying to bring a great round into the barn despite the distracting downpour. Cotton, twenty-three, had visited the United States for the first time in November 1928. He played the winter golf circuit and did fairly well but could not come close to winning, because the Tall Boy from Missouri owned first place. That was the winter that H. Smith won eleven tournaments, which made him the center of attention. He didn't exactly bloom in that hothouse of country-club dinners and cocktail parties, however. Henry observed Horton at a social function that the star of the tour could not avoid. A pretty young woman offered him a cigarette.

"No, I don't smoke."

"You don't drink either?"

"No!" replied Smith, with feeling.

"Then you have no vices?" the woman asked with a suggestive smile.

"Oh, yes," Horton said. "I'm often short with my long putts." The conversation hit a lull at that point.

While Smith toweled off, Cotton hit his ball in the drenched sand of bunkers on Dun, Royal, and Stand. Still, he shot a 70 and tied for the lead with Jones.

The day's most remarkable performances came from that twosome who teed off just as the thunder and deluge began, and they did it with leather grips and without rain suits or golf gloves. Long Jim Barnes—an American by way of England, six feet three, forty-three, and 170 pounds—shot 71. And Mac Smith! Mac birdied the second, third, and eighth holes and kept his round together until the end. His 70 tied Jones and Cotton for the overnight lead. Tolley shot himself out of it with an 84, but all the other big names lurked.

Thursday, June 19

The *Atlanta Journal* masthead contained a daily reminder of its mission and its value: "We Cover Dixie Like the Dew." Covering Dixie like the dew meant covering Bobby Jones above the fold on page one and giving news of his exploits banner headlines on the first page and the sports page. Three Bobby stories often ran side by side by side during the big events: a factual game story about what had happened that day in the Open or whatever; Jones's column; and Keeler's smart country-boy musings about what it all meant. The column was called "O.O.'s" by O.B.—an O.O. being a once-over.

Keeler's virtually unlimited access to the man of the hour gave his writing a tremendous authority. Everyone—even Darwin—quoted O.B. quoting Jones. This week, his words would reach more people than ever: The Associated Press had hired him to give the more or less official account of the event for the hundreds of newspapers that subscribed to its service. On top of that, the National Broadcasting Company set him up with headphones, a microphone, and an engineer so that he could file nightly fifteen-minute radio reports from the tournament. His relationship with Bobby made an oracle of Keeler, and contemporary and future golf journalists—not to mention his newspaper, magazine, and radio audiences—accepted his opinions as Truth. Thus, his errors of fact or emphasis rippled like a big rock thrown in a little pond.

Ignoring the evidence of Bobby's scores and his standing relative to the other guys, O.B. wrote and said repeatedly in books and magazine articles still unwritten that Bobby played poorly in the 1930 British Open. Perhaps because he played atrociously himself, Keeler didn't grasp the first rule of golf, which may also be the first rule of all sports with a scoreboard or a scorecard: It's not how, it's how many. Bobby wasn't hitting the ball well; to O.B. this meant he wasn't doing well. His study of Latin and Greek in high school may have encouraged him to imagine a Platonic ideal of championship-level play: In Keeler's mind, every drive should be long and in the fairway, every iron on the green, and so on. But golf doesn't require perfect striking to be great. Golf doesn't require anything—just numbers. And the numbers don't have to be gaudy either, just better than those put up by the other guys.

Jones began his second round with bad numbers. Mindful of the grass sea to the right and of his poor tee shot the previous day, he knocked a careful brassie into the first fairway. But his pulled four-iron into the rough near the green resulted in another opening bogey. The second hole at Hoylake looked benign compared to the first, just a gentle dogleg right, a two-shotter of 369 yards. You had to be careful with your second shot because the green didn't hold, but that was no big deal with a niblick in your hands. Jones hit his second so poorly, however, that it landed short of the intervening greenside bunker and jumped over it onto the green, a piece of luck that got him a nervous par.

An ancient, brown stone wall surrounded the third tee, and five thousand interested spectators surrounded the wall. Low, dense trees prevented actual sightings, but a rush of fractured air and sudden metallic clanking reminded you from time to time that another train was arriving at Hoylake Station. The fairway on the short but intimidating 480-yard par five swung sharply to the left about 230 yards out and then, from the vantage point of the tee, disappeared to nothing. Jones lined up his drive over a large gorse planting on his left, a needed shortcut if he wanted to hit an iron second to the green. Hatless spectators shielded their eyes from the sun with their hands. Jones swung his loose, wristy, not-a-care-in-the-world swing. The ball flew high as ordered but hooked too much and bounced out of the fast fairway. From the healthy rough on the left, Bobby hit to the lush rough on the right. He left his pitch short of the green, chipped, putted, and putted again. He had a 5-4-6 start against par of 4-4-5.

At this critical juncture, Jones's short-game radar turned on and locked in. Keeler didn't recognize the beauty of Bobby's eight one-putt greens in the last fifteen, but his scrambling produced lovely numbers. He holed ten-footers on eight and nine for birdie and par, he hit the par-five fourteenth in two for a two-putt birdie, and he didn't hurt himself on Dun-Royal-Stand. The off-center striking ratcheted up the pressure on his fraying nerves and nervous stomach, but the black-and-white result was an even-par 72 and the thirty-six-hole lead.

The other eighteen-hole leaders—the sad-faced Silent Scot and suave Henry Cotton of Langley Park, England—suffered serious misadventures. Mac Smith seemingly missed every putt, causing a 77. Cotton woke the morning of the second day with his right wrist so stiff that he couldn't bend it in any direction without sharp pain. He found a doctor who told him to get it massaged. He found a masseur to rub it for thirty minutes. He ran to the train station and hustled to the first tee. And shot 43-36—79. "I could have cried when I read 'Cotton Blows Up,' " he recalled. "[But] it was no use telling the world my wrist was not normal *after* 79."

Fred Robson, Horton Smith, and Clem Todd provided additional excitement. Robson, age forty-five, a journeyman English pro rejuvenated by the miracle of steel shafts in his woods, shot 72 and trailed Jones by one. Smith played well again, although he hit his second shot on seventeen almost into Ball's hotel, and Darwin swooned, as usual, over the "ridiculous ease" of Horton's stroke. Mr. Todd, a spectator from Sheffield, England, dropped dead.

The leader board by the red brick clubhouse looked something like this after two rounds (note that the honorific "Mr." preceded amateurs' names, English pros' clubs were carefully noted, and the affiliations of foreign professionals were listed haphazardly, if at all):

Mr. R. T. Jones, Atlanta, U.S.A.	70-72—142
F. Robson, Cooden Beach	71-72—143
Horton Smith, Cragston, U.S.A.	72-73—145
L. Diegel, Mexico	74-73—147
A. Compston, Coombe Hill	74-73—147
J. Barnes, U.S.A.	71-77—148
Mr. C. J. H. Tolley, Royal and Ancient	84-71—155

Jones returned to the Adelphi and ordered dinner from room service, had a few drinks, and took a long bath, with another drink within reach of the tub. He also wrote the flattest, dullest column of his life. It was even inaccurate, starting with the first sentence. "The second round of the British open," he wrote, "was played under as perfect conditions as the first." Did he forget about the thunderstorm on the first day?

As much as the circles under his eyes, Jones's unusually poor writing effort indicated that his burnout had accelerated. He had one day left of this Open, thirty-six more holes, approximately eight hours of pain.

Friday, June 20, Morning

The Black Cat teed off at 10:30, about an hour after Jones. When word filtered back to the clubhouse that the leader had for the third consecutive day started very slowly, it became clear that the tournament was there for someone with the guts to grab it. Archie Compston was such a man. He had a gambler's cool nerves, that was certain. Two British PGA championships and his mind-boggling win over Hagen showed that he could handle pressure and an audience. At Coombe Hill, the course near London where he was the pro, he'd taken so many pounds and pence in golf wagers with his members that the tax man tried to get a piece. Archie could have settled with the government, but he rolled the dice and let a court decide. To his own delight and that of his many friends, Compston won again.

Supported by a number of the lads who had come up from Coombe Hill, Compston marched off in double-time: par-birdie-birdie-birdie. The shouts and growing size of his gallery made him impossible to miss. Jones heard the commotion perfectly well, and the golf course grapevine told him what it all meant. With his own dismal start of par-bogey-bogey and a par on the short fourth, he'd lost five shots to Archie in the first four holes. They were tied for the lead.

As graying Fred Robson stumbled to a 78, Compston became the English hope. The big, blond Black Cat seemed ebulliently American: He swung hard, walked fast after his drives, putted aggressively, and grinned when his partisans cheered. In this drama, Jones played the reserved—almost depressed—Brit. He seemed tired and acted peevish. "Jones had been nervous all along," wrote the correspondent for *Time* magazine. "[He] snapped at photographers, hooked into the long grass again and again, missed short putts, and puckered his lips angrily when he missed a shot."

"One of the greatest throngs in the history of tournament play" looked on, according to the Associated Press, despite unpleasant weather. A fresh breeze blew throughout the day, and rain fell on and off and hard and soft. Jones, in a light blue cashmere sweater, a dark tie, a white shirt, a flat white cloth cap, light-colored woolen plus fours, and two-tone brown-and-white shoes, righted his ship in the middle of his round with a long series of threes and fours that included birdies on eight and ten. But he slumped at the end with 5-5-5-5-4, two over par, on the concluding holes that had previously been so good for him. He'd heard Compston's people about five holes behind him, as everyone on the course could, because on ten through thirteen Archie went birdie-par-birdie-birdie, building a crescendo of support. His third-round 74 complete, Jones walked to the second floor of the clubhouse. He asked a waiter for a ham sandwich and tea. He looked out the window. On the broad battleground of Royal Liverpool, various small parades proceeded here and there, but an army marched in the company of one aggressive general.

"Compston was truly striding after the ball as if he could not wait to vent his fury on it," Jones wrote in his memoir thirty years later. He imagined that as Archie swept past the sixteenth green, everything and everyone that was not tied down might be swept into the air in his wake, like dust behind a speeding car.

What eating Jones could do, he'd done. As Jones walked to the first tee to start his final round, Compston passed on his way to the clubhouse and lunch, with a smile a mile wide, photographers in front and friends behind, their hands slapping his broad back. He'd shot 68, a course record. He had the lead by one. As the giant walked by, his metal spikes scraping the unpaved path, Jones scanned him with the appraising look he used on opponents on the first tee. He thought that he had never seen a happier man. He also decided that Archie simply couldn't play as well in the fourth round as he had in the third.

After fifty-four holes, one important competitor had left the race for first and another had joined it. A 78 did in Horton Smith, but a one-under-par 71 reasserted the claim of that crazy man who jumped and ran and putted like he'd caught his tie in his fly: Diegel.

Compston	74-73-68—215
Jones	70-72-74—216
Diegel	74-73-71—218

Of all Jones's rivals, none played more aggressively than Leo Diegel,
the tightly wound pro from Detroit.

Friday, June 20, Afternoon

The sky darkened. Mist filled the air in a long prelude before rain. After a par four on the first, Jones hit a tee shot on the second that seemed to hang in the air forever. As the ball descended to the right toward deep rough and trouble, Jones observed in the gray light that it was on a collision course with a man wearing the red skullcap that identified him as a gallery marshal. The ball hit the man flush on his hat and rebounded as if it had hit concrete. History does not record if the man remained standing; all eyes were on the ball. The awesome flight of the Spalding took it back toward the sky once more, way to the right, over the rough on the second, over the tee on the fifteenth, and into a bunker in front of the fourteenth green—at least fifty yards from skull to sand. As he took his unexpected walk toward the fourteenth from the second, Jones wondered what in hell that man's head was made of.

The marshal wasn't hurt, and neither was Jones. Although the incredible carom didn't gain him any yards, it hadn't cost him any either, and now he had a clean lie in sand instead of who-knows-what in the deep rough. Jones quickly realized that the shot in front of him was practically identical to the one he'd holed for an eagle on the fourth hole in his first match in the British Amateur. With that positive thought, he played the same club and the same punch shot as in the match with Sid Roper at St. Andrews. The ball finished on the green twenty feet from the hole. He made the putt—a turning point, the first of several. His step a little lighter, Jones played the next five holes in one over, which wasn't at all bad. He arrived at the tee of the long eighth needing two fours for a one-under 35. He felt sure he could do it.

Compston would have heard of Jones's renaissance by the time he began his final round. He hit a perfect drive off the first, then an iron that was not quite perfect, and a mediocre putt from the edge of the green. Estimates of the length of the remaining real estate ranged from a foot and a half to thirty inches, but no one argued about the look on Archie's face after he missed: stunned. An avalanche of little mistakes followed; England's hope managed only 5-5-5-4-5-5 against a par of 4-4-5-3-4-4. His supporters and members of the news media began to look away from him, as if he was disfigured. At the end of the day, the writers recorded only his score, a sorry 82.

Jones had the lead—as the efficient golf course grapevine had probably informed him, via his caddie—when he played the 482-yard eighth. The smell of sea salt got in your nose on the Far, as they call the eighth at Royal Liverpool, a beautifully wild-looking hole with a big valley in the center of the fairway and waves in its ground imitating the nearby Irish Sea. Giant mounds dominated the right edge of the fairway and provided the strategic guide: miss the mounds. Jones did. He hit a spoon second up the hill toward the plateau green to a good spot ten to fifteen yards short. Although the fairway and fringe were mowed as close as felt and the raised green repelled water and, thus, golf balls, this shot presented no real problems for a short-game master like Jones—unless he got too fancy or lost his head.

He did both. Attempting to run the ball up the slope, as opposed to lofting it, and making it die just onto the edge of the green, Jones hit it fat. The leading edge of his iron contacted earth before ball, and the shot came up woefully short. A low groan from the crowd and a second chip, this one not much better, still ten feet from the hole. The birdie he'd counted on now gone, he went for the par and missed. Another group groan. Angry now, and the par he'd counted on gone, he tapped the ball for its final journey, from a foot, a formality. And then the world went blank.

Jones walked up the grass-covered sand dune overlooking the Dee to the ninth tee. Had he really missed that tap-in, really made a seven? He had, and the dull realization that he had put him in a profound daze. Darwin remarked famously that a little old lady with a croquet mallet could have saved him two strokes. For Jones, sixty-one holes of labor had been lost. Diegel and now, suddenly, Mac Smith were back in the running. The high, swaying rough and the coffinlike bunkers of the ninth hole loomed before the shaken golfer.

Jones recalled this moment rather bloodlessly in *Golf Is My Game*, making no effort to describe the shimmering force field of emotion in the air when he turned a four or five into a seven. "My reaction was precisely this," Jones wrote. "I was completely incapable of making any calculation either of what score I might ultimately achieve or of what it would be necessary to do to stave off the challenge of others. Since I could not think, I did what I think nine persons out of ten would have done under similar circumstances. I simply resolved to keep on hitting the ball as best I could. . . . I had no more thought of attacking or defending or of being over par or under par, but merely of finishing."

Like a boxer on the ropes, Jones bought time until he could clear his head, less a strategy than mere survival. On autopilot for the next eight holes, he scraped out four pars, three bogeys, and a birdie. In the aftermath, he could hardly recall a single one of these shots. But consciousness returned and fatigue departed after he bogeyed fifteen. For the last time, Jones came to the sixteenth and that field.

Desperate, Diegel tried to close his two-stroke deficit but made no headway, playing the front nine in the same two-over-par 38 as Jones. He diegeled brilliantly coming home, however, and reached sixteen roughly an hour after Bobby, one shot from the lead.

The sixteenth at Royal Liverpool, the Dun, was a mirror image of the first, but longer; both wrapped around the practice ground like tentacles. At about 270 yards from the tee, the fairway narrowed and turned right toward the green. Left meant safety. Jones went right. In an all-out effort for a birdie four, he wanted to hug the out-of-bounds line formed by the edge of the field, a line that would save scores of yards. It worked, a brave shot for a man struggling with his driver. Now Jones could think about reaching the surface in two on the 582-yard hole. He took another lusty swing, this with a three-wood. His ball soared over the field and landed in safety, but rolled unluckily into the most inconvenient position possible.

With his own gallery mixed with thousands of refugees from Compston's sad show, Jones approached his seventieth green like an actor entering a stage. He'd pulled his spoon just enough for his ball to scurry into a bunker to the left of the green. He had about twenty-five yards to the hole, a good lie in the smooth sand—but no room to hit the damn thing. The ball had stopped so close to the far wall that Jones would have to stand with his right foot on the bank out of the bunker and manufacture an extreme up-and-down swing. He frowned. His supporters muttered. A desperate time calling for a desperate measure, Jones took the one club from his bag he didn't know very well: the massive soupspoon on a stick, his concave-faced sand wedge. Up to this point, he'd only used it in competition for two relatively inconsequential shots—a hack out of a gorse bush at St. Andrews and a pitch to the first green in the first or second round at Hoylake.

Keeler's account of what happened next was inaccurate; Jones's was dispassionate; and Darwin didn't see it, at least not up close. But George Trevor in *The Sportsman* saved the day:

> "My sand wedge, please," says Bobby, turning toward his Scottish caddie, adding, by way of explanation, "That extra-heavy niblick with the steel fin."
>
> Thus armed, Mr. Jones settles his feet firmly in the deep sand. That grotesque niblick flashes as it catches the sun—a rare visitor to foggy Hoylake. Out pops the ball, garlanded in sand; it plumps on the green so close to the cup that the gallery squeals as the rubber core rolls around the rim, finally sitting down contentedly three inches from the lip!
>
> ... The gallery, scrupulously well behaved heretofore, after the fashion of English golf crowds, now hummed with whispered inquiry. Everyone wanted to know what manner of weapon had extricated Bobby from chancery. . . .
>
> No protests against Mr. Jones's use of the sand wedge at Hoylake have come to the writer's ears.

Jones would call it one of the best shots of his life, and it undoubtedly was, regardless of the shovel he used to do it. But after his tap-in birdie, he still had two tough holes to play and physical and mental reserves that he'd drained almost to nothing. He saved par with a putt of a yard or two on Royal and scored a routine four on Stand. It was over. He'd shot 75. Given the weather and the pressure and the seven and his waning mental health, it was a damn good round by a gutsy, resourceful competitor. His 291 total was three over par. Would it be enough?

Jones made his weary way to the clubhouse to await the result—win, loss, or playoff tomorrow. He hid out in the club secretary's office. Someone handed him a glass of whiskey, the first of several. He didn't talk much. To Darwin, Bobby looked wasted and unhealthy. "Seeing him nearly past speech," he wrote, "I thought that the time had come to call a halt and that this game could not much longer be worth such an agonizing candle."

Keeler popped in and out to give Jones scoring updates and to ask a few questions for the record. On one of these occasions, he asked the man who was like a son to him when he was going to give up this damned foolishness. As much as he loved reflected glory, O.B. hated to see Bobby suffer. "It's my last shot at the British open," Keeler wrote that Jones told him, although Bobby's ability to deliver an oration at this moment seems doubtful. "This tournament has taken more out of me than any other I ever played in. It's quite too thick for me. . . . This was my hardest tournament, win or lose. I feel that I'm not strong enough to play in another one. I'm happy to win, if I should win with Leo and Mac still out and going strong. And if I should win after all, I'm the luckiest fellow in the world."

Jones-centric accounts of the denouement of the 1930 British Open never acknowledge how much Diegel and Smith wanted to win, too. The siren call of validation, recognition, and immortality lured them as much as they summoned Bobby. The two pros had the powerful additional motivations of prize money, coupled with a desire to obliterate histories of frequent and frustrating near misses in the biggest events.

Time dripped slowly for Jones as he awaited the verdict. "Those of us who were with him in one of the smaller rooms of the clubhouse united in assuring Bobby that all was well, as he wandered restlessly about holding a glass in two hands," Darwin recalled. "And then came a suggestion that all might not be well. . . ."

Starting the final nine with a rush, Diegel had arrived at the sixteenth tee needing three fours to tie Jones. Surely, at this point, the journalists and the

Jones takes the Double. His wins in the 1930 British Amateur and Open
were considered the greatest-ever achievement in golf. A parade awaited
in New York City.

tournament leader went upstairs to the windows. Ringing the wall behind
them were portraits of every captain who had ever commanded at Royal Liverpool, all wearing red jackets. Men on tiptoes, men spilling gin, waiters,
wives, all of them encircled with blue tobacco smoke: They all watched
through the glass as the tense little athlete from Detroit bent to place a ball
on one of his extra-long wooden pegs. He swung his unusually steep swing.
The observers seven hundred yards distant on the second floor of the clubhouse would have found it hard to pick up his golf ball in the air, but little
Leo's body language provided a reliable indicator of his shot's direction and
how he liked it. He hit, then leaned to the right; his semaphore indicated disgust. Fearing the field, he'd played too safely to the left, and his ball rolled
into a fairway bunker. He could not recover. He bunkered his third shot,
came out well—but then missed his shortish putt for par. Diegel fell two
shots behind.

When Leo did not make a three on the seventeenth or a two on the eighteenth—he took two par fours—his race was run.

Jones had been in purgatory for two hours when, finally, Smith came into view, a yacht to Diegel's speedboat. Everyone on the grounds turned their eyes to the Silent Scot. Mac progressed slowly from tee to green on sixteen, stretching out the drama. He took his usual full dress rehearsal practice swing before each shot; he took a good look at his target; he took his time. He arranged his feet very carefully and swung his full, round swing, lovely to behold. He played the sixteenth flawlessly in birdie four, taking a very long time to hole out. Now everyone knew the score: Like Leo a few minutes earlier, Mac needed two threes to tie Bobby. He parred seventeen and now needed a two. After a perfect drive on eighteen, Smith asked a steward to run up to the green and tend the flagstick. The Silent Scot's iron shot landed dead on line—then rolled past the hole.

Jones had done what John Ball Jr. did in 1890, the greatest achievement in golf history: the Double.

A man in tweed shushed the crowd then spoke into the microphone. "Another championship, the British Open championship, is completed. This is the fifty-eighth occasion upon which this cup has been played for. I must congratulate Mr. Robert T. Jones on having won not only the Amateur championship at St. Andrews, but being here amongst us this evening, as winner of the British Open championship."

The tournament winner stepped forward. As a roar of approval filled the air, the secretary of the R and A shook the champion golfer's hand frantically, as if it were a pump handle and they were all dying of thirst. Bobby Jones accepted the Claret Jug and cradled it in his left arm. His smile obscured but did not hide the circles under his eyes.

For the umpteenth time, Keeler (at left) and Jones (center) prepare to board a Pullman car.

Smokin'

Tobacco is a dirty weed. I like it.

It satisfies no normal need. I like it.

It makes you thin, it makes you lean,

It takes the hair right off your bean.

It's the worst darn stuff I've ever seen.

I like it.

—Graham Lee Hemminger,
Penn State Froth, November 1915

ones won the Double, and the world went crazy. New York City mayor Jimmy Walker and police commissioner Grover Aloysius Whalen fired up the machinery for America's official hero's welcome, a ticker-tape parade. They danced in the streets—literally—in some parts of Atlanta. Major John Cohen, publisher of the *Atlanta Journal*, convened a meeting of many of the leading citizens of the city, then announced that for those who desired to travel the eight hundred miles to New York to greet Bobby, a special train had been secured. The second section of the Southern Railways Crescent Limited would be dedicated to the welcome party and would depart Terminal Station just after noon on June 30 and stop ten minutes later to pick up more passengers at Brookwood. Discounted round-trip tickets would cost $50.75, Pullman sleeper accommodations and tips not included. Major Cohen's people had also secured a great rate at a good Times Square hotel: The Vanderbilt on Forty-seventh Street in midtown Manhattan had extended a rate of $4 per night per Georgian.

Excitement about the big party grew every day. Mr. and Mrs. Asa Candler, of the Coca-Cola Candlers, made headlines when it got out that they were going to *fly* to New York to help organize logistical details. And wait a minute—the proud citizens of Atlanta asked each other—shouldn't we be planning our own parade when Bobby comes marching home again in July, after the U.S. Open? You're damn right, they decided, they should, and they would.

Meanwhile, U.S. Open officials in Minneapolis expressed apprehension and joy. With Bobby's Double, their event would be bigger than ever—but could they handle the crowds? "Bobby to Draw 10,000 Persons to Golf Event" headlined the *Minneapolis Tribune*. Embedded in the front-page story was a photo of a very worried-looking man, D. C. Edwards, the chairman of U.S. Open crowd control. Minneapolis also discussed in its newspapers the need to welcome Jones to town in some grand way. A red carpet, a band, something.

In the week before he and Mary sailed, Jones followed through on promises he'd made to help some friends raise money for charity. On Saturday, June 21, he played an exhibition match at Blackwell, a delicious golf course in Worcestershire, near Birmingham. Jones and Dr. William Tweddell, the 1927 British Amateur champion, defeated Stanley Lunt and Eric Fiddian three and two. It's hard to imagine that Jones really wanted to play in front of another audience less than twenty-four hours after his exhausting win in the Open, but he'd pledged this day to Tweddell in 1928, when the doctor was in the States for the Walker Cup at the Chicago Golf Club.

A second promise made and kept was to English golf stalwart Ted Ray, who had asked during the Open if Bob might come to his home club, Oxhey Park, a sporty little course in Watford, in suburban London. Big Ted got two other aging golf gods to complete the foursome, James Braid and Harry Vardon. About three thousand people paid a few bob to watch—and what a shame none of them had camcorders. Ray, age sixty, easily the most boisterous one of the group, always wore a golf suit and a sort of formal felt hat, never a cap, and tried to hit a home run with every swing of his driver. Tall, thin, and Scottish, Braid, also sixty, owned a vast mustache and dignity that a judge would envy. "No one could be as wise as James Braid looks," someone said, a line that stuck to him as tightly as his facial hair. Vardon, like Ray, kept a straight-stemmed pipe in his mouth while speaking and when hitting a golf ball—and while winning the Open six times (Braid had won the Open five times; Ray, once). Harry had been the greatest player in the world until Jones hit his stride, but now he was fifty-three and tubercular; he would live less than seven more years. He and Jones got along famously. Vardon always called the younger man "Master Bobby."

The written record at Oxhey Park states that Bobby shot 66 on their 5,602-yard par 73, while Jones would remember it as a 68. Whatever—Jones played great and had fun. "The recollection of the game at Oxhey was a very good thing to take on the boat with me," Jones wrote. "I had played entirely up to the form I had had at Augusta. Perhaps I should not have to work so hard in the tournaments back home." But the feeling wouldn't last.

Friday, June 27
Leaving England

The Atlanta group laid low in London for a few days after the exhibitions and then took the boat train to the coast for the voyage to New York. Judging by the figure he showed in a photograph taken a week after the Open, Jones had gotten serious with his effort to replace the circumference he lost during the tournament. Keeler had not been there to eat cold mutton and boiled potatoes with his closest friend; he and Mrs. Keeler had gone back to Paris for a few more days. In O.B.'s stead was another delightful man, Cyril Tolley, who would be playing in the American Open and Amateur.

Tolley looked as though he'd just stepped out of his haberdasher on Saville Row when he and Bobby boarded the train. Every inch the gentleman, Mr. Tolley wore a gray three-piece pinstripe with a pocket handkerchief, French cuffs, and a dark derby that set off the gray of his hair. He carried a newspaper in his left hand; a cane hooked his right forearm. Bobby stood on the platform next to Cyril while a photographer snapped. Half a head shorter, thicker in the middle, and obviously less vital than the English gentleman, Jones suffered by comparison. His dark blue double-breasted topped by a gray homburg wasn't bad, although with his foreshortened form he looked a lot better in a sweater and plus fours. And in contrast to Tolley's confident gaze at the camera, Jones's tired eyes regarded something or nothing far away.

Bob, Mary, and Cyril settled into a compartment. Cyril said something, Bobby gave it credence by repeating it in print, Keeler used it again and again, and thus it became written in stone. But it was hogwash.

"Bob, how long have you been over here?"

"About six weeks."

"Do you suppose you have ever played so badly for so long a period, and yet you have won both our championships?"

Jones bought into the idea to a degree because, he wrote, "my game was never once near peak efficiency." Who cares? Peak efficiency was not the goal in golf, and it didn't matter how you won; it mattered *that* you won. Besides, it was a relative game, not an absolute one like the times and distances in track and field, such as the four-minute mile and the fifteen-foot pole vault. Jones often got more credit than he deserved for a lot of things, but because of this piece of inverted logic, his invasion of Europe in 1930 got less.

But his determination, his resourcefulness, and his *results* in the Amateur and the Open were nothing short of flawless.

Looked at another way, however, the assertion by Jones and his press agent that Bobby had won with his worst stuff, a mile from his A game, was breathtakingly arrogant.

Keeler rejoined the group in Southampton, and they all got on board the S.S. *Europa*.

Saturday, June 28

"Bobby Sails for Home without His Clubs"

Hundreds of papers picked up a report by the Associated Press "that the golf clubs which rendered him such glorious service in winning the British open and amateur championships didn't sail with him." Apparently, Jones checked out of his hotel in London but left his sticks behind in the hubbub of farewells; a bellman raced the clubs to the station but arrived as the train was leaving the station; another near miss at Southampton required the cargo to be placed aboard the *Aquitania*. The leather bag holding his hickory sticks would arrive in New York a day after Bobby did, the AP reported, but someone would whisk them to him before he left for the U.S. Open. What a story!

None of it was true, however; Jones had his clubs with him all along. Possibly the unusually detailed and widely distributed fable illustrated how hungry they were back in the States for something, anything, about Bobby. Even the announcement of his first two starting times in the U.S. Open in two weeks rated a feature treatment in some newspapers. He would begin the first round at 9:45 on Thursday, July 10, and the second on Friday, July 11, at 12:50 . . . he would be paired with Jock Hutchison of Chicago . . . It was thin thread with which to weave six paragraphs.

Almost everyone missed the best hook. Bobby didn't mention it in his retrospectives on the Open, and neither did Keeler, nor did the wire services—

but the idea that Jones might win *all four* majors this year finally got a little traction. Lloyd's Insurance Exchange in London led the way; moments after Jones had won the first two, Lloyd's lowered the odds on his winning all four from fifty to one to twenty-five to one. Next came Grantland Rice, the widely read syndicated columnist. "He has a good chance now to win the four premier crowns of the game in one year against the best professionals and the greatest amateurs of the world," Grannie wrote in the seventh paragraph of his June 22 essay, two days after Hoylake. "His appearance at Interlachen Country Club, Minneapolis, in July, will make this championship one of the most notable competitions in the history of sport."

The June 30 issue of *Time* magazine stated the intriguing possibility most plainly. Jones had wanted the Double, *Time* said, and was quite pleased to be the first-ever simultaneous holder of the U.S. Open, the British Amateur, and the British Open: "And his ambition goes even further—to hold the four major titles of England and the United States at the same time."

Sunday, June 29
At Sea

The German-owned and -operated *Europa* was built for speed more than comfort—at least compared to the opulent *Mauretania*, the outbound ship. Still, the first-class passengers lived in a luxurious world of great food and deck chairs and not much to do. But Keeler (definitely) and Jones (probably) pecked at a typewriter during the five days at sea. "Starting back for home after a rather strenuous campaign in Great Britain, there are a number of reflections which assail me," the attorney began aridly in the "Bobby Jones Says" column published on July 5. The foremost assailing reflection was the case for the stymie, an oddly arcane topic, given the circumstances. Yet it wouldn't have been like Jones to invade his own privacy by sharing what people really wanted to know—the state of his mental and physical health, for example, or his plans or what he thought about in the Royal Liverpool clubhouse while waiting to see if he'd won the Open. His modesty prevented him from talking about himself too explicitly. He just couldn't do it.

Before Keeler got to his heavy lifting—four thousand words on a tight deadline for *The American Golfer*—he wrote two shorter pieces. The first was a telegram responding to the storm of congratulatory messages from the folks back home:

> Warmest appreciation from Bobby and all of us. Party includes Bobby, Mr. and Mrs. Hurt, Mrs. James C. Cross, Tom Payne, Cyril Tolley, Tom Potter, Don Moe, Johnny Dawson and me. Dead tired but happy. Love to everybody.

He'd forgotten to mention Mary.

Keeler's second short subject attempted to scotch reports that Bob was unwell. Diegel had had a good look at Jones after finishing second to him at Hoylake, and he'd mentioned to a reporter how ragged the new champion appeared. No byline appeared beneath the "Bobby in Perfect Health" headlines—it was an Associated Press story—but O.B. had been freelancing for AP and was in a position to know how Jones felt, so he had to be the author. "Bobby Jones, recently crowned British open and amateur golf champion is in perfect health," Keeler wrote, "but somewhat nervous and apprehensive over reports that a big welcome is awaiting him when he lands in New York."

O.B.'s major opus on board the *Europa* was "The Battle at Hoylake," in which he repeated the canard that "Bobby won the British open playing at very nearly his worst" and that "he got more out of a worse game than he ever has managed before in an important competition." Near the end of the piece, Keeler wandered off in an interesting direction: the whispering and jealousy of the other boys.

"They have said he was the pet of the United States Golf Association; he was favored in the matter of starting times, and partners, in the open events, that sort of thing," O.B. wrote. "One or two writers have even been guilty of the absurd reflection that he has been favored in rulings on matters of fact, in play-offs—that sort of thing."

Keeler put forth an odd defense for the petty attacks he had brought to light. In Great Britain, "where they pull everything out of the hat—starting times, partners and all," Bobby had won the last four big events in which he'd competed. Therefore, Keeler concluded, in Scotland and England, where they were most transparently fair, Bobby actually did better than in the United States.

Odder still, infinitely odder, was that in two and a half weeks some of Jones's most respected peers would be saying—loudly, for the record, not whispering—that Bobby was the pet of the USGA and favored in rulings on matters of fact—that sort of thing.

Beneath the water, the two huge screws in the *Europa*'s hull turned furiously, plunging the ship toward New York.

Monday, June 30
From Atlanta to New York

Pilot Beeler Blevins touched down at Newark Airport at 11:15 A.M. local time, after a flight of four hours and forty-five minutes. The vanguard of the Welcome Home Bobby Jones committee crawled out of the Candler's cramped little airship: Mr. and Mrs. Asa Candler; Hunter Perry, a real estate man; and Ralph Smith, a columnist for the *Atlanta Journal*. At their subsequent meeting at the Hotel Vanderbilt, the Atlantans and their New York counterparts worked on the guest list for the banquet on Wednesday night after the parade. They went big: Governor and Mrs. Franklin D. Roosevelt; ex-governor and Mrs. Al Smith; Will Rogers; and Adolph Ochs, the publisher of the *New York Times*.

The Candlers announced that they'd radioed an invitation to Bob and Mary to fly them to the next engagement, in Minneapolis. It wouldn't happen; Bobby, it turned out, disliked flying and had made other arrangements, and Mary wasn't going to the Open. She'd be heading back to Atlanta to reunite with the children, Clara, age five, and Bob III, three.

After a dining car and several Pullman sleepers had been attached, the express train to New York chugged out of Atlanta. Mayor and Mrs. I. N. Ragsdale; Robert and Clara Jones, Bobby's parents; and John Malone, Mary's father, were among the one hundred revelers on board. The train would stop in Washington, D.C., to pick up U.S. Senators William J. Harris and Walter F. George and Congressman Robert Ramspeck. The party arrived in New York at noon, after twenty-four hours on the rails and God-knows-how-many bottles of Prohibition beer, wine, and whiskey.

Meanwhile, a bit of weather had come up in the North Atlantic. As the sky turned to iron and the seas got rough, the *Europa* slowed.

Tuesday, July 1
At Sea

Jones woke at 7:00, as he had throughout the voyage, and wrapped himself around a big breakfast. Afterward he did not hit golf balls off the deck against a net or into the ocean; in fact, not once during the five-day crossing did he pick up one of his supposedly missing clubs.

Instead he ate, rested, ate some more, and talked with Keeler and Tolley and the others. Cyril may well have already broached the subject of his lawsuit, but these five days together would have provided a chance to discuss the thing in depth. Perhaps they leaned on the deck railing six stories above the sea, while Tolley talked about those damned difficult chaps at J. S. Fry. Tolley had sued the English candy manufacturer for defamation after Fry ran print ads in 1929 using a caricature of him hitting a golf ball. A rhyme accompanying the visual compared "this excellent shot/to Fry's excellent choc-o-late." Tolley complained that the commercial message had the appearance of an endorsement by him, something the rules of golf prohibited for amateurs. The makers of Five Boys chocolate bars and Crunchie should be made to pay and to apologize, said Cyril's solicitor. Four lower-level Law Lords agreed, but Lord Blanesburgh did not. The suit was ridiculous, the lord said; no one who knew Tolley would have suspected that he had anything to do with an advert for candy. Case dismissed.

Bobby's sympathetic ear may be presumed. He was always being asked to participate in one business scheme or another, some of which would surely get him in dutch with the USGA. It wouldn't be surprising if Jones knew Amateur Definition, Interpretations 1 and 2, by heart; they were on page 74 of the rule book. "The Committee rules that the following constitute a forfeiture of Amateur standing: 1—Lending one's name or likeness for the advertisement or sale of anything except as a dealer, manufacturer or inventor thereof in the usual course of business; 2—Permitting one's name to be advertised or published for pay as the author of books or articles on golf of which one is not actually the author."

In a couple of months, someone would approach him during the U.S. Amateur to ask if he'd be interested in making golf movies. How would the USGA view that? If he controlled the content as the de facto "author" of the golf film, that should be okay, shouldn't it? But he didn't even think about it then. He sent the movie man on his way.

While hewing to the rules of amateur status could be tricky, harder still was the matter of making a living. Tolley knew; 1930 was a terrible year to be a stockbroker. Jones's own situation seemed almost as tenuous. He made a few bucks from his column, and Rice surely paid him well for his articles in *The American Golfer*. The Atlanta Crackers minor-league baseball team may have delivered a stipend in addition to season tickets, and the First National Bank of Atlanta had made Bobby a director during his campaign in Europe. A little more money trickled down from the family business in Canton, but any wealth he had was more inherited than merited. Grandpa had paid for his house. His father had paid most of his expenses over the years. They made him a partner on his first day at his daddy's law firm, but he was the kind of partner who took eight to ten weeks of vacation each year and left work at noon on Wednesdays. He wasn't pulling his weight, and he knew it. His desire to make his own way financially weighed on his mind.

A few hundred miles to the west, the *Europa*'s progress weighed on the minds of the parade organizers. A flurry of shore-to-ship messages asked the captain for updates on the estimated time of arrival, the messages arriving with the clatter of metal keys striking one-inch-wide strips of paper called ticker tape. This would be the stuff they'd be throwing out the high windows on Broadway tomorrow afternoon. Jones knew the drill; he'd already had a ticker-tape parade, when he returned to the States after winning the Open in '26. Once again, a tugboat carrying his most ardent supporters would come out in the harbor to greet the ship. He would transfer from the mother ship to the tug. There would be press and photographers and so many handshakes and backslaps that he'd get sore. They would land at the Battery, on the southern tip of the island. He would get in a convertible—in '26, he'd walked—and be surrounded by police in dress blues and outriders on horses and a marching band. The parade would roll slowly through the concrete corridor of the financial district to the steps of City Hall. The sight of streamers and confetti falling from the summer sky would have a hypnotic look. Rebel yells from the Georgians and the sudden bang of firecrackers would fill the air. Mayor Jimmy Walker, that leprechaun, would give a speech. Then Bobby would have to give a speech.

The whole thing embarrassed him. He hadn't enjoyed the public display of affection in '26, and he wouldn't like it tomorrow. "Sometimes he tells me it's the regret of his life that he has to be famous just for his proficiency at a sport," Keeler had once told Westbrook Pegler of the *Chicago Tribune*. "He could enjoy all this if they were following him because of some great achievement in some thoughtful line of work, such as writing or healing. . . . He never will be pleased with the idea that he was famous only for what he did in sport."

Pegler recalled the conversation as he waited with thousands of others in New York for the ship to come in. "When Bobby comes back," he wrote, "and the speeches are going out over the air Wednesday night he will be sitting there behind his purplish tan complexion and his hard-boiled shirt front still telling himself that he is very much overrated and only a champion golfer after all."

The weather cleared, and the mammoth *Europa* charged ahead at its maximum speed, twenty-nine knots. Experienced passengers could sense the slight change in the sound and the feel of the ship.

Wednesday, July 2
New York City

Three boats, not one, intercepted the *Europa* in the bay; the members of the Foxhills Golf Club of Staten Island got so fired up about the return of Bobby that they hired their own vessel, a little tug called the *Eugene F. Moran*, to accompany the municipal yacht *Macom* and a four-tiered excursion steamer, the *Mandalay*. Between the aural assault of horns and whistles from scores of watercraft, two big bands—one from the sanitation department, one from the police—played three songs: "Valencia," "Home Sweet Home," and "Dixie." The Atlantans—most of them on the *Mandalay*—raised holy hell. Planes swooped overhead. Fireboats squirted such impressive streams of water into the air that Tolley remarked that they seemed to be trying to put out the sun. Which would have been welcome—it was boiling hot.

Bobby's mother and father wept as they hugged their son when he walked down a gangplank and came aboard the *Macom*. He wore his blue suit. Hundreds of passengers stood high above them by the deck rails of the *Europa*, adding their applause to that from the other boats.

"What are your plans after the U.S. Amateur, Bob?" shouted a reporter aboard the *Macom*. A man from NBC Radio held out a microphone; they were broadcasting the Jones homecoming live, nationwide.

"I have got to get back to work and make a living," Jones replied, smiling. Suppose you win all four major titles this year—will you quit golf then?

"I have given no thought to winning all four. Not a thought."

What about defending your titles in Great Britain in '31?

"It will be absolutely impossible for me to go back next year, for you see, I have to work some time."

Newsreel cameras caught Jones looking his modest, smiling best, but the *Atlanta Journal* described Jones in midparade as "fairly gasping for breath and looking almost wildly as if for some avenue of escape." A bit later—or an eternity later if you were Jones propped up like a beauty queen in the convertible or a policeman sweating buckets inside a blue woolen uniform—Mayor Walker warmed up his vocal cords. A little flyweight boxer of a man, the mayor stood on the marble courthouse steps in front of at least six microphones—NBC broadcast this, too—a handful or two of still photographers, several policemen, and a man furiously cranking a movie camera. Walker had done this very duty two weeks before, when Rear Admiral Byrd, the polar explorer, had been given a parade. Linking the previous event with the present one in his grand style and New York accent, Walker praised Byrd's "scientific accomplishment, his unusual courage, and the additional thanks that he has brought the two poles together."

The orator paused, obviously enjoying himself. He turned slightly toward Jones. "Now today *you've* come, and New York is happy. New York is gay. New York is proud of you and your accomplishments. But it was not foreseen nor expected that your coming would bring two *other* poles together." Recognizing the setup for a joke, Jones's tight smile widened a bit. Mary stood behind her husband, looking exhausted, a fashionable dark cloche as tight as a tourniquet on her head.

"Namely, the world's greatest golfa to be welcomed by the world's *worst* golfa." Laughter and applause, and it was Bobby's turn.

"Usually, you know, when someone else is makin' a speech, I get a chance to think about what I'm going to say, but, uh, you rather put me off my game," Jones said. "Because I was listening to you this time. There's nothing that I can say which will express my feelings half as well as saying, simply, I am grateful to you and the city of New York and the people of Atlanta from the bottom of my heart. I've never been so impressed by anything in my life as the way you've turned out today. You've been so kind. There's nothing really I can say. Thank you."

As reported in the July 3 issue of the *Atlanta Journal*:

> One member of the Atlanta contingent couldn't get to the celebrations. He is "Geechee," negro waiter of an Atlanta club, who came up on the Bobby Jones Special to take care of his "white folks." And so busy was he at that, that he feared he might get lost in New York, a fear which he allayed by pinning a white tag to his coat, which read: "If lost, return to Hotel Vanderbilt, Room 802."

At 8:30 that evening, Jones and 500 of his friends dined in the Della Robia Room in the Vanderbilt. USGA president Findlay Douglas was among the speakers. They gave the man of the hour a gold cigarette case.

Thursday, July 3
New York to Chicago

The 3:00 P.M. departure of Bobby's train allowed his Atlanta fans to reconvene at Penn Station for another demonstration of love and admiration. Mary accompanied her husband the few blocks from the hotel and kissed him goodbye; she and her father would leave the next day for Atlanta. Jones and the others got on board, and they closed the doors—but no Tolley. The conductor delayed the Broadway Limited for two minutes at Jones's request, but Cyril didn't show and the train chugged away without him. As newspapers across the country explained the next day, the Englishman had gone to the wrong station, Grand Central instead of Penn, so he caught another train and met everyone in Chicago the next morning.

Keeler sat with Jones for a few minutes to get some grist for the mill of his column.

What about your health, Bob?

"That ocean trip was a fine thing. I ate a lot of food and I got a lot of sleep . . . the big breakfasts certainly put the weight back on me. I'll have to begin cutting down on them now. But as soon as a tournament starts, I won't have to exercise any restraint; I rarely want any breakfast at all, then."

Much later he described the crossing as tedious and then terrifying, as he contemplated the mob scene in his honor in New York.

Considering those wins in Great Britain, Keeler asked—are you proud of yourself?

"If I should win that little event in Minneapolis, I'd be."

How about that incredible reception in New York?

"It made me feel that maybe I had amounted to something after all. . . . and that the best part of any journey was getting back home again. I mean home to Atlanta."

Clickety-clack, clickety-clack. . . . Bobby and O.B. and Big Bob and Clara chatted over the train's unceasing metallic sound track. From a scenic point of view, the best part of the trip was its beginning. The concrete and crowds of the big city disappeared quickly as the Broadway Limited rolled north through the Hudson River Valley. Mansions dotted the riverbanks and high plateaus, and West Point stood like a gray fortress in the wild, green country. But after those vistas of gorges and the river, it was Albany, Syracuse, Rochester, Buffalo, Erie, Cleveland . . . and for someone staring out the window, no great disappointment when darkness fell.

Chicagoans were anticipating Jones's arrival on the following day. As reported in the *Chicago Daily News* on July 3: "Bill Hay, broadcaster for WMAQ, will interview Bobby Jones tomorrow on his arrival in Chicago over the Broadway Limited. Wires have been strung from the *Daily News* studio to the Union Station to provide the broadcast which will go on at 10 A.M."

Friday, July 4
Chicago

Howard Berry wrote his account of Jones's visit in the July 5 issue of the *Chicago Tribune:*

Bobby Jones, a young man who has become world famous without ceasing to be himself, stepped off a train from New York yesterday at the Union Station and was besieged immediately by a buzzing group which wished to shake his hand, get his autograph, take his picture, and listen to him talk.

. . . the way in which he handled the situation might be the key to his popularity. The man who holds three golf titles which no one has ever held simultaneously, was ingratiating to no one and snubbed no one. When a meek messenger boy halted Bobby on his march through the station and asked him to write some little message on a slip of paper as a keepsake, the golf king of the world paused and did so with the same casual courtesy with which he would have done a favor for the Prince of Wales or the mayor of New York.

Why Chicago?

When Jones was a student at Harvard and the USGA wanted him on its Walker Cup team, Melvin Traylor was the president of the USGA. Mr. Traylor had gone politely to bat for the scholar athlete—to no avail, as it turned out, but it had been a lovely gesture. That was Traylor handing Bobby the U.S. Amateur trophy in 1928, and Traylor taking Bobby's side when his supporters wanted to buy him a house. They hunted birds together. When Bobby started his own golf club in 1932, Mel was a founding member and the first vice president. Since they'd made Jones a committeeman in '28, the Chicago banker and the Atlanta lawyer had been colleagues as well as friends. Therefore, when Traylor had called Bobby in New York to invite him to pause on his long trip to Minneapolis to play his course, he had said, Yes, Mel, I'd be delighted, and thank you very much.

They played at old-money Old Elm, a men-only Donald Ross–designed club on the north side, in Highland Park. Tolley, Don Moe, Bob Gardner, and Jones formed the foursome; Traylor, the host, may have made the fifth or he may have only watched (Old Elm kept no record, and the Chicago papers did not cover this private game). But surely Mel and Bob got together afterward for drinks or dinner or to look at fireworks bursting in the dark sky over Lake Michigan. Nothing sinister attached to a meeting between these important gentlemen of the USGA, of course. But did either of them find it odd that Bobby was both management and labor in that organization, both a judge in its biggest competition and a participant? Of the fact that Jones operated on the decision-making level there could be no doubt. He'd started the year by traveling to USGA headquarters in wintry New York City; after the annual meeting, Jones had his picture taken holding the just-announced tournament schedule. While conflicts of interest seemed possible, even likely, the relationship was also symbiotic: Jones was the most successful USGA competitor in history and enjoyed friendships and contacts with people like Traylor. And in Jones, the USGA had the perfect public face. They loved Bobby in the USGA as much as those people on the parade route did—maybe more, because they knew him better.

The next morning the Jones party checked out of the Blackstone Hotel, the Michigan Avenue landmark where at the Republican convention of 1920 the phrase "smoke-filled room" was first applied to describe closed-door deal making. On the train to Minneapolis, Jones refused to say a few words into a radio microphone. Keeler filled in.

Minnesota in the summer sounded cool, but such an unusually fierce heat wave gripped the upper Midwest that Minnesota's ten thousand lakes could easily have been imagined as hellish pits of sulfur. Crops were wilting. No one had air-conditioning. People were dying.

Saturday, July 5
Woodhill Country Club, Minneapolis

"We're so sorry, but we're very busy," they said at Interlachen. "We squeezed in one group of U.S. Open players yesterday, but our golf season is short, and the Fourth of July weekend is a real highlight at the club, doncha know. So please tell Bobby Jones he can't play here today. But check back with us tomorrow, and we'll see what we can do, eh?"

At Interlachen they liked to say they were prestigious without being pretentious, qualities which would one day apply to the club's most famous member—then a twelve-year-old girl—Patty Berg. The Old Course and Royal Liverpool had more famous golf courses, but Interlachen could have taught them both a few things about the American way of golf. At this classic American country club, great swimming, tennis, dining, and a big, fancy clubhouse complemented an excellent Donald Ross–redesigned golf course. Thursday, maid's night off, always meant dinner at the club. Sunday tea was an institution. "You and your juniors are welcome on any evening," read a club bulletin. "Come out to the club for a private dance with our phonograph, no charge. . . . but the juniors must come early and go home early."

With Interlachen unavailable to them, Jones, Tolley, and Harrison "Jimmy" Johnston played at nearby Woodhill Country Club. Bobby shot 69, two under par, but his face looked lined, and his shoulders drooped in the afternoon heat.

"I have hopes that I will be able to win the four major golf titles this year," he told a reporter for the United Press, at last acknowledging the obvious. "After that, I have no plans for the future."

Sunday, July 6
Interlachen Country Club, Minneapolis

Jones motored west from the Nicollet Hotel in downtown Minneapolis through quiet streets to suburban Edina, which rhymed with "china," not "emphysema." Rolling down a leafy residential street in the morning cool, he passed side streets named Hankerson, Skyline, Cooper, and Rolling Green. On the right he saw the big Tudor clubhouse, set magnificently on a hill, and below it some of the golf course. And—this was interesting—more golf course on the other side of the road. Highway 100—Interlachen Boulevard—bisected Interlachen Country Club like a part dividing hair.

Oaks, elms, hills, soft green grass, and freshwater ponds: Interlachen presented an entirely different look and feel from the stern treeless acres and salty air of St. Andrews and Royal Liverpool. And instead of a reserved older gentleman in a tie introducing himself as his caddie, Jones shook the hand of an enthusiastic teenager in a T-shirt. By virtue of his job this week, Donovan Dale, age seventeen, was about to become a celebrity, with his picture and his comments in the paper. He'd won his spot when the caddie master drew his name out of a hat in a lottery involving Interlachen's top sixteen caddies.

The club was open for member play, but Willie Kidd, the pro, squeezed in Jones, Tolley, Johnston, and Moe. They played thirty-six holes, thirty-six dramatic departures from the courses they'd recently played overseas. While the golfer toiling around the Old Course and Hoylake could always see the sea and six other holes, each of Interlachen's eighteen holes was a self-contained world, like a science project in a shoebox. Tight, little bunkers framed smallish greens, rough framed the doglegs and fairways, and trees framed the perimeters. Jones liked the close quarters and the definition; East Lake, the course he grew up on, wasn't substantially different from this. He shot 72-72, a good handful below the second-best score in the group, and a performance that commentators considered to be outstanding. Two hundred spectators watched.

Someone with a pad and a pen waylaid Donovan Dale afterward. "He's a swell guy!" the caddie said. Did he speak with you, the reporter asked. Yes, twice, Donovan said. What did he say? " 'What's your name?' and 'Where's the water?' "

Monday, July 7
Interlachen Country Club

Three days before the U.S. Open: Jones felt the pressure growing on his gut, on his temples, and on his brain at night, a force so real that it might have been measurable in pounds per square inch. His suite at the Nicollet was an oven. It was hard to sleep but easy to obsess that this might be his final appearance on this particular stage. How should he exit? There was only one way: He had to win. But he was tired, a little overweight, and his clubs felt somehow strange; he should have at least picked them up on the *Europa*. In short, Jones knew that he didn't have his mind right to compete. And each day on the golf course was a cauldron. On Wednesday, Minneapolis suffered its eighth fatality from the heat. In the region, over one hundred had died.

The ninth green at Interlachen. This is roughly the view Jones had when he hit the most famous shot of his career during the second round of the 1930 U.S. Open.

Jones responded to the stress in several sensible ways. First, he played the course a lot. Second, he bore down exceptionally hard in practice. Interlachen was no mysterious game of pinball that took years to learn—like the Old at St. Andrews—but neither was it an open book. During his practice rounds, he hit lots of experimental shots into and out of the rough and to one side of the fairway and the other off the tees. He learned that an almost-invisible lagoon lurked to the right of the first green and that while the first and fourteenth were supposed to be the toughest holes on the course, the par threes were murderous. He discovered that seventeen played shorter than its yardage, but eighteen played longer. He ingrained a thousand details. His opponents were doing the same thing, of course, but Jones was a better student.

He played this day with a handkerchief wrapped around his sunburned neck and a coating of unguent that made him smell like a pine tree. He and Diegel played together, and both shot two-under-par 70, a new course record. Both smoked. Leo even hit shots with a cigarette between his lips.

Bobby had used tobacco for years. His consumption level on the golf course varied: Sometimes he lit up not at all, and sometimes he smoked like a Pittsburgh steel mill. When Walter Hagen clobbered him in a challenge match in Florida in 1926, some wag noted that Walter went around in sixty-nine strokes and Bobby in sixty-nine cigarettes. No data exists on how many cigarettes Bobby burned at this tournament, but newsreels and photographs showed him at Interlachen cupping butts in his right hand and pulling hard, in the manner of a soldier in a foxhole. Cigarette consumption in the United States roughly doubled between 1919 and 1930, and Bobby helped.

The tobacco companies' ads in 1930 often featured professional golfers, including at least nine who would be competing at Interlachen. Tommy Armour, Wild Bill Mehlhorn, and Leo Diegel all took the Old Gold blindfold test to prove that Old Golds were "smoother . . . better . . . not a cough in a carload." Although he was well known as a nonsmoker, a photograph of Horton Smith in full follow-through also appeared in the Old Gold campaign. The ad copy finessed the issue. "Nature simply made him a winner," it read. "And that's the only answer to the swift success of another champion: Old Gold." Oil portraits of Walter Hagen and Johnny Farrell grinned inside oval frames for their Lucky Strike ads, which offered this advice: "For a slender figure—reach for a Lucky instead of a sweet." Jock Hutchison,

Jones's playing partner in the first two rounds, endorsed Omars (Omar *means* aroma!). Jock's magazine spot featured his disembodied left hand holding a thick, white cylinder of the nineteen tobaccos in the allegedly best-smelling cigarette. The best-selling cigarette, R. J. Reynolds's Camel, employed entertaining six-panel cartoons depicting athletes—such as Sarazen—in action, with wonderfully hokey commentary.

Spectator A: Gene dropped that trap-shot three inches from the pin!

Spectator B: That cinched it! Gene's lighting up a Camel!

While no one would posit that cigarettes did Jones any good in the long term, the ritual of opening the pack (or the cigarette case)—shaking one out—lighting one up calmed many people under stress, just by giving them something to do with their hands. At the same time, inhaled nicotine, a stimulant, caused the heart to beat faster, which pushed more blood to the extremities. Some people felt more sensitivity in their hands when they smoked. It's entirely possible that cigarette smoking was good for Jones at Interlachen.

A pack of twenty ready-rolled smokes cost about twelve cents in 1930. As the economy grew worse and worse, an appetite-suppressing cigarette became for some a cheap alternative to a meal.

Another consumer product came to mind as the U.S. Open began in a whirl of hot, sweaty bodies. Despite the swelter, few of the thousands of men on Interlachen's cozy acreage dared not wear a tie, and virtually every woman wore a dress. Everyone tried to beat the heat with white cotton, but cotton fabric was coarser in those days and didn't breathe as well as the modern high-thread-count stuff. Therefore, Saturday's peak attendance of fifteen thousand probably meant thirty thousand bacteria-trapping armpits in need of deodorant. Unfortunately, Odo-Ro-No, the first national brand, had achieved only a limited market acceptance and only with women. Getting the word out hadn't been easy. When the company placed its first ad in the

Ladies' Home Journal, a chaste essay entitled "Within the curve of a woman's arm," several hundred women cancelled their subscriptions in their outrage at seeing such a delicate topic discussed so openly. Nonusers of Odo-Ro-No relied on soap, talcum powder, baking soda, or, all too frequently, nothing at all. This would be a bad week for B.O. Minnesotans were used to sweating, but never like this.

Adding to the humanity getting off the Como-Hopkins streetcar near the first green were 141 tournament players, 226 writers, 100 Western Union employees, the personnel from two radio stations, and officials and volunteers no one bothered to count. Of the volunteers, probably the most crucial and overmatched committee was Crowd Control. Before play began, each of eleven men, all members of Interlachen, was handed a fifteen-foot bamboo pole and received instructions from the USGA on its use. Hold them back like this, the stick men were told. Say, "Fore, please" or "Quiet, please." Try to keep the gallery walking; when they start to run, that's when things get out of hand. The job sounded like fun. It wasn't. "Everyone was expected to do *something* for the tournament," recalled Harlan Strong, "but I was low on seniority. Only been a member five months. So I drew the cane pole patrol. It was three days in 98-degree heat with my back to the golf. I didn't get to see anything."

Among the players—possibly even including Jones—Hagen held the most fascination. The theatrical king of the pros and the worrywart king of amateurs amused each other, and they certainly had a history. Probably the highlight occurred in Florida in 1926. The story of how they came together by the Gulf of Mexico that winter is a little complicated: Bobby had come home from Harvard with a second undergraduate degree but without much idea of what to do with it. Into the breach stepped George Adair, one of Big Bob's best friends and an heir to one of the South's biggest post–Civil War land speculators, George Washington Adair. (Already an important man in Bobby's life, Adair had taken Colonel Jones's fourteen-year-old son to play with his own son, seventeen-year-old Perry, in their first national championship, the U.S. Amateur of 1916, at Merion.) George hired the out-of-work college boy to sell real estate, eventually relocating him to his big project, Whitfield Estates, an early golf course community in Sarasota. Jones didn't spend a lot of time selling lots; he and the pro, Tommy Armour, played golf every day.

It occurred to someone that a match between Jones and the suave, varnish-haired Hagen, who represented Pasadena Country Club in nearby St. Petersburg, would raise the profile of both courses. The match was arranged. To familiarize Bobby with Walter's home track—and to pad the pockets of the pros—a warmup fourball match was scheduled two weeks before the big Hagen-Jones duel. An hour before the match, Hagen called in sick, but Jones didn't believe the famous gamesman. "If he doesn't play, I don't play," Bobby said. Mad as hell and really sick with the flu, Hagen got out of bed and played. Predictably, Jones and Armour won easily, taking Hagen and Gil Nicholls four and three. Without shaking hands with anyone afterward, Walter got back in his car and went home to bed. He planned a simple re-venge: When they played head-to-head, he'd give Jones the beating of his life.

He did. Jones lit the first of many cigarettes on the first tee and then lost the first of many holes. Eight up after the first thirty-six on the Whitfield Es-tates club, Walter ended the contest twelve up, eleven to play, at Pasadena. Flamboyantly gracious in victory, Sir Walter gave $5,000 of the $11,800 gate to the local hospital and bought Bobby a pair of gold cuff links with some of the change. No hard feelings surfaced publicly on either side, but each man loved to beat the other.

In addition to the first duel of the year between Hagen and Jones, one other aspect of the field could not be missed, although the Minnesota papers chose to ignore it: Not a single British professional showed, and only one top British amateur, Tolley, made the trip. The USGA gave exemptions from qualifying to the appropriate English and Scottish golf experts, so it could not be blamed. The snub might cause some to draw big conclusions re-garding the relative importance of their Open versus ours, but the problem was probably more basic than that. It was the economy. If things continued to slide, entertainment—including golf—would be the first thing people would cut from their budgets. Some clubs had already started to teeter financially, and many of them would close before the cloud lifted. Golf pros on both sides of the Atlantic were justifiably nervous.

The blue bloods running this red-hot tournament were not immune from such concerns. But Prescott Sheldon Bush, the thirty-five-year-old secretary of the USGA, surely worried less than any golf pro. Business had been very, very good at Harriman and Company, one of Wall Street's first and most successful private banks. Although things had been uncertain since Black Tuesday, Harriman operated in an unregulated wonderland, and if they couldn't make money in the United States, they could—and did—make it in Europe, especially in Germany. Furthermore, natural leaders like Bush seemed destined to survive and thrive in any circumstance. At Yale he'd been on the golf team and in the glee club, played a great first base for the baseball team, and been elected to Skull and Bones, the secret society for the most favored few. In a bizarre incident in 1918, the year after he graduated, Bush demonstrated both his leadership and the lawlessness that often comes with privilege.

Late one night he and two friends with shovels crept into a Fort Sill, Oklahoma, graveyard and crept out with, they thought, the skull of Geronimo, the famous Apache Indian chief. What a trophy for Skull and Bones! In the words of *Pittsburgh Post-Gazette* columnist Dennis Roddy, "The head was taken out, spiffed and forwarded to New Haven, where it was given pride of place for goofy rituals that have been attended by generations of Bushes and a veritable army of powerful types."

Like Jones, Bush had been a USGA executive committeeman for two years. His credentials were impeccable. He had Yale, of course, and a big Wall Street job, a good-to-excellent golf game, and the presidency of Round Hill Country Club in Greenwich, Connecticut. And the topper: He'd married Dorothy Walker in 1921, whose father was the Walker in the Walker Cup. George Herbert Walker was also his son-in-law's boss. He made young Prescott Bush a vice president of Harriman and Company in 1924.

Prescott had a couple of kids, one of them named George.

At Interlachen, Bush would act as a rules official. But he wouldn't act as if he knew what he was doing.

Wednesday, July 9
Lake Minnetonka

Hot as hell.

From long habit on the day before a big event, Jones planned to do nothing but rest. But as he lay in bed that morning, the sun also rose, and unfiltered heat and saturating humidity slowly crept into his room, removing any chance of comfort and naps. Jones called Harrison "Jimmy" Johnston, who lived in tropical Minneapolis, and asked if he'd take him fishing. Although he caught two little bass, the fish in the warm, brown water of Lake Minnetonka seemed as enervated as the humans above it, and Jones found himself worrying about the state of his golf game. They put away the fishing gear and went out to Interlachen for a final nine holes of practice.

Someone asked Gene Sarazen for a prediction. "This is the toughest test since Oakmont," he said, referring to the U.S. Open of 1927, won by Tommy Armour. "And you will recall that Oakmont is one course Bobby Jones never has been able to conquer."

As Jones wrote in his column of July 16:

All open championships tell very nearly the same story. . . . it goes something like this:

At the start of the first round everyone is nervous and uncertain. They begin by feeling their way along, ready to throw away strokes or pick them up as the breaks of luck decide.

. . . Then the second round, and some of those who began well continue in more or less the same vein, but some who struggled around in

77 or 78 the first day, now relieved of the strain to some extent, begin to crack off 68s and 70s.

Starting the last day . . . there are always left as possible three kinds of players—the leaders, who have done two good rounds; those only a few strokes behind who have done a bad round and a good one; and a few just within striking distance.

At this stage, something usually happens. . . .

Thursday, July 10
Interlachen Country Club

With ten thousand figures in white wandering in the shimmering heat, Interlachen looked like a dream. A thermometer in the clubhouse verandah hit 101 degrees. Ten spectators fainted. Someone (Hagen) drew a bigger gallery than Jones. The dye in his red tie and the paint from the red tees in his pocket stained Jones's white shirt and pale-colored plus fours like war wounds. Jock Hutchison, his playing partner, shot 84. Al Espinosa hit a reasonable drive on the ninth hole, a gentle-dogleg-right par five with a pond from a Monet painting about three hundred yards from the tee. Al decided to play straight for the green, over the hazard—but he skulled the long-iron shot right into the water, and for a furious second he was sure he had turned a birdie into a bogey or worse. But no—the ball skipped like a stone off the water and into the fairway, and Al chipped, putted, and got a four.

If Walter J. Bemish or some other unknown had led the 1930 U.S. Open at the end of the day, it would have made the unreality of the day complete. Instead, the players at the top of the leader board were utterly predictable. Mac Smith and Armour shot 70; Jones, 71; and Hagen and Horton Smith, 72.

"We started pretty well today—I mean Bobby Jones did," wrote caddie Donovan Dale in his story for the Associated Press (the alleged author's prose style sounded suspiciously AP). "And considering the heat at Interlachen and the big gallery which shut out every breath of fresh air, the champion's 71 seemed to me to be especially outstanding.

"Bobby used fifteen of his seventeen clubs. Only his No. 1 iron and big niblick got a rest.

"Bobby had little to say—only [that] he wondered if it would be possible to play thirty-six holes on a day like this."

As he always did when surrounded by big crowds, Jones had recruited two friends to walk at his side—sometimes they hooked elbows—to insulate him from autograph seekers and conversationalists; the cane pole patrol couldn't possibly keep everyone away, nor did they try. When he putted, the wingmen scurried off to fill vacuum bottles of water for the boss and to chat with Big Bob, a little man sweating beneath his straw boater. At the end of his round, Bobby's neckwear was so wet with sweat that it couldn't be untied, and Keeler cut it off in the locker room with a pocketknife, an incident much beloved by chroniclers of that day.

And so they all left Interlachen for cool baths and long drinks of water and delicious illicit beer. But you wonder what Louis Bataglia did that evening, and Albert Anderson, William Johnson, and Emma Lindstrom. It was the last night of their lives. They and several others from the Twin Cities died the next day from the heat.

Friday, July 11

Just as he had the day before, Al Espinosa hit a reasonable drive on the par-five ninth, and again he didn't debate about what to do: He'd whack it directly over the pond and, hopefully, onto the green. And just as he had the day before, he looked up and skulled the damn thing in the water. But—stop us if you've heard this before—the ball skipped like it had hit ice and bounced up on the opposite bank. It seemed so unlikely, almost physically impossible, because Lake Espinosa sat a good deal lower than the fairway, and the drought had made it lower still. Al got a par.

Jones came to the 485-yard ninth in the hot middle of the afternoon, dragging with him something like five or six thousand people dressed in white. He'd been playing cautiously. "Somebody may go crazy and shoot [even par] 288," he'd said on Tuesday, when asked to predict the winning score. "If they do, they will win with no trouble at all." Keeler noticed that his boy had not gone after a single long putt or tried for distance out of the rough, and he hadn't aimed at a single pin if the shot was at all difficult. Through the first twenty-eight holes, the strategy was working: Jones was one under for the day and two under for the tournament as he walked with his guards through the heat and humanity.

He stood by his Spalding ball and Donovan Dale near the right edge of the fairway. Up ahead, Horton Smith arched his wrists forward and stroked a twenty-foot putt for eagle. On the tee behind him, Gene Sarazen waited to hit. Smith's putt fell in. While they applauded and yelled up at the green, the Jones gallery stared at Bobby while slowly shuffling into corridor formation to watch this interesting shot over water. A light breeze blew left to right, and his lie wasn't very good, but if Jones could fade a spoon, he could get it close. He withdrew the three-wood from the brown leather bag and took his stance. But the crowd was not nearly ready; some of the spectators on the fairway and up by the green stood directly between him and the hole. A few of them were shooed back, but others seemed to like their vantage point so much that they stayed put. When waves and body language wouldn't budge them, Jones tried again. He began his brief preshot ritual—from behind the ball, a look at the target, half a practice swing, another glance at the target, then the stance. But a couple of members of the restive gallery scampered across his line, and he had to back off once more. Why was he playing so fast? Keeler wondered. A third time he tried. He swung—and hit the most famous shot of his career.

As Jones told the story thirty years later, at the top of his backswing, two little girls in the gallery on the right jab-stepped like basketball players, as if to run across the fairway. They didn't—apparently a parent or guardian pulled them back—but he noticed the movement and flinched. The flinch caused him to hit an ugly, low line drive right into the drink. Caddie Donovan Dale confirmed the story—"someone stepped up," he said.

Keeler saw it a little differently. "When Jones stood up to his ball," he wrote that day, "a large angle of the gallery stood directly between him and the pin . . . He paused for a moment to see if the way could be cleared but, when nothing was done, he decided to play a wide slice over the lake . . . It was a daring and apparently a foolish chance." Asked for an explanation after the round, Jones didn't mention the two mystery girls.

Whatever the cause, the effect was the same. The ball hit the middle of the lake, took two long skips and a couple of short ones, and finished its journey drying in the sun on the opposite bank. Sarazen said the ball hit a lily pad— which it didn't and he couldn't have seen the shot anyway—but thereafter Bobby's skip across Lake Espinosa was known as the Lily Pad Shot. From thirty yards he pitched to within a step of the hole and made the putt for a birdie four.

Jones struggled on the holes across the street—the eleventh through the seventeenth. "The fifteenth made me so mad I didn't know what to do," he told reporters in the locker room, still looking and sounding peevish. "I played like an old woman on the second nine." He'd suffered a typical U.S. Open double bogey on fifteen, going from the rough to the rough to the rough, and bogeyed the very long—262 yards—but downhill par-three seventeenth. Hutchison, his playing partner, put the finishing touches on his sour second nine by blasting two balls out-of-bounds from a bunker on seventeen, at which point, he quit.

"For the first time in my life, I found myself in an important competition with only one instinct and desire," Jones told Keeler afterward, "to get the round over as soon as possible. It was terrible out there."

The top ten were:

Horton Smith, 72-70—142, who told reporters, "I'm overrated."

Bobby Jones, 71-73—144, who remarked that it was so hot that, "I think we'd be justified to play in pajamas."

Harry Cooper, 72-72—144, possibly the fastest player in golf history, who said he was hitting the ball perfectly. His nickname saluted his speed: "Lighthorse."

Charles Lacey, 74-70—144, age twenty-three, a native of London, who kept alive the U.S. Open tradition of an unknown golfer doing well.

Mac Smith, 70-75—145, who complained about missed short putts.

Tommy Armour, 70-76—146, who said the same things as Mac, with the same Scottish accent.

Wilfred "Wiffy" Cox, 71-75—146, who was always referred to as "the public links pro from Brooklyn."

Johnny Farrell, 74-72—146, who was in the hunt despite starting the tournament with a quadruple bogey eight on the first hole.

Johnny Golden, 74-73—147, who worked at a club in Connecticut.

Walter Hagen, 74-73—147, who had praised Jones at every opportunity all week and didn't talk about himself much.

Although Hagen had been the first competitor to arrive at Interlachen, a week of practice couldn't make up for the fact that for months he'd been training on whiskey, constant travel, and meaningless competition. The U.S. Open was his first big event of 1930, and thus his only chance to reassert himself against Jones. But things weren't going all that well. Even mild exercise in hot, saturated air bothers heavy drinkers, and Hagen always had a flask in his golf bag or on his hip. The thirty-six-hole finale on Saturday did not look promising for Sir Walter.

Hagen may have labored under one other lifestyle burden: "I'm ready to state this for the record," he wrote in his autobiography, "those second- and third-generation Norwegian, Swedish and Danish girls [in Minneapolis] were among the most beautiful and the healthiest I've ever met. Nicollet Avenue and the

Flame Room of the Radisson glowed with their fresh blonde beauty . . . Nothing gave me more pleasure than catering to those healthy appetites."

As Tolley walked to the shower, Keeler picked up his pile of wet clothes and put them on a scale. He estimated his golf costume had six pounds of sweat in it.

As Jones walked to the shower, a diminutive fan from Winnipeg who had slipped into the locker room asked the naked man if he could shake his hand. He could. He did.

Saturday, July 12, Morning

Jones was right: Something happened.

Blessed rain fell for fifteen minutes on the heads of the first few starters, and the nine-day heat wave broke. But it was still warm enough and the walk was long enough to make the double round a test of physical and mental fitness—and of golf under pressure, of course.

Jones started more than an hour ahead of the tournament leader on the gray day, giving him a chance to charge while Horton Smith waited at the gate. "This was the one time that I played at my very best in a championship," Jones wrote with fond nostalgia in *Golf Is My Game.* "I felt as I think a good halfback must feel when he bursts through a line of scrimmage and finds the safety man pulled out of position, sees an open field ahead of him, and feels confident he has the speed to reach his goal."

But the honeyed memories from thirty years later often don't mesh with the reality of the moment. Contemporary accounts described Jones as "tight-lipped and frowning," "grim-faced," and "intent." The *Minneapolis Tribune* reported that "all the pleasure was gone from the game for him." A sports/humor columnist in the *Minneapolis Journal* named Jack Quinlan, whose humor would not survive the years, zipped off half a dozen Bobby one-liners. For example: "When Mr. Jones arrived at the clubhouse . . . he was as congenial as a young tiger with its first set of good teeth . . . He made three practice swings on the first tee and the Red Cross nurses carried off four pneumonia victims who were caught in the draft . . . After witnessing Mr. Jones's homicidal mood, some of the other players paid off their caddies and called for their railroad tickets back home."

Smith stood on the practice putting green with a good view of Bobby's huge gallery advancing up the ninth like an army. Horton had already lost the lead. Jones was three under for the day and for the tournament; Smith was minus two.

Neither Jones nor Espinosa provided thrills on nine to compare with the previous two days, but aficionados murmured when Bobby prepared to play his third from a bunker to the left of the green: He'd taken that strange scoop of a niblick out of his brown leather golf bag. But he didn't duplicate the magic of the sixteenth at Hoylake with the controversial concave club. He splashed out an unimpressive twenty feet from the jar and two-putted for par. He'd shot 33; behind him, Horton Smith scored nine fours for a 36.

With a rarely seen combination of powerful, accurate striking and a surgeon's precision with the putter—ten one-putts!—Jones came to the seventeenth tee at six under par. He needed two pars for a 66 that would break about five records. He knew he had the lead by more than a little; he'd learned from field reports that Horton Smith had started to make bogeys. History does not record if Jones said hello to the rules official on seventeen, Prescott Bush, but we're fairly sure he hit a wood into the bunker short and left of the green (the *Chicago Tribune* put him in heavy rough, not sand). At any rate, his second shot wasn't close to the hole. Bogey.

The midday heat increased. Jones walked across the shady, two-lane road, then had to exert himself like a mountain climber to reach the elevated tee. The 402-yard eighteenth distilled all of Interlachen's subtle challenges into a single hole. You played from one hill through a gently right-bending valley and up another hill to the green. You wanted to keep it left off the tee, but too far left could be a disaster because of the ball-swatting arms of a big oak. You got a better look at the green from the right side of the fairway, but mounds, high rough, and more trees made that a risky line to take. The second shot was equally thought provoking: Short or right, and the ball would roll down the shaved bank of the hill; trees on the left practically grew on the green; and the green itself had two tiers as pronounced as stair steps. The evil excellent eighteenth at Interlachen played like two par threes. Delays were common.

Jones drove behind a tree, clipped a branch coming out, missed the green long, and one-putted for a bogey. Despite the hiccups at the end, he'd shot 68, a score none of his challengers approached. With one round to play, he led by five over Harry Cooper, a second-generation golf pro from Dallas, and by seven over sad, resolute Mac Smith.

Sixty-eight! Everyone was talking about it. "I think I'll turn amateur!" one of the pros said to Hagen.

"My boy," said Sir Walter, "you're not good enough!"

Big Bob got comfortable in the clubhouse during the intermission and decided not to venture out into the white-clad crowd to watch his son win the U.S. Open. He'd been walking this course with thousands of others for three days, and he was tired. Besides: a five shot lead. . . . It was over, wasn't it?

Saturday, July 12, Afternoon

Something else happened.

In the most amazing twenty-four hours of an amazing life in golf, Jones had had his luckiest break—the Lily Pad Shot—and followed it with possibly his best-ever competitive round. But the final day of the 1930 U.S. Open held two more shockers, incidents that Jones, Keeler, Grantland Rice, and their see-no-evil successors would never commit to paper. Even Dick Miller, a slightly less adulatory biographer, missed or ignored the most important, controversial ten minutes of the Slam.

From nerves, fatigue—he'd lost seventeen pounds this week—or too much Interlachen, Jones began to wobble like a top at the end of its spin. He bogeyed the second and doubled the par-three third, with three-putts on both. Playing too safe on nine, he blasted his second shot over the water and over the green and onto the putting green. As he surveyed the situation, he inhaled a cigarette as if tobacco smoke were oxygen. He took a big divot out of the practice green on his pitch back to the flagstick, and he made a par. On thirteen, a very difficult par three for a hooker like Jones, he bunkered his tee shot and left it in the sand on his first escape attempt. "The crowd gasped, knowing that he would now go four over par on the last final round," reported the *Minneapolis Journal*, "but Bobby only let his hands come to rest upon his hips and stood looking silently down upon the ball with his bronzed face masking whatever emotion he was experiencing." It couldn't have been a pleasant emotion; he took another double. But he mixed in a couple of birdies, too, protecting a shrinking lead over Mac Smith. Twenty years after he'd tied his brother for first in the U.S. Open, the forty-two-year-old Silent Scot charged for a major one last time.

When Jones birdied the short sharp-dogleg-left sixteenth, he put the tournament in his pocket. Then he trudged up the ski slope to the seventeenth tee, swung, and gave the U.S. Open away.

A running hook landed short of the green was the shot to play on the 262-yard hole, but Jones hit the ball so far in the heel of his wood—probably a brassie—that it flew dead right, fifty yards off line, toward a grove of trees. Beyond the trees lay a low, marshy pond. No one—not Jones, his playing partner Joe Turnesa, Donovan Dale, the gallery marshals, Prescott Bush, or the eight thousand in the gallery—saw where Bobby's Spalding returned to earth.

One of the most impressive search parties in golf history fanned out. The rules-savvy among them knew they had no more than five minutes; after that, the ball was officially lost. Here was a situation unique in sports, in which a mere spectator could have a profound effect on the outcome of a big event (and not in a negative way, like the moron who reaches out of the stands to interfere with a baseball). Who would be the hero to find Bobby's ball? The eager searchers circled trees, studied the ground as if reading fine print, and even looked up into the trees. The hundreds milling around the pond crunched the hollow stems of monocotyledonous plants. Everyone grew more nervous as feet snapped reeds and the clock ticked . . .

"Found it!" A portion of the crowd moved excitedly toward a man who had spotted a ball in the mud.

Jones walked through the crowd to the water's edge. "I think we better make sure that that's my ball," he said. He sounded very calm. He wore a long-sleeve white shirt and a matching flat cloth cap. His skin looked brown against the pale background of his clothes.

He reached down into the mud and water and held it up for Bush to see. Bobby was a scant five feet eight, and the USGA secretary stood six feet four, so he really did have to hold it up. It wasn't his ball. Time was up. He'd have to go back to the tee.

They'd be applying one of golf's oldest but not necessarily best-understood rules, first put in writing in 1860 by the King James VI, a Scottish club by the banks of the river Tay:

> Should a ball be driven into the Tay and seen by both parties, it is not lost; if not seen by both parties, it is lost.

The distinction between in the river and simply lost was key because the penalties were different. Water usually meant a drop by the hazard's edge, and lost meant going back to the tee. A one-shot penalty applied in both instances, but the lost ball cost more because you had to give up the distance gained on the first swing.

What do I do now? Jones asked. And the future United States senator from the great state of Connecticut said, *Bob, drop it here,* or words to that effect. Author Robert Sommers, in *The U.S. Open Golf's Ultimate Challenge,* quotes Bush exactly: "You are permitted to drop a ball in the fairway opposite where the ball crossed the margin of the hazard." Bush gestured to a spot in the short grass, at least fifty yards from the swamp. It was an incredible ruling, without precedent and possibly without merit.

Jones might have argued either against the instruction *that* he could drop or *where* he could drop; rules officials make mistakes. But golfers rarely argue against rulings favorable to themselves. Jones himself did, at the U.S. Open in 1925, when he saw a microscopic movement of his ball in the rough, and officials on the scene said no you didn't. Bobby was sure, and he was a sportsman, so he called a one-shot penalty. But now he didn't seem sure at all. As a lawyer and the best player in the world, he knew the rules as well as anyone, and apparently it seemed reasonable to him and to Bush that the ball had gone in the water. The only problem was that no one had actually *seen* it go in: no splash, no ripple. Some accounts written way after the fact indicated that some spectators were sure the ball hit a tree and landed in the water. But if any among the throng had come forward with evidence that the ball swam with the fishes in Lake Bush, then why the search? But there *was* a search, and the ball had not been found. The rule was explicit: When you can't find your ball, it's lost. In other words, you were not allowed to presume a missing ball went into a hazard unless there was reasonable evidence that it had. According to USGA rules, an unsuccessful search by itself did not constitute such evidence.

The decision by the future president of the USGA was therefore simply wrong, even unjust, and the relationship between the man making the call and the man receiving it had to be considered.

"The ball wheeled far off line to the right into a marsh whence a local rule permitted me to drop in the fairway," Jones would write in *Golf Is My Game*, a shove-it-under-the-carpet dismissal of the episode.

After the sweetheart ruling, Bobby knocked a fifty-yard niblick up on the green and two-putted for a five, his third double on a par three in the final round. If he'd applied the lost-ball penalty and gone back to the tee and played his second ball from there, he'd probably have had the same score. Probably. But with a double bogey in his last practice round, bogeys on this hole in the second and third rounds, and now this, a six or more was a distinct possibility. Or, with his unearthly ability to rise to the occasion, he might have made a birdie two with his second ball.

He now stood four over for the day, even par for the tournament, one ahead of Mac Smith—and leaking oil like an old LaSalle.

A river of murmuring humanity padded across Interlachen Boulevard to the eighteenth hole. Bush accompanied Jones as he made the vertical climb to the tee. If he'd given Bobby a piggyback ride up the hill, it wouldn't have been more outrageous than his next move. *Gentlemen,* Prescott said to the competitors waiting on the tee, *this match is playing through*—or words to that effect. And Jones and Turnesa did indeed cut in line in front of a couple of groups, including the twosome of Johnny Farrell and Charles Guest—thus avoiding a long, stressful wait on the tee of the final hole of the U.S. Open for one group while prolonging it for everyone else.

"You can't *do* that," commented PGA Tour rules official Vaughn Moise in 2004. "It's Rules Administration 101, first page. You treat everybody in the field exactly the same, and then you have a true champion at the end. Sometimes a group will be told to play through for pace-of-play reasons, but not because there's a wait on the tee or because an official wants a certain group to finish first. Letting someone play through like that gives him an advantage over the rest of the field. You just don't do that."

Jones slapped a weak drive in the fairway on the 402-yard hole and then surveyed the awkward shot from and over uneven terrain to an uninviting target. He'd have to fly his ball about 180 yards uphill through the usual corridor of excited fans and try like hell to avoid going left, right, short, or long. People peered down the hill from the windows in the clubhouse, from the clubhouse roof, from trees, and from borrowed photographer's stepladders. Radiomen spoke softly into microphones. The man in white swung his three-iron. The ball hung in the air, a thrilling sight . . .

And plopped down on the front edge of the green and stayed there. After a minute's pause, the massed humanity on the hill above enjoyed another unforgettable scene, as Jones emerged through his gallery to walk alone onto the green. There was a thunder of applause.

He surveyed his putt. The ball lay seventeen of Bobby's short steps from the hole, about forty-five feet. Jones had avoided the array of long grass and bunkers, but now he had to figure out a way to get down in two. The green sloped upward gradually, then dramatically, then broke to the right. But topography wasn't the problem. After that through-the-looking-glass experience on seventeen, Jones's mind and body had collapsed. Confidence had left him and probably his will to live. His breathing came in gasps. He was, as he recalled much later, "quivering in every muscle."

"Quiet, please," a loud voice said.

Jones slowly evaluated his putt, but he was only going through the motions, only buying time until some of his legendary composure returned. In silence, Donovan Dale stood with the bag on his right shoulder, while he tended the flagstick with his left hand. When Jones couldn't delay any longer, he set his club in front of the ball, then behind it, then rapped the putt up the hill.

Something happened. A reporter from the *Minneapolis Journal* described it: "When he hit the ball the mounting cheer that followed its course rose to a deafening roar as it found its way over successive yards of bumpy green and dropped squarely into the cup."

Pandemonium. The gallery shouted and screamed and threw hats into the air but was restrained from rushing out onto the green; there were more players on the course, and one of them still had a chance to win.

When Mac Smith came to the eighteenth hole a while later, Prescott Bush again took the law into his own hands and allowed him to play through the groups waiting on the tee, who could only watch like lapped runners. But it was too much for Mac. Just as at Royal Liverpool, the Silent Scot needed a two to tie. When he didn't do it, Jones had won the Open.

Exhaustion paints Jones's face a few days before
the final leg of the Slam, the U.S. Amateur at Merion.

6

I 'Spec He Is

Do I contradict myself?

Very well then I contradict myself,

(I am large, I contain multitudes.)

—*Walt Whitman, "Song of Myself"*

he champion came out last, a few dramatic minutes after everyone else. He walked down the green hill from the big Tudor clubhouse and took his place in the semicircle of chairs that had been placed on the practice putting green. The exhausted, happy spectators on the hillside could see the black dollar-bill-sized hole in the green, the unfilled divot from Bobby's third shot to the ninth hole during the final round.

With the U.S. Open champion finally settled, a tall, bald man with a fringe of gray hair rose to speak. Plainly flustered and unhappy, USGA president Findlay Douglas had undoubtedly gotten an earful of anger and disgust from the professional golfers who'd heard about the Jones ruling on the seventy-first hole.

"And I am now going to ask Mr. Robert T. Jones to come and accept this champion-shick-chip cup," Douglas said, "representative of the, uh . . . open championship of the United States of America."

Amid applause and cheers, Jones rose to his feet from his chair behind the podium. He wore a gray double-breasted coat, gray socks, gray patterned tie, his usual two-toned shoes, white plus fours, and a smile. His hair was perfect. The blue-blazered Douglas handed him the trophy, then dug around in his pocket to find the gold medal that went with it. Jones looked expectantly at the president for eye contact or a handshake but got neither. He put the trophy on the table and gripped it while he spoke. Bobby had had a drink or two, but it didn't show in the least.

"I do want to say just two things," he said, speaking rather quickly. "One of them is that I consider myself exceedingly lucky to have won this championship and the second one is that I want to thank you all for a very considerate way in which you've all behaved this week. I've never played in a place where the galleries are so kind to the playah and so anxious to get out of the way. You know how hard it is for you and we know how hard it is for us. I want to thank you very much."

Mac Smith accepted his second-place check for $1,000 and tried to sit back down without addressing the crowd, but several loud people yelled, "Speech! Speech!" and Mac had no choice. He said a few mostly inaudible words, something about how pleased he was to be here and that he had tried his best. Horton Smith, the third-place finisher, showed the most flair of any of the orators. "We did our best to corner the elusive Mr. Jones, but again we failed," he said. "We'd all rather beat him than do anything else in the world, but so far we haven't had that experience."

When it was over a few minutes later, reporters and fans surrounded the magnetic champion like iron filings, and it took two policemen to get him back up the hill and into the clubhouse. What are your plans, Bobby? "I'm going back to business," he said, "until it's time for the national amateur in September."

Keeler went on the radio after the ceremony, but Bobby declined to be interviewed. From years of practice, O.B. knew what to do. He told the audience that he'd talked to the champion right after his round, and this was what he said: "I'm very happy. I'm happy to have won but most of all I'm happy because I'm going back to Atlanta—going home. I played my shots better today than I ever have in an open championship," and blah-blah-blah that sounded like Keeler winging it.

Bob and his parents and the others did not hang around. They hustled to the railroad station and left town that night on the 10:20 train.

Sunday, July 13
Southbound

The Lily Pad Shot got five paragraphs in his memoir, but except for that brief line in *Golf Is My Game*, Jones never spoke or wrote for the record about the ruling at Lake Bush. And who would want to bring it up in conversation and thereby challenge his dearest possession, his honor? "Tainted," the professionals in the Open had said. "The USGA gave him this championship," Gene Sarazen, the 1922 U.S. Open champion, wrote in a column, and Gene was a friend. Friends or not, publicly suggesting that a score (or a win) was not deserved was the very worst thing you could say to a golfer. Jones was not just any golfer, of course. With his deserved reputation for fair play and his adherence to the chivalrous moral code of the Old South, he held himself, as he said, "beyond the letter of the law." Had he really done something wrong? Did he worry about it? He didn't say.

If Sarazen and the others were right, Jones had not adhered to Note 2 of Rule 33 (a ball may not be presumed to be in a water hazard without reasonable evidence to that effect). Therefore, he'd played under a wrong rule and should have been penalized two strokes under 21-3b, the wrong rule Rule. And then he'd signed his scorecard that showed a 75 instead of the 77 he would have had with the penalty. You didn't have to speak the USGA's ridiculous legalese to know what that meant: golf's death penalty, disqualification.

But practically speaking, the point was moot. Any mistake had been Bush's, not Bobby's. If an official caused an error, the player did not pay. It's the only situation in which golf's rules can be broken with impunity.

So while there wasn't any legal stain on Jones or his magnificent win, Prescott Bush had some explaining to do. His defense at the next USGA Executive Committee meeting would surely be that he'd only tried to be fair. "Here's fair," Findlay Douglas would say just as surely, throwing a rulebook in front of him. "You're fired, Prescott."

Interestingly, Bush's unilateral, breathtakingly perverse decision to allow Jones, and later Smith, to play through on the final hole did not get a public hearing. If not for the memories of Interlachen old-timers, such as Bill Sherman, a member, and Bill Kidd—the son of the pro and himself the professional at Interlachen for forty years—that most bizarre part of the narrative might have been lost forever. Kidd's father, a competitor in the '30 Open, talked about it but didn't see it. "I know it's true," said Kidd in 2004, "because Les Bolstad was in one of the twosomes Jones went through, and he told me." In *The U.S. Open*, author Robert Sommers mentions Smith getting the green light on eighteen, but apparently no one else ever wrote about it.

Probably the more crucial events on seventeen overshadowed it.

And that didn't cause a public furor either; there was no mention of the incident in the Atlanta papers. But in Minneapolis, while not playing it up, they couldn't ignore it. In the midst of subheads in the *Tribune* game story, such as "Wind Gives Mac a Bad Break" and "Johnny Goodman Is Second Place Amateur," readers found "Indignation Arises among Professionals" "over a ruling of the USGA which gave Bobby Jones a one-stroke penalty, a chance to play his third shot from the fairway and a five on the hole after his drive had hit a tree and lost itself in rushes on the border of the swamp.

"The rule which governed the case was a special one drawn to suit Interlachen which provided that any player finding a water hazard paralleling a fairway could play his penalty shot from the adjoining fairway.

"The professional contention appears to be that they were not informed of the rule and that Jones's ball was not in the water hazard but in the long grass between the hazard and the fairway. They contend that Jones should have been playing three from the tee instead of from fifty yards short of the green."

Here was another tangle in the web: No one had heard about this special rule, and it was apparently applied only once all week. The USGA responded that all its scorers knew about the unusual procedure and would have applied it for any competitor, not just Jones. Its *scorers* knew? That was the wrong answer. Rules people always tell the *players* about something as extraordinary as a fairway drop for a ball in a distant water hazard because only the *player* is responsible for his score. The reason for the local rule must have sounded lame even as it came out of the spokesman's mouth: high grass around some of the water hazards. Every aspect of the USGA's reply to the professionals' objections sounded like butt covering for itself and Prescott Bush.

Anyway, the explanation didn't address the fundamental issue: Why was the lost ball deemed a water ball?

Donovan Dale thought he knew what happened to the missing Spalding. "[The crowds] were terrible; there was no one to hold them back," the caddie wrote in his as-told-to column. "They did steal balls. We set out with the pocket [in the golf bag] full, and I had all I could do to get one for myself." In another story, Donovan stated flatly that someone had picked up Bobby's ball on seventeen. "There is more than a possibility that some souvenir hunter cost Bobby Jones a penalty," the *Minneapolis Journal* concluded. "There was a possibility that [the ball] had sunk beneath the ground before anyone saw it—but there was also a possibility that some spectator has that ball today." In either case—gone underground or gone in a pocket—the lost-ball penalty, stroke and distance, was supposed to apply.

"Let's put all this into perspective," commented PGA Tour rules official

Vaughn Moise in 2004. "Things like this will always happen whenever you have an event conducted by volunteers that have *some* knowledge of the rules and mostly good intentions. I'll bet that Bush knew that that 'local member convenience rule' on seventeen [the drop in the fairway] was contrary to the rules of golf, but he thought it was fair. And I'll bet that in his heart he thought that playing through noncompetitive groups was the fair thing to do for the championship.

"Trying to be fair is what gets amateur rules officials in trouble. It's not easy to say, 'Yes, I believe your ball is *probably* in the hazard' or 'Yes, I believe someone in the gallery *probably* picked the ball up as a souvenir.' But you have to have actual, visible proof."

Meanwhile, not a whiff reached Atlanta. Not from Keeler's radio broadcast, of course, nor from the local papers. *Au contraire:* "Even among the professionals, his greatest rivals, there was a feeling that [Jones's win] was quite all right," spun Francis J. Powers in the *Atlanta Journal*, without referring specifically to the incident on seventeen. "The professional stars wanted, in their heart of hearts, to see Bobby win.

"I have seen him in every American championship since 1920 and there never was a title more honestly won."

The train rolled southeast through the heart of the country. Big Bob's immense pride made him humble and quiet. Chick Ridley, who'd held one of Bobby's elbows with one hand while clearing the gallery with the other, now could not keep his hands off the U.S. Open cup; the joke on the train was that he was sleeping with it. Charlie Cox, an amiable officer in the Georgia National Guard, had been the man on the other elbow. He had carried another kind of hardware for Bobby during the Open, a big thermos bottle filled with cool water. Now the victorious Atlantans drank a little firewater and let the miles roll by. "Bob rested easily on the trip southward," wrote an *Atlanta Journal* reporter on board the *President Lincoln*. "He easily was the most comfortable member of the party."

If he felt conflicted, he didn't show it; a stoic, Jones was the kind of man who could (and did) hole a forty-five-foot putt to win the U.S. Open and walk to retrieve his ball like he was strolling to the curb to get the paper. Although the perfect achievement of his goals this summer made him proud in a way he was too modest to say, and in a day he'd be reunited with his desperately missed children, some mental storm clouds must have scudded by. There was Sarazen's accusation; the challenge of getting up for one more tournament, the U.S. Amateur; and his deep weariness with everything involved in big-time golf. After that steam bath in Minnesota, he'd face more brutal heat when he got off the train (it had been 103 degrees in Atlanta the day before, its highest-ever recorded temperature). Worse, much worse, the town fathers had declared the day of Bobby's return a legal holiday. They were sending airplanes to fly over his train when it approached the city limits. He'd have to endure another parade.

Monday, July 14
Atlanta

To avoid a mob scene at the Atlanta station, Mary and the kids sneaked Jones off the train at about 9:30 A.M. at the Chattahoochee station. They hugged his neck and motored him home. He'd barely had time to hang up his coat when a reporter and a photographer from the *Journal* rolled up the driveway. The newsies beheld the pale pink brick of the symmetrical, architecturally perfect two-story L-shaped mansion, with the chimneys at either end jutting out of the dark slate roof and the ornate white-painted wooden scrollwork above the front door. But what most impressed the writer, Ernest Rogers, was the quiet.

Rogers rang the bell. As he recalled it, "the Negro maid answered the alarm. 'Is Mr. Jones at home?' I asked.

" 'Yes, sir,' " she replied with a great big smile. 'I 'spec he is.'

" . . . and then the American Open champion, British Amateur and Open champion stepped through the door. He was browned to a rich nut color and looked in the finest physical condition. He extended his hand with a smile and asked our mission."

After a brief chat and a few snaps of Jones holding his doorknob, the South's greatest hero since Robert E. Lee excused himself. He had to get ready.

Atlanta turned out, ten deep on both sides of Peachtree, yelling at the sheer joy of having Bobby. He'd honored them, and he'd done so with pure Southern class; the people clogging the streets returned the favor with wonderful passion. They loved him. But he didn't love them; he couldn't. Crowds drained him. But Jones kept a smile on his face and kept a wink and a wave ready.

Grandiosity reigned in the newspapers ("never before has the city been stirred to such concert pitch as this year when his flashing blade has carved his name deeper than ever in the immortal scroll of sport"). Businesses closed, bands played, sirens and loud speakers blared, planes flew overhead with the thin drone of insects, paper poured out of windows, and everyone wanted to watch or march in Bobby's parade. Jones and his family were to stand on the porch of the Capital City Club, in the manner of a royal family reviewing marching troops, although it's not clear that they did this. They may have merely sat in a car and brought up the rear of the march to City Hall.

It was Carnival in Rio or Mardi Gras in New Orleans, only rated G. Little girls in the crowd carried tiny golf clubs with ribbons. Men wore lapel buttons with Bobby's picture on them. The heat was an issue: Shaded patches of sidewalk on the parade route filled up early, and quite a few spectators parked themselves in front of movie theatres to feel the rush of refrigerated air when the doors opened. Sirens wailed, loud speakers blared the WSB radio coverage, and then you heard the pulse-quickening drums and horns of the Double Eagle March. Police motorcycles led the parade, followed by the 122nd Infantry National Guard marching band, followed by some trucks from the fire department, then Kiwanis, Rotary, City Club, Loew's Atlanta Cinema, Exchange Club, Atlanta Woman's Club, American Legion Drum Corps, American Legion, the Atlanta Women's Golf Association, Georgia Tech, Atlanta Athletic Club, the Venetian Athletic Club, the Greeters Club, the Atlanta Hotel Men's Association, Gulf Refining, Georgia Power. There were floats and double-decker buses. Uniformed Atlanta Crackers baseball players walked along, inspiring applause as they tipped their hats.

Caddies from Druid Hills and East Lake marched, too, all of them black. The East Lake caddies carried signs reading "Mr. Bob Done It" and "Mr. Bob and Calamity Jane Done Brought the Bacon Home Again." Then came a flatbed truck with Mr. Bob's three newest trophies flashing in the sun, with a man in a straw boater in each corner. A sign on the side of the trophy truck read "Bob Is Home—Here's the Bacon." In that juxtaposition of bacon signs—and the belittling language imposed by their employers on the caddies' banner—were the ham hands of someone who listened to *Amos 'n' Andy* for ten minutes, six days a week, like everybody else. But to a lot of people there then, it was funny.

Finally, the Jones car rolled into view. Newsreel men from Paramount and Pathé News trailed like dogs after a fire truck. They cranked their cameras and tried not to miss a thing.

"As they ascended the City Hall steps it was evident that Bobby had crowd fright," the *Journal* noted. "He wished that he could have been welcomed a little more quietly."

After the speeches . . .

"Mr. and Mrs. Jones
Given Luncheon
by Friends"

The society page covered the story in a disciplined style that was a pleasure to read after all the hyperventilating by the sports and feature writers.

"Luncheon was served buffet," the *Journal* noted. "The central table had as its decoration a mound of ice in the center of which were gorgeous pink roses and pink lights reflecting from the table."

Wednesday, July 30
Canton, Georgia

Probably Big Bob or one of his brothers persuaded Bobby to take his afternoon off up in Cherokee County. Inspired, perhaps, by their famous nephew, Uncles Albert, Louis, Paul, and Rube had hacked a golf course out of a North Canton cow pasture in 1927. In May 1930, they'd rounded up enough enthusiasts to form a club. Twenty-six players signed up for their inaugural tournament, with Rev. Dixon the winner and Dr. Coker the runner-up. A visit by Bobby would surely be another step forward for the Canton Golf Club.

Cows and what cows left behind were CGC's greatest hazard; each of its nine sand greens was encircled by a strand of wire that was supposed to keep the bovines away. Bobby held his nose and watched his step and played a few holes or at least hit a few shots; the record is unclear. But he clearly didn't enjoy himself. One of the founding members asked Jones what they should do with their humble golf club.

"Move it," he said.

Even though it was a pre-home-air-conditioning hellhole in the summer, a lot of people—especially Atlantans—still thought Atlanta was *the* place to be. Once a Civil War battleground, it had evolved into a city of go-getters with an unusual tolerance of Yankees. The Chamber of Commerce launched a three-year campaign in 1925, called Forward Atlanta, whose purpose was to attract new business to the Athens of the South. In an incredible success, 762 new businesses came to town in three years. Atlanta's athletes amplified local pride: Jones; the 1928 Rose Bowl champion Georgia Tech football team; the Crackers of the minor-league Southern Association; and the Black Crackers of the Negro league. Most of all, Atlanta had Robert Woodruff, the genius who was making Coca-Cola the first world brand.

Jones not only fit in—belonging to the best social clubs, attending upper-crusty civic and charity fund-raising dinners with Mary—he was the perfect citizen of his hometown and its symbol. While maintaining a gentility no Yankee could ever fully understand or duplicate, he operated with complete effectiveness throughout the country and the world.

Except for one exhibition match at East Lake, he stayed out of the news during the long hiatus between the U.S. Open and the U.S. Amateur. He went to work at the law office, wrote his column, and attended some Crackers games. At night he had a drink on the porch and listened to the crickets. Nothing in his column revealed a mind or a man melting down from pressure. He stuck to instructional themes, for the most part: "Jones Moves Head in All Full Shots"; "Bobby Declares Fixed Head Idea in Golf Is Fallacy Even in Putting" and "Jones Takes Issue with 'Eye on the Ball' "; "Bobby Says Concentrated Stare Is Harmful and Often Upsets Rhythm of Swing."

At last, on August 11, he wrote about Interlachen and the big decision of the USGA there. But instead of his thoughts on what happened and why at the seventy-first hole, Jones revealed to a waiting nation his unequivocal support of bunker rakes. But they had to be regular rakes, said Bobby, not those awful long-tined ones that created ridges in the sand, "which have been the curse of almost every championship since [the U.S. Open at] Oakmont."

A column called "The Locker Room" in the August issue of *The American Golfer* finally discussed the ruling at Lake Bush. There was no byline on the one-thousand-word piece, but in its dryness and equivocation was the hand of the USGA—the thing certainly contained none of the breezy sports-writerese of the magazine's editor, Grantland Rice. "Cards calling attention to the existence of the parallel hazard were given to all starters," the story pointed out, which was an excellent point. But overall the arguments in the piece were subtle, specious, and crafty; while it addressed the difficult logic of applying water hazard rules to a ball that may not have even gotten wet, there was only a weak line about allowing Bobby to drop his ball in the fairway when Lake Bush was so far away. "The decision in the Jones case was made by an official of the association, and it is presumed he followed the precedent of the club in the matter of the limits within which a ball could be dropped."

In the final sentence, a touch of regret: "If there was any doubt about it to the legality of allowing the ball to be dropped out, it would have been well to have Jones play another ball from the tee and hole out both balls, with the final decision reserved for the committee at the end of the round."

And then the matter died, an unfortunate incident that would never be discussed.

Jones played golf at East Lake during the two-month interregnum between the U.S. Open and Amateur, which was the one spot on earth where he felt and acted most like himself. The contrast between Bob at his leisure and the correct and contained Robert T. Jones Jr. at Hoylake or Interlachen could not have been greater. If you gave him a mask or a phony mustache, you might even believe they weren't the same person. His partners and opponents on his home course were his best friends in the world, including his father. They called each other "son-of-a-bitch," and they called the ball the same or worse. They played for seventy-five cents. They paid their caddies well, seventy-five cents plus a quarter tip. Jones threw clubs and broke them and sometimes threw the pieces in the lake. Liquor was involved. Most golfers are disgusted by such behavior and have it thrown off their course when it surfaces, but Jones biographers always found his feudin' and fussin' forgivable, even charming. See how human he is, they said. Playing golf this way must have felt like a delicious joke to Bobby after the solemn, church-like procession in the big tournaments.

Probably the first national exposure to the way the private Bobby played was provided by Paul Gallico in the October 26, 1929, issue of *Liberty Magazine*, a general-interest rag that called itself "A Weekly for Everybody." Gallico was one of the original participatory journalists: While covering a Jack

Dempsey training camp, he invited himself into the ring with the champ and got knocked out in less than two minutes—but he had his story. The bespectacled writer was about as much a golfer as he was a fighter, but he got inside the ropes one day with Jones and his pals at East Lake. "Jones throws them," he wrote, meaning his clubs.

> Jones apostrophizes them. Jones screams at his ball in anguish during its flight. Jones bellows at it from the tee demanding that it come around and reviews its ancestry when it doesn't. Jones plays a bad shot over again. Jones gashes the side of a bunker with his niblick to celebrate an unsatisfactory shot. Jones grows irritable when his caddie moves momentarily like an idiot. . . . Jones squabbles with his partners over strokes taken and holes won and who is up and handicaps given. In short, [he] behaves very much like a human being.

After the novice from New York hit what was intended to be a full three-iron only six feet, and dead right at that, he took his cue from the others and broke his club. "Bobby looked on with quiet approval," Gallico wrote. "Jones declared he would have done the same thing himself and that he would not have thought that highly of anyone, who having made a similar shot, had not immediately destroyed himself or the instrument."

Gallico offered opinions why the polite golf hero acted like he did behind the gates at East Lake. Career disappointment: "law is a mental hair shirt . . . He admits frankly that he doesn't like to work. . . . [and] admits a great longing for financial independence from the routine of desk slavery." Constant, unwelcome public display: "[he's] a sort of civic institution at the mercy of every self-estimated bigwig to come to town" with whom he has to meet or even play golf with. And before the Crackers season opener, he consented to making the locals whistle by driving six golf balls from home plate over the center-field fence.

Jones told Gallico about a recent incident that had scared him to death: Bobby's fun-loving group had completed nine holes when storm clouds boiled up in the southwest. They played the tenth and the eleventh with their eyes on the sky and then arrows of lightning started to pierce the golf course. After Jones felt a tingle of electricity through his spikes as the first bolt hit the tenth fairway, just forty yards away, they ran for it. More white five-inch-wide flashes of pure energy exploded around them as they ran through the wild downpour, and another hit a chimney on the roof just as they reached the clubhouse. A chunk of brick and mortar flew through the air and landed on Bobby's umbrella, collapsing it. The meteor tore the back of his shirt, from the shoulder to the waist, and gave him a superficial six-inch scratch. If the block had fallen an inch or two this way, he'd never play golf again. An inch or two that way, and he wouldn't breathe again . . .

In his memoir, Jones would recall this near-death experience as having occurred in July or August 1930, as evidence that perhaps fate did not intend for him to win the Grand Slam. The anecdote added to his faintly saintlike myth and became part of the agreed-upon fable. But—obviously, since he told a writer about it in 1929—the big lightning strike at East Lake actually took place a year before. Probably this was a harmless error by an older man conflating time. On the other hand, he put it between hard covers and with a specificity that made people believe it.

"It was only a few weeks after my brush with the chimney at East Lake that I had my second narrow escape from a serious accident," Jones wrote. As he recalled it, the second near-death experience that summer occurred at noon one day as he walked from the office of Jones, Evins, Powers, and Jones in the Atlanta Trust Company Building at 31 Broad Street to have lunch at the Town House of the Atlanta Athletic Club at 166 Carnegie Way. This was a well-worn path for Jones, and he was lost in thought as he turned the corner of Cone and started left onto Carnegie Way. Midway between the corner and the club entrance, he was startled to hear a voice behind him call out, "Look out, Mister." At that moment a driverless car mounted the sidewalk and came straight for him. Jones jumped out of the way, and the car rolled right over the spot from which he'd jumped, then crashed into the wall of the clubhouse. "Apparently, it had been carelessly parked at the top of the hill some one and a half blocks away."

His inaccuracy regarding the lightning incident gives reason to doubt Jones's second story and its tone. A little footwork reveals that the corner of Cone and Carnegie Way in Atlanta does not resemble the corner of Larkin and California Streets in San Francisco. This was a mild grade, in other words, not a steep one. A Model A could easily have been induced to roll but not very fast.

In the pages of the *Philadelphia Evening Bulletin* in late July, Odo-Ro-No asked, "Why bear the humiliation of offensive underarm odor any longer?" Sears offered tropical-weight men's suits—with two pairs of pants—for $11.95. The manager of the Phillies blamed the jeering, unmerciful fans for the team's last-place standing in the National League. "They do not come to the park to see us win," said Burt Shotton. "They come to see us lose." Police raided a meeting of a choral society in a house near the corner of Broad and Oxford, arrested two men, and seized their "alleged wine." Government officials and economists were now routinely using the word "depression."

Twenties craziness spread. Someone spent thirteen days in a tree, the *Evening Bulletin* reported, and another attention-seeker sat in a rocking chair for one hundred hours. Miniature golf boomed: for $2,800, James J. Andrien of Upper Darby, Pennsylvania, offered to build eighteen holes and throw in fifty-eight shrubs, nine "rustic" chairs, two umbrellas, and one hundred putters and balls. "Now I know why they call it miniature golf," said Mutt in a "Mutt and Jeff" cartoon. "In a miniature through!" (In a minute, you're through.) Aviators flew all over the paper: There was a girl student flier; daredevils taking planes up at night; a new airline flying ten-passenger Stinson tri-motors to New York and Washington beginning on August 15; and crashes, crashes, crashes.

The *Evening Bulletin* began to pick up Jones's column and gave it a prominent place on its sports page. U.S. Amateur preview stories—starring Jones—ran nearby. In a report on the new four-mile-long underground sprinkling system at Merion Golf Club, reporter Joe Dey declared that because of Bobby, the tournament "has assumed proportions of staggering importance. . . . Jones needs but the American amateur diadem to round out the greatest record ever achieved." Like other sportswriters around the country, Dey was addicted to the word *diadem*, which means "crown." Diadem seemed to appear in sports pages as often as the phrase "grand slam."

"Grand slam" did not appear anywhere in a golf context in the summer of '30, however, except in ads run by Hillerich and Bradbury, the Louisville, Kentucky, manufacturer of baseball bats and the new Grand Slam golf clubs. To orient the consumer about what that meant, H and B always included an image of a hand holding thirteen cards in its ad. In bridge and other card games, a grand slam was a perfect hand.

But winning four of the biggest golf tournaments had no name, no logo, no identity—probably because, even as it was occurring, people could not believe it was possible. New York went bonkers because Jones won the Double, and Atlanta planned its celebration for the same reason. Bobby's victory in the U.S. Open only iced the cake Atlanta had already baked. No one bothered to enshrine the Big Triple or the Triple Play or the Thunderbolt Threesome, because, my God, Jones had another tournament left this year and it looked like he'd make it four. "Today he began his bid for a 'grand slam,' " a Philadelphia newspaper reporter would write on September 22. New York sportswriter George Trevor coined "impregnable quadrilateral," an odious phrase that called more attention to Trevor or those who quoted Trevor than to the achievement itself.

Monday, September 15
Northbound

Motion . . .

All year Jones seemed to be going to a tournament or home from one. He'd crossed the Atlantic on ships that gave little sense of progress, and he'd rolled to Augusta in a motor that made him feel too acutely every inch of

Georgia along the way. Mostly he'd remember the clatter and sway of the train, and changing trains, and the station names: Savannah, Victoria, Leuchars, Saint-Placide, Saint-Michel, Lime Street, Crewe, Euston, Penn, Union, Milwaukee, Brookwood. . . . The English countryside meant mossy roofs and hedgerows. Paris resembled a fashion model in its beauty and self-absorption. Scotland looked molded by a gentle God; the sudden sharp tang of manure through the window reminded that those cows and sheep on the round green hills were not mere decorations. Rolling through his own vast country on steel wheels alternately bored him to tears and inspired him to deep thinking.

Now Jones began the long last trip of the year. With a handful of his homeboys, including, as ever, Keeler, he set out for Philadelphia for the U.S. Amateur, with a late stop in Chevy Chase, Maryland, to play an exhibition. He saw no scenery on this trip. Within two hours after the train chugged out of Atlanta, poor Bobby passed out in his berth, and he didn't awaken until the arrival in Washington the next morning. He was ill, with what, no one could say for sure. He'd seen a doctor the day before. He was finding it difficult to eat, and, notwithstanding his sixteen-hour nap, to sleep.

Tuesday, September 16
The White House, Washington, D.C.

Rain drummed the roof of the sleeper car when Jones awoke, and fell hard all day. But that afternoon thirty-five hundred people appeared at Columbia Country Club in Chevy Chase to watch Fred MacLeod, the pro at the host club, and Mac Smith, play Jones and his partner, Roland MacKenzie. The gate would go to Bobby McWatt, who had been MacLeod's assistant, until he'd been horribly injured in a motor accident two years before. The amateurs beat the pros one up. Bobby and Mac Smith shot 70, even par; MacKenzie had 71; and MacLeod, 73.

Writer Joe Dey from the *Evening Bulletin* came down from Philly to watch Jones. Dey asked the great man the obvious question: How do you think you'll do in the Amateur next week?

"If I should qualify and win two eighteen-hole matches on Wednesday, then I'll have high hopes," Jones replied. "Wednesday is the toughest day of the tournament."

All that—the golf and the interview—happened in the afternoon. The first thing Jones had done upon his arrival in the District of Columbia area was to get cleaned up and put on his best suit and get to 1600 Pennsylvania Avenue. President Herbert Hoover wanted to meet him.

The kindly son of a Quaker blacksmith was on his way to becoming probably the least popular president of the twentieth century. Like Jones, Hoover had trained as an engineer (Stanford, class of '91); unlike Bobby, he was good at it and had made his living from it. But circumstance was overwhelming his talent for planning and logistics. After a mild summer rally, September stock prices had fallen disastrously. Drought had prostrated hundreds of farm communities. About one thousand banks would fail before the year was over, leaving depositors in the lurch. Hoover acted decisively and often wisely in response to the disintegration of the economy, but mob psychology and his lack of political skill doomed his efforts. His opponents in Congress were painting him as cold and callous, which helped make the president the human symbol of the Depression. The shantytowns for the newly homeless were called Hoovervilles.

They met in the White House at noon. The president praised Jones for appearing for such a worthy cause and said that if the money raised for the injured pro was used to build him a miniature golf course, they might all have fun getting together again. "The old boy looked a bit fagged [tired], to me," wrote the ubiquitous O.B. in his column that day. "I suppose it is quite a job being president of these United States. But honestly, I liked better than anything else the manner in which his embarrassment matched that of Bobby Jones—the two of them seemed to me a couple of very plain and quite substantial Americans, going through with a formality which neither of them had actually wished. . . . And it is very funny, really, that they looked alike at their meeting at the White House. They are both on the plump side, for one thing."

And both were worrying full-time, for another. But with the differences in their ages—at fifty-six, Mr. Hoover was twice as old as Bobby—it was telling that Keeler saw a resemblance.

Wednesday, September 17
Philadelphia

Philadelphia aimed for magnificence in its public buildings like no other city in the United States. Its midcity train station, for example, resembled arched and spired Westminster Abbey. Jones arrived in the awesome Gothic on Broad Street at 8:50 in the morning, his worn-out appearance a sharp counterpoint to the architecture. He stood for a moment on the platform while a photographer snapped. The dark, shiny half-circles under his eyes gave him away. He looked beat up. He looked like hell.

Often Jones had had a collapsed, stressed-out appearance at the *end* of a big tournament. It was strange to see after he'd had a long rest; possibly his long rest had not been that restful. Had Mary ratcheted up the pressure for him to quit? Had his will to win the unnamed Slam become desperation?

Those haunted, weary eyes plainly needed sleep, but rest during a tournament had become elusive in recent years. "I have a good, big dinner in the evening in my room, prefaced by two good, stiff highballs, the first taken in a tub of hot water," he and Keeler had written in the first Jones memoir, *Down the Fairway,* which was published in 1927, when Jones was twenty-five. Whiskey, a bath, and a lot of food, Jones wrote, were "the finest relaxing combination I know; and then a few cigarettes and a bit of conversation, and bed at nine o'clock. And usually I sleep well."

But with his fourth consecutive major on the line, there was nothing usual about this week. The usual remedies would not chase his insomnia, so he drank more highballs and stiffer ones. Keeler watched over him like a nurse until his patient drifted off. Dry-mouthed, head-throbbing mornings required hair-of-the-dog.

From Broad Street Station, Jones motored the four or five blocks to the hotel in which he would not sleep. The Barclay had nice, big bathtubs; Ben Hogan, another ritual soaker, would reside there in 1951, during his famous battle with Merion in the U.S. Open.

That afternoon, Jones saw another doctor, an osteopath. He had a pain in his neck.

Jones rhapsodized about the Old Course at St. Andrews, but Merion meant the world to him. He'd become a national figure there in 1916, when Mr. Adair took him and his son, Perry, to play in the U.S. Amateur. Jones was a chunky fourteen-year-old boy with clunky shoes who didn't know any better than to shoot at the funny flagsticks that had bulb-shaped wicker tops instead of flags. Drawling L'il Bobby's unawed style and appealing manner succeeded brilliantly for a while. He qualified for match play and won a couple of times, but then the growing crowds observed that the charming adolescent was merely a talented brat, probably with an indulgent father back in Atlanta. He threw clubs; he swore audibly. He was not ready for the big time.

Eight years later, when the Amateur returned to Merion, Jones *was* ready. Scores of exhibition matches for the Red Cross during World War I had taught him how to play in front of a crowd, a dozen or two tournament defeats showed him how to win, and he outgrew his temper like teenage acne. Merion showcased his strength, which was absence of weakness. Merion examined your ability and guts thoroughly: It required slugging and precision, conservative play and gambling, very clear thinking, and a diamond-cutter's touch on the greens. And endurance, because the last five holes were so tough. Jones took his final two matches in the '24 U.S. Amateur, over Ouimet and von Elm, by eleven and ten and nine and eight, massacre scores. He'd won his first national tournament. He was on his way.

Now, on a cool, bright September morning, Emperor Jones walked up the path to the big, white clubhouse and up the stairs to the locker room. Mike McFadden, the attendant, showed him to his locker and said, whatever you need, Mr. Jones. Meanwhile, caddie master Joe Markey pointed at a young man named Howard Rexford and then pointed at Bobby's brown leather bag. Rexford started to tremble all over. He'd won the caddie lottery.

A polite, well-spoken young man of nineteen with perfectly pomaded light brown hair, Rexford had been selected from the 350 caddies available, all of whom wanted that one bag. Inside his yellow sweater, Rexford's heart beat like a parakeet's as he walked through the hundreds of people milling around the first tee. Virtually every spectator on the grounds—there were eventually about two thousand—wanted to see Howard's new boss. As one of the writers said, it was Bobby-this and Bobby-that at Merion.

"When he started out, he asked me my name," the ink manufacturer's son revealed during a break between the two eighteen-hole practice rounds Jones played. "He called me Howard . . . He doesn't want you to hand him a club, except his putter—he makes his own selection for each shot. He wants you to be perfectly quiet and to stand off to the right, out of his line of vision. . . . He doesn't ask what sort of a club should be used for a certain shot. He did that only once during the round and I didn't answer—[his partner] did the answering."

Not at his best, Jones shot 73 and 78 and didn't make a birdie in either round. By the end of the day, he was plainly disgusted with his play and with his large, undisciplined gallery. On the fifth hole of the second round, he hit his third shot with a niblick into a creek and threw the club to the ground.

On Thursday, his gallery doubled to four thousand. After poor iron shots, Jones would have liked to hit a second ball, but that was impossible: After each of his full swings, the crowd surging in front of him looked like the start of the Boston Marathon. He played with tight lips and frowns. Afterward, he told reporters that he was going to lay off golf the next day. And do what? they asked. "Take a trolley ride," Jones replied.

Friday, September 19
Pine Valley Golf Club, Clementon, New Jersey

Reporters patrolled outside the Barclay that morning, paparazzi-style. A luxury motor pulled up to the entrance. Jones came out of the hotel and got inside the car.

"Where are you going, Bobby?"

"Just going for a ride."

"There seem to be some bags of golf clubs in the car with you."

Jones smiled but didn't reply as the getaway car sped away from Rittenhouse Square, with Thomas D. Paine of the USGA behind the wheel and O. B. Keeler in the backseat. They drove southeast for about an hour to Clementon, New Jersey, whose claim to fame was its golf course, possibly the toughest in the world. Although Pine Valley did not seem to be the place to rest from the rigors of Merion, at least there shouldn't be a crowd. But even on an unannounced mission at this most private club, a gallery appeared (no one there that day estimated its size). Jones played poorly on the front nine and picked up three times but shot a two-under 33 on the back. He and English amateur Dale Bourne lost by one hole to Tolley and Jess Sweetser.

After lunch at the clubhouse, the Pine Valley boys motored back up to Philadelphia to take in a baseball game. John A. Brown, the founder, president, and patriarch of Pine Valley, a giant of six feet five inches, joined the group. They arrived at the Baker Bowl, a cozy cigar box of a ballpark, during the third inning and took their well-placed seats on the first-base side. An enterprising writer from the *Evening Bulletin* positioned himself close enough to Jones to record everything he said and did during the final six innings. The paper ran the story—"Phils Disappoint 'King of Golfdom' "—above the fold in the center of the front page, between an account of a double murder in Minnesota and a ferry boat crash on the Delaware River.

"Bobby arrived very quietly with a group who knows what's what in the golf world. He bought a score card, took a seat in the second row of section K, and leaned forward in regular baseball fannish attitude, waiting for thrills." The paper reported various knowing comments made by the executive vice president of the Atlanta Crackers—regarding the short right-field fence, how seldom anyone threw out a runner from center field nowadays, and "I see Chicago is beating Boston." The golfers stayed to the last out, but the first-place St. Louis Cardinals beat the last-place Phils, 7 to 3.

After the game, a kid came up and asked Jones for an autograph. He signed. He yawned.

Saturday, September 20
Merion Golf Club, Ardmore, Pennsylvania

The newsreel account of the U.S. Amateur by Fox Movietone News began with a headline: "Bobby's Hardest Test." Well, that was food for thought, because in so many ways this looked just the opposite, the most certain victory of his life. The U.S. Amateur was Jones's strongest event; he'd won it four times. In the previous six years, he'd been first, first, second (to George von Elm, in 1926, the last time he'd lost a thirty-six-hole match), first, first again, and then that shocking opening-round loss to Goodman at Pebble Beach. In the field this week, only Harrison "Jimmy" Johnston, Tolley, and George Voigt had given him trouble this year, at the British Amateur back in May—but none of them had contended in the two big Opens since then, both wins by Jones.

He had momentum on his side. He loved the golf course. He had a great draw; with one or two exceptions, he'd be playing nervous, sweaty young men in over their heads. Even the format favored him. Although his record in eighteen-hole matches since 1926 was seventeen and two, Jones feared the short form. But he'd only have to survive two of those on Wednesday to move on to the quarterfinals. If all that didn't work, emotion seemed sure to. The vibes from the gallery were always stronger and more important in match play than in stroke competitions; crowd support during man-to-man combat could be almost tangible, an invisible hand pushing a favorite along while holding his opponent back. And everyone wanted Bobby to win—even the other players.

"If I can't repeat, then there's nothing I'd rather see than victory for Bob Jones," defending champion Johnston said.

On the other hand, maybe the newsreel was right. A lot was going against him, too.

The Jones psychodrama contained enough elements for a three-act play. The simultaneous pressure to win and to quit; no Hagen, Sarazen, or other star to deflect some of the fans and media; a golf course that could discourage even the strongest player if he didn't have his best stuff; and his deteriorating physical and mental condition. The costars in the play were Keeler, Big Bob, Howard Rexford, and Mary on the phone every other night. The supporting cast would be a faceless army of golfers, fans, officials, reporters, and cameramen—and Mike McFadden, getting him a towel and brushing his shoes and watching in amazement as Bobby started his day with a glass of whiskey.

Five thousand fans watched Jones shoot 74 on Saturday. He was playing fairly well, but regular lapses into mediocre play made him a bit uneasy. Probably all he needed was rest—which he'd try to get on Sunday. With the exception of that emergency nine at Interlachen, when his room was too hot for comfort, Jones rarely if ever played the day before a big event.

Sunday, September 21

According to legend, USGA president Findlay Douglas called on Jones in person in his suite at the Barclay. He asked a special favor: Would Bobby come out and play?

Both men were in a tough spot. Naturally, Douglas knew Jones's pregame ritual, and he could see that he was stressed and tired. To ask a man on the verge of making history to sacrifice his rest was asking a lot. But crowds and gate receipts would materialize if Jones came out and performed, and the

USGA needed money. For reasons he kept to himself, Jones assented, an extraordinary gesture under the circumstances.

He and R. A. "Dick" Jones of Westchester Hills, New York, played Voigt and Watts Gunn, Bobby's old protégé. The Joneses won, three and two, and Bobby shot 69, which put him in a better mood for the first day of qualifying, but at some cost to his diminishing supply of energy. And the USGA made money. According to Desmond Tolhurst in *Golf at Merion*, the receipts for the U.S. Amateur in 1930 totaled $55,000, compared to just $17,000 in 1964.

Monday, September 22

Except for an afternoon breeze that some players found inconvenient, the weather was perfect. About seven thousand attended, most of whom walked in the Jones gallery. *New York Times* reporter William D. Richardson was one of these, and he fell under Bobby's spell. Like Fred Astaire, B. B. King, or Itzhak Perlman—pick your virtuoso—he made a very difficult thing look easy. "After watching Bobby Jones produce a 69, one under par, at the Merion Cricket Club," Richardson wrote, "one could not refrain from wondering why only thirteen other players in this most select field could score 75s or better and why Jess Sweetser, the 1922 champion, took 81; Cyril Tolley, former British amateur champion, 82; and Harrison R. Johnston, the defending titleholder, 83."

Jones's 69 looked even more impressive when you noticed that of the 169 who teed off, only sixty-one broke 80. After two rounds, the lowest thirty-two scores would qualify for match play.

Laura Lee, a reporter for the *Evening Bulletin* and obviously no golfer, produced a wonderful picture of the day, painted only with short declarative sentences, most of them in the second person. "It looks dull," Lee wrote.

You wish you hadn't come. You wonder where all the marines came from and why there are so many officials with badges and brilliant red caps and arm bands. . . . 9:08 o'clock. Bobby appears at last, seven minutes ahead of schedule and very much at home. Respectful applause greets him, no cheers. Bobby good-naturedly faces a line of excited camera men. Bobby proves himself an able comedian. He rates two great laughs with the funny, serious, sheepish way he shakes hands with his partner, Emory Stratton. You suddenly notice a tremendous crowd. They are tense and quiet, their eyes glued to Bobby. Bobby has his stick in his hand. You begin to feel that the air is charged with electricity. This is a good show, after all. . . .

No one speaks above a whisper. "Isn't he darling?" "Look how calm he is." "He's certainly getting plump." "Doesn't he look young?" "Isn't his caddie cute?" "No, the thin one in the yellow sweater . . ."

The galleryites are brimming over with sympathy for everyone. "It's a shame the crowd doesn't even wait to see the other boy drive," thinks the lady in the red hat with lips and finger nails to match . . .

You wait, five thousand of you, for Bobby to putt. Now even the whispers have stopped. You get a thrill out of the concentrated, tense, silence. No sound but the heavy breathing of the gallery. Short applause and silence again. . . .

You decide that the most popular fall color is rust or red, with brown a close second. You see Red Hat again with a new pair of lips. She is excited because Bobby got the birdie. You wish she would talk English.

You like the way Bobby whams the balls. Must be fun to do it . . . A vast circle ten deep around the greens. "Gangway!" The multitude divides and lets the Emperor through, followed by faithful yellow sweater and a retinue of father, reporters, and officials. . . .

More mountains to climb. The great thick woods look most inviting. But you are held to the game, fascinated. . . .

Suddenly, it is all over. "Sixty-nine" is on all lips. . . . the boys at the gate sell "photygraphs of Bobby Jones." The cool ride home. Idea for a theme song: "Bobby made a golfer out of me."

Tuesday, September 23

With a 73 on Tuesday, Jones led all qualifiers, and his 142 tied the lowest number ever in U.S. Amateur qualifying. But he finished with two bogeys and showed plenty of angry body language over the delays caused by the ten thousand fans who watched. Ten thousand, most of them on one hole, was way too many for snug Merion. Not that it was only the gallery's fault, but the wait on the seventeenth tee was twenty-three minutes. Getting this army out of the way on each hole made it seem, Jones said, "like driving off eighteen first tees."

Tolley's 82-81 didn't come close to making the low thirty-two, and defending champion Johnston's 83-73 was one shot too many.

Wednesday, September 24

Now the real tournament began, with a dangerous day of two eighteen-hole matches—if, of course, you got past your first opponent. For Jones that was C. Ross "Sandy" Somerville of London, Ontario; if he beat Somerville in their 9:00 match, he'd face the winner from the 9:08 twosome, F. G. Hoblitzel of Toronto or Ellis Knowles of New York.

The weather again was perfect. Virtually every spectator followed the Jones match. The *Bulletin* estimated the crowd at fifteen thousand, a number the paper said was conservative but was still hard to imagine.

Somerville had game, as everybody knew. He would win the Canadian Amateur three times, and the U.S. Amateur in 1932. He hung with Jones for the first third and was only one down, but on seven Jones holed from eight feet on downhill ice, and Somerville's caress from one foot closer just missed on the high side. Then, the deluge: Birdies from Bobby on eight and nine, a four-up lead, and a four-under nine holes. Old Man Par, indeed. Jones won five and four in two hours and ten minutes.

Hoblitzel fell like a tree in the afternoon; his first nine 44 allowed Jones to bumble to the turn with a 41 and still lead by three holes. Jones wrote later that he was "just so tired" that he "was not equal to a steady performance." But not so fatigued that he couldn't beat Fred Hoblitzel by another five and four.

Meanwhile, von Elm, Ouimet, Goodman, and Gunn lost. Only one other man who had ever beaten Jones survived to the final eight: Jess Sweetser. In the 1922 U.S. Amateur, Jess had thrashed Bobby eight and seven. They'd had no matches since.

Thursday, September 25

Jones played a young man from California named Fay Coleman. A dreary match: Bobby snored through the first eighteen holes; in something closer to 80 than 70 (he had a "newspaper" 76), with a ball hooked out-of-bounds on the fifteenth. But pars on the quarry holes, Merion's legendarily difficult final three, resulted in two wins and a two-up lead at lunch.

Did he go to his locker at this point for a glass of liquid courage? McFadden, the locker room man, told his friends that that was Mr. Jones's habit. "A big chug of that corn liquor in the morning, he told me, and another shot for lunch with a chicken sandwich on white," recalled Bud Lewis in 2004. "Mike waited on him there in the lower locker room, said he was a great guy. And Rexford said the same. Jesus. Jones was all Rexford talked about, and he never stopped talking."

Lewis, the golf professional at Manufacturer's Country Club in suburban Philadelphia from 1943 to 1979, would gain a mighty reputation as an instructor. In 1930, he was a twelve-year-old caddie at Llanerch, another area club, and a nonpaying spectator at the U.S. Amateur at Merion.

"Yeah, Jones inspired me. I think he inspired everyone who saw him. He hit it dead straight off the tee; just hit and walk down the middle. But he was loose at the top. Too loose. Wouldn't stand up today."

Before the afternoon round against Coleman, Jones walked through the buffet line. "My stomach has been jumping around like jack rabbits all week," he'd told his friends. Now he deposited two hard rolls on his plate, a slice of tongue, and a slice of chicken. He drank iced tea, one sugar. "Bobby Jones eats less than any contestant remaining in the national amateur golf championship," wrote a local reporter, who saw the nearly empty plate as the symbol of a purposeful and healthy diet. But, he wrote, Bobby "apparently puts no limit on the number of cigarettes he smokes around the course. Jones consumed many cigarettes while making his round with Coleman."

By staying close to par, Jones smoked Coleman in the afternoon. Fay shot a third nine of 42, and that was that. Bobby won six and five. He'd face Sweetser in the semifinals.

Friday, September 26

It rained late Thursday, then rained some more overnight. When the morning sun came out in the cloudless sky, it produced an Interlachen-like sauna so oppressive that Jones exchanged his gray flannel plus fours for Wimbledon whites, and he didn't wear a tie. He didn't look right without one.

This would be Jones's first real match, various experts declared. Sweetser had won big events before—the U.S. Amateur in '22 and the 1926 British Amateur, both with Jones in the field. The head-back, hands-in-his-pockets way he posed with his opponent for the prematch first-tee photograph showed a confident, even cocky competitor ready to let the clubs do the talking.

"Sweets"—his ironic nickname—had not been in a good mood. In previous matches, he'd set himself to hit a shot, discover a distracting movement, then glare in the direction of the guilty party. "Always highly irritable in a golf match, [Sweetser] seems to be even more so now than ever before," reported the *Evening Bulletin.* "In a few instances it was excusable for the space is badly cramped at Merion and the galleries that follow Jones seem to have absolutely no consideration for any of the other players."

Merion Golf Club, as seen from above.

About ten thousand persons convened around the first tee, and about five thousand more joined during the day. Despite the heat, a lot of them ran from green to tee and from tee to fairway. They jumped over creeks and scurried up hills in the almost desperate competition to get a glimpse of Bobby. They knew he'd won three big ones in a row, and they'd read the rumors that this might be his last tournament. They were a spectacle.

Except for a brief interval in the middle, the thundering army didn't see much of a match. Almost immediately, Merion and the occasion found out Sweetser. Since his glory year in 1926, respiratory illness and business had put golf on Jess's back burner. Jones's idolaters would always refer to him as a part-time golfer, but in 1930 he'd been anything but that; he devoted a lot more time and energy to the game than Sweetser did. Bobby quickly went four up, lost three of the lead, then gained it back with solid pars around the quarry.

Although no one in it had a chance to win the Grand Slam, the other semi-final match was much more interesting. Charles Seaver, age nineteen, of Los Angeles, had the square, handsome face of a male model in an aftershave ad and the tousled blond hair of a surfer. A great athlete, he would sire another great athlete, his son, Tom, the Hall of Fame pitcher. With his big hands and muscular torso, Seaver bombed the ball, usually pretty straight, and he raced to a five-up lead over his foe, Eugene V. Homans of Englewood, New Jersey. But the mild-looking Homans, age twenty-two, possessing steel shafts, steel-rimmed glasses, and a dippy swing, would not give up.

Charles and Eugene looked like the homecoming king and the nerd who helped him with his homework. They'd become good friends: Early in the week, they'd been introduced and discovered that they were staying in the same hotel. Since then, they'd shared rides to and from the golf course and had gone to the movies together several times; *All Quiet on the Western Front* was playing at the nearby Ardmore Theatre. Now they concentrated on the fight to have the honor of being beaten by Bobby Jones.

Jones nursed his four-up lunchtime lead for a while, then he started to make putts. He made a thrilling side-hiller on the fifth, then slightly straighter and shorter putts fell in on seven and nine. He won the eighth with a par and won the match by pitching close on ten, for his fourth birdie in the final six holes. Jones beat Sweetser nine and eight, to make the finals of his final tournament.

The other match went down to the wire. Both men played to type. Seaver kept blasting and played fairly well, but his colorless, conservative opponent pecked away. Homans diligently kept it in the fairway and knocked it on the green. He completed his determined comeback on the seventeenth green, when he wiggled in a par putt around a partial stymie. Now all square with one to play, Homans hit a driver and a three-wood onto the eighteenth green. Seaver hit his usual much longer drive but hooked his second shot badly and couldn't recover. The tortoise two-putted and beat the hare, one up.

Later, in the locker room, Charlie kidded Gene about how long he was taking to get dressed. Then the two pals left Merion together.

Saturday, September 27

This twenty-five-hour day, the last day of daylight savings time, was bright and sunny with a cool west wind.

They shook hands for the photographers at about 10:00. Both wore sweaters; Jones's was sleeveless and his neck tieless. Outwardly as serene as Buddha, Jones gripped the hand, looked into the eyes, and might have asked pleasantly do you prefer Gene or Eugene? Homans looked down at his shorter, sturdier, much more famous adversary and drew his lips back from his teeth, the uncertain smile before the first parachute jump.

The younger man stood six feet one and weighed 155 pounds. It appeared that he would benefit from orthodontia. He came from money: He'd prepped at Choate, played golf at Maidstone, and attended (but didn't graduate from) Princeton—solid credentials to be an officer in the USGA or to run for Congress. His making the final of the U.S. Amateur was no surprise to the cognoscenti; he'd shot an excellent even-par 70 in the second eighteen against Seaver, and earlier in the year, he'd won the North and South, one of the biggest U.S. amateur tournaments. What would winning *the* U.S. Amateur mean for Eugene Vanderpool Homans? He'd be starting work at his father's insurance office in New York in two weeks—would the world beat a path to his door to buy a policy? Would the conqueror of Jones become the new Bobby Jones and write a syndicated column and ride in the back of a convertible in a ticker-tape parade?

No. Even if all the angels and saints stepped aside for a few hours and they handed Homans the bigger trophy at the end of the day, he *couldn't* win. Something Joe Dey had written early in the week rang true: "Bobby overshadows all the others by such a wide margin, that even if he were to lose, which doesn't appear very likely, the man who beat him would be considered lucky and not get any great amount of recognition for his victory."

The game began at 10:07. Mr. Jones took his spoon from the sagging leather bag held by solemn Howard Rexford. The breeze ruffled Bobby's hair. The audience hushed. Even without thousands of Pennsylvanians straining to see every preshot twitch and gesture, the first swing at Merion often induced a strangely intense stage fright. The tee was so intimate, with the dining facility under the big awning attached to the clubhouse, that a golfer could smell the turtle in the snapper soup and hear the diners' teeth chewing the lettuce in their club sandwiches. Then, sudden silence. You tried to ignore the diners' eyes on your back and hit a useful shot between the bunkers and not in the rough on a slightly uphill, gentle-dogleg-right 360-yard par four with a pear-shaped green that undulated like a belly dancer.

With no easy-looking shots until the tenth hole, that Merion first-tee fear could stay with you until it was too late.

The pattern of the match was set immediately. Both men hit the fairway on the first, but Jones was both straight off the tee and long, easily outdriving Homans, even though he'd used a three-wood. Gene hit a weak shot to the right, into the chalk white sand in a greenside bunker, then hit an irresolute bunker shot, then missed his thirty-foot putt for par. Bobby hit it on, rolled it close from twenty feet, and was one up after one. The duelists walked across Ardmore Avenue to the second tee; just like at Interlachen, a fairly busy two-lane road bisected the course.

Bobby hit a full-blooded two-iron onto the green on the hilltop-to-hilltop par-three third; with his swing and that ball flight, the shot was something beautiful to behold. Gene pulled his spoon—three-wood—into a bunker on the left; he feathered a good soft niblick from the pit to about eight feet. Rexford took out the flagstick, which was heavy as lead with the red-orange basket on top instead of a flag. Homans missed. Jones two-putted and went two up.

On the fourth, one of only two par fives at Merion, Bobby hit the shot of the day. He drove into a bunker on the right. Gene hit a very good tee ball past him and in the fairway. Then Jones showed his profound understanding that each hole is a little tournament in match play, and that when you're two up after three and you've seen fear in your opponent's eyes, it could be a good time to gamble. So Jones played the low-percentage shot, a spoon from the sand—and nailed it. The ball hung in the air on its exceptionally long and high flight down the fairway; the gallery of about eighteen thousand oohed and ahhed as if it had seen fireworks. Jones made par. After that knife in the side, Homans contrived to bogey the hole and fell three down.

It was a death march for Eugene after that. Jones shot a one-under-par 33 on the second nine, with birdies on eleven and fifteen and a bogey on seventeen, and plucked off hole after hole like grapes. "It was terrible to watch," reported the *Evening Bulletin*, "with the dogged youth in spectacles staggering along with that hopeless look on his face." After eighteen holes, Jones stood seven up. He'd shot 72.

High above the Merion clubhouse, a daring young man in a flying machine performed aerobatic stunts during halftime.

The end began after lunch and about an hour of golf. Jones hit that concave-faced sand wedge from the bunker on three. He not only almost holed it, he laid poor Gene a partial stymie; when he couldn't get around it from two feet, Homans lost with a bogey four. The next hole showed what eighteen thousand people looked like: Spectators ten or twelve deep lined both sides of its 595 yards in a solid wall and surrounded both the tee and the green.

A push-pull of halved holes ensued, shortening Homans's rope. At least one account had Jones driving the green on the narrow par-four eighth, an incredible and incredibly lucky shot if true, which had never been accomplished before or since. Walking up the railroad-tie steps on the steep hill to the tenth tee, Jones led by eight holes. In the fairway up by the green, a little dog scooted back and forth, obviously excited to be surrounded by so many people. When Bobby bombed his tee ball over the ravine and damn near hit the dog, the throng cooed a sympathetic "Ooh," and the dog ran away.

Theoretically a birdie opportunity because it was only 335 yards long and not particularly tight, the tenth at Merion still had bunkers, trees, rough, and a green like a frozen pond; enough problems, in other words, to cause an infuriating five or six. Which was exactly what happened to Bobby and Gene—except for the anger part. Jones looped a circle around the two sixes on the scorecard and wrote a rueful "ha ha." Here was information to win a bar bet: With a chance to win the Grand Slam with a bogey, Jones pitched his ball straight into a bunker already occupied by his opponent. Bobby left his ball in the silicon, Gene skulled his over the green into another bunker, and both men chopped their way to double bogeys on the drive-and-pitch par four.

Now Jones was dormie eight—eight up, eight to play.

Most of those in the know agreed that the eleventh was a more suitable hole than the tenth on which to end the drama. Certainly, it more closely epitomized Merion: A hole of modest length—378 yards—the eleventh was absolutely terrifying if you didn't hit it in the right place—twice. The fairway hid out there between bunkers and rough, and a stream crossed the righteous path about eighty yards in front of the green. Two deep bunkers and the aptly named Baffling Brook guarded the tiny plateau where a wicker bulb, like a bee's nest, sat on a pole. Mature oaks, gums, and beeches framed the target. High above the trees to the right of the green, two brooding Tudor mansions perched on top of a stone cliff. These big, brown houses on Golfview Road had verandahs with tables and umbrellas and a perfect view of the incredible sight below. Spectators lined the hole twelve deep from the tee to the green.

Off a conceded birdie two on the ninth, Homans had the honor. As usual, his head dipped down on his backswing and came back up at impact; he drove very well into the right side of the fairway. Now the hero teed up a ball, his brown skin and white clothing vivid in the sun. Jones's full, balletic swing with a hickory stick produced a muffled *whomp*, the sound of a broom beating a carpet. He killed this final drive, into the left center of the fairway and about 290 yards out.

With a mashie, Homans hit and held the back left of the green, a pretty good shot but leaving a probably unmakeable putt. Jones knitted his eyebrows and flicked a niblick to a safe spot twenty feet below the hole. There was no need to gamble; all he needed was a tie. "Bobby, looking a little haggard and drawn, walked over to his ball after his caddie had handed him his pet putter," William D. Richardson wrote in the *New York Times*. "One of those quizzical glances that he gives the hole, the familiar cocking of the Jones head, a slight movement of the wrists, as they brought the club back and then forward." The cautious ball rolled to within ten inches. Because of the possibility of a stymie, Homans did not give him the putt.

Jones with the trophies of the four major championships, all of which he won during his last year of competitive golf, his year of glory, 1930.

Gene would have to make his eighteen-footer or block Bobby's ball for the match to continue. Nothing in his body language indicated that he thought he could do it. He played quickly, missed quickly, and before his ball had even stopped rolling, he extended his hand. Jones had won the Grand Slam.

The eighteen thousand roared, the sound concentrated by the natural amphitheatre around the green. Then they charged—or some of them did—but were rebuffed by the marines. A hurricane of emotions rushed through Jones, clear to his soul. "All at once I felt the release from tension and relaxation I had wanted so badly for so long a time," he would write. "Nothing more remained to be done."

It took a few minutes for the guards to create enough of a hole in the humanity for the golfers to begin the half-mile walk back to the clubhouse. They cheered Jones on his victory march, of course, but his face remained blank. He looked completely spent.

In November, Jones shocked the sports world
by retiring from competition. His new job: movie star.

7

Glory's Reward

"We're overpaying him but he's worth it."

—*Samuel Goldwyn (Samuel Goldfish),*
Polish-born U.S. film producer

ack and Harry Warner hated one another with the loathing attainable only by brothers who are also business partners. Flashy Jack wore loud sports jackets, patent leather shoes, and a big smile. He had a wife, girlfriends, another wife—this one, to his brother's horror, a gentile—and more girlfriends. Among his several annoying habits were the little soft-shoe dance he performed when meeting someone and the tasteless jokes he delivered in his loud, clanging voice. For example: Standing before a table of Asian women at a banquet for Madame Chiang Kai-shek, whose husband was the president of China and later of Taiwan, classy Jack exclaimed, "Holy Cow! I forgot to pick up my laundry." More shtick when Albert Einstein visited the studio: "I have a theory about relatives, too," he told the great physicist. "Don't hire them."

Older brother Harry, on the other hand, rarely smiled. A devout Jew, he kept kosher and always lived within walking distance of the temple, so he could follow the decree in the Talmud that you must not ride on the Sabbath. Promoting tolerance in race and religion became his mission; Harry wanted Warner Brothers to make movies with a moral, while Jack just wanted entertainment as loud as his clothes. Although they barely spoke and each detested what the other stood for, they worked it out. One of their most brilliant gambits was betting big on a new technology: sound. For the first real "talkie," Warner Brothers adapted a stage play called *The Jazz Singer,* the plot of which contained elements that appealed to both men. Harry liked the story of a Jew's assimilation into American life, and Jack was intrigued by the songs and dialogue synchronized to Al Jolson's lips. Both were right: *The Jazz Singer* opened on October 6, 1927, and it was a huge hit. The film effectively ended the silent era and made the nine sons and daughters of the immigrant Polish peasant Benjamin Warner wealthy.

They were smart, those Warner boys: They diversified into record companies, radio stations, and Broadway plays, and they invested a lot of their skyrocketing profits in the latest sound equipment for their studio and theatres. They owned over five hundred theatres and in the first six months of 1930 added an average of one a day to their chain. But like everyone else, they were hurt by the stock market crash. Less than half as many movie tickets were sold industrywide in 1930 as in 1929, and Warner's profits fell from $14 million to $7 million. What this new market wanted, the feuding brothers and the others decided, was more reality but with a good story. Gangster films, something like that.

Atlanta was a major city with no major-league sports, but it had one big show: Georgia Tech football. No school had a better fight song:

I'm a Ramblin' Wreck from Georgia Tech
And a hell of an engineer
A helluva, helluva, helluva, hell of an engineer

Like all the jolly good fellows
I drink my whiskey clear
I'm a Ramblin' wreck from Georgia Tech . . .

Especially for an alumnus like Bobby Jones, those home games on sunny Saturday afternoons simply could not be missed. From the optional pregame party or a meal at the world's biggest drive-in, the Varsity, a.k.a. the Greasy V, you walked through the green oasis of the Tech campus to the stadium, and you heard the band a hundred yards down Techwood Drive. Freshmen in their yellow RAT caps—Recruits at Tech—ran out on the field to form a human tunnel for the team to run through before the kickoff. "To Hell with Georgia"—that is, the University of Georgia—was always a popular sentiment on hats and signs regardless of the opponent. Tech football had a score of such traditions and rituals, including whispering the "hells" in the fight song, but none of them were more delightful than winning.

They knew what that was like. Under coach Bill Alexander, the Golden Tornadoes—a.k.a. the Yellow Jackets—won every single game in 1928, including the Rose Bowl, where they beat California 9-7. But the '28 national champs slipped to a 3-6 record in '29. In the fall of 1930, by God, Tech would return to the mountaintop. They won the home opener on October 4 over South Carolina, 45-0. After a bad loss at Penn, the boys won again in Atlanta over Auburn, 14-12. Now that was more like it. "I'm a Ramblin' Wreck from Georgia Tech and a hell of an engineer . . ."

Season ticket holder Jones was one of those superinvolved, pain-in-the-ass fans who wrote to the coach—explaining in one letter that in football, as in golf, it was foolhardy to attempt to sit on a lead. In the years to come, he would be president of the Alumni Association and serve on the Athletic Department executive board—but for the most part, he enjoyed being a spectator for a change and not the spectated. After those football games in the fall of 1930, his mind was free to resume thinking about his two problems: how to make some serious money while retaining his dignity and despite the Depression; and what to do about golf.

After the win at Hoylake, several observers were sure that they'd never see Bonnie Bobby in competition again. After the win at Interlachen, a number of writers were given to understand that he was finished; Keeler later wrote that before the trophy presentation, while Bobby sat in a small room upstairs in the clubhouse, he had decided to finally quit (but O.B. also wrote that it would be good for Bobby to give up the more stressful opens and just play the amateurs). In short, the situation was confused. At Merion, after finishing the Grand Slam, Jones addressed the retirement issue. Sort of: His statement was a masterpiece of lawyerly equivocation.

> I have no definite plans either to retire or as to when and where I may continue in competition. I might play next year and lay off in 1932. I might stay out next season and feel like another tournament the following year. What I want most right now is to be free of any obligation, express or implied, to continue playing each year in both major [U.S.] championships.

Then one day that fall clarity arrived in Jones's life like a bolt of lightning. A charming 1910 Tech graduate named Young Frank Freeman—friends called him Frank, not Young—was sitting in the law office of Jones, Evins, Powers, and Jones, gabbing with Bobby as he did almost every day. Their favorite topic was Georgia Tech football, but sometimes the topic strayed to the Crackers or to business. Frank worked for S. A. Lynch Enterprises, a film distribution company. Effectively, he was a wheeler-dealer, a middleman who found theatres for films or found films for the few independent theatres. But that wasn't all he could do.

"One day we started talking about doing some motion pictures designed to teach people how to play golf," Jones recalled in *Golf Is My Game*. "The more we talked, the better we both liked the idea."

The well-connected Y. Frank Freeman got on the phone. It was a pleasant thing to get Frank's call, just to hear the music and the y'alls in his Georgia drawl. Harry Warner was one of those Freeman talked to, and he liked what he heard. Golf instruction? From the star of the newsreels, the greatest golfer in history? Now that would be realism. Why don't you gentlemen come up to my office and we'll discuss. The first week of November, after Tech lost at home to Vanderbilt 6-0, Freeman and Jones took a train to New York and took a meeting with the solemn, devout Mr. Warner. A week later, after Tech lost again, Jones returned to New York and signed a contract to star in a series of twelve one-reel films. After the success of the first twelve, Jones returned to Hollywood and did six more.

Suddenly, he was very rich.

The Bobby Jones story was turned on its ear.

One day he was a financial naïf suffering for his art, and the next he was a considerable man who really belonged in that big house in Atlanta's fanciest neighborhood. With Harvard, the USGA, and now money, his ascent into the Club was complete. How much money? In up-front cash and royalties,

The Jones home in Atlanta. The servants' wing was in the back.

Jones put $250,000 from Warner Brothers in his pocket during the next couple of years. In 2005 terms, that was at least $18 million, according to Wall Street veteran William Earley. "That's conservative," Earley said in 2004. "If you figure interest at seven percent a year, which is not unreasonable, the present value is about $37.5 million."

(Jones put half of his $120,000 advance into a trust fund for the children. The IRS refused to treat the trust as a deduction and taxed the entire amount as simple income; he sued in federal court and lost.)

The movie deal represented the denouement of Bobby's year, and of the Grand Slam, and the end of the first act of his life. Harry and Jack Warner had dramatically and irrevocably taken care of Jones's financial uncertainty. Had they simultaneously answered his other big question? Now Jones had a big handful of reasons to retire from golf's main stage:

He'd achieved four huge goals in one calendar year, an accomplishment no one had ever dreamed of or come close to. What grander way to end a career than with the Grand Slam?

He knew he couldn't do it again. The far-flung, six-tournament campaign of 1930 had burned him out.

It hadn't been fun, not even close.

Mary was drumming her fingers, making plain her readiness for the end of the travel, stress, and intrusive adoration of her husband.

Then there was the sticky issue of his amateur status. Although, amazingly, Jones didn't easily concede the point, all that money gave him an aroma of professional athlete you could smell a mile away. But to Bobby, a golf pro was a grown-up caddie who bought shirts for $2 and sold them for $5, a working-class man who hung out a shingle, opened a shop, and took care of the clubs and the backswings of his social betters. That's what the pro at East Lake, Stewart Maiden, had done and what Bobby would never do. Making movies didn't make you a pro, did it? After all, the USGA had let him get paid for writing about golf—was it such a leap to make films about his sport? Jones wasn't sure. This was new ground for him and everyone else.

On the other hand, the law seemed clear. On page seventy-three of the

1930 Rules of Golf, the USGA declared plainly what a professional is and what an amateur is not: "A Professional Golfer is any player who has played for a money prize or has received payment for playing or teaching the game." And "An Amateur Golfer is one who, after attaining the age of eighteen years, has not (a) Carried clubs for hire (b) Received any consideration either directly or indirectly, for playing or teaching the game . . ."

Finally, Jones had to have thought about what people would say if he kept the money and attempted to pass himself off as an amateur. Only three years before, he'd gone through a similar crisis when the Friends of Bob in Atlanta bought him a house. Although he and the USGA had said the home fund was okay—stretching the "received any consideration" clause to the breaking point—public opinion had compelled Jones to give the money back. If the USGA again stood with him, those whispers that he was the organization's pet might become shouts. The seventy-first hole at Interlachen might be re-called, in detail this time, and with more pros than Sarazen taking a loud stand.

No, Jones decided, that would not do. He would quit.

He signed his deal with Warner Brothers on November 13 in New York City. The USGA headquarters at 110 East Forty-second Street was just a cab ride away. Did he consult with his colleagues there, before or after signing the movie contract? It seemed likely, but if a meeting occurred, the participants left no paper trail.

You picture Jones on the train back to Atlanta, crafting his brilliantly worded retirement announcement. It began with a paragraph that contradicted his statement at Merion and might have prompted a trial lawyer to ask a classic question: Were you lying then or are you lying now?

> Upon the close of the 1930 golfing season I determined immediately that I would withdraw entirely from golfing competition of a serious nature. Fourteen years of intensive tournament play in this country and abroad had given me about all I wanted in the way of hard work in the game. I had reached a point where I felt that my profession required

more of my time and effort, leaving golf in its proper place, a means of obtaining recreation and enjoyment.

He hadn't planned on making an announcement, but merely to fade away, like an old soldier, by not sending in his entry to the big events. But now he felt he needed to explain himself. The explanation not only provided a wonderful blast of advance publicity for the films, it made his movie deal appear to be a selfless thing, almost a public service, like planting a tree on Arbor Day.

On November 13, 1930, I signed a contract with Warner Bros. Pictures to make a series of twelve one-reel motion pictures, devoted entirely to exhibiting and explaining the methods which I employ in playing the shots ordinarily required in playing a round of golf. These pictures are to be purely educational in character, and it is the ardent hope of both parties that they will be of some value, first, by improving the play and thereby increasing the enjoyment of the vast number of people already interested in the game, and, second, by creating an interest where none exists now among the many who may find enjoyment and beneficial exercise on the golf course.

And then he expressed the extraordinary opinion that accepting the modern equivalent of something between $18 million and $37.5 million did not make him a pro:

I am not certain that the step I am taking is in a strict sense a violation of the amateur rule. I think a lot might be said on either side. But I am so far convinced that it is contrary to the spirit of amateurism that I am prepared to accept and even endorse a ruling that it is an infringement . . . The rules of the game, whatever they were, I have respected, sometimes even beyond the letter. I certainly shall never become a professional golfer. But since I am no longer a competitor, I feel able to act entirely outside the amateur rule, as my judgment and conscience may decide.

This was the masterstroke. By resigning from competition at the instant he took all that money, Jones had not technically violated the amateur code he'd always held so dear. Moreover, the question of what to do in 1931 as the defending champion in four big competitions was dramatically and finally answered. Leaving golf and the way he spun his leaving allowed him to take the moral high ground, which he would occupy forevermore. He'd wanted to quit anyway, but it appeared that he'd retired for the good of the game. No cynic emerged to point out that it also worked out for the good of Bobby Jones.

Jones put his pen down and felt the train rumble on toward Atlanta, and home, and the start of his new life. On November 17, he released his statement to the press. Despite the warnings and rumors all year, the Jones retirement shocked most people and made headlines around the English-speaking world. Many writers compared his leaving to a king abdicating his throne, but even that metaphor wasn't quite enough. No athlete ever left his sport from such a summit.

Even in retirement, Bobby Jones won. It was a final victory in the greatest year a guy ever had.

Coda

What Ever Happened To . . .

In a sense, <u>amateur golf</u> retired with Jones. At the instant Bobby left the scene, a pleasant but thoroughly anonymous young man from Texas named Gus Moreland may have suddenly become the best not-for-pay player in the United States. Although Lawson Little and others developed high-profile names and golf games, Jones's departure left a hole that would never be filled.

Jones did, however, demonstrate that golf could fill an amateur golfer's pockets. Charlie Coe, Harvey Ward, Bill Hyndman, Jay Sigel, and other great players could afford to compete for mere trophies around the world because their name in the paper helped them sell insurance, cars, or real estate. That clause in the USGA bylaws—an amateur may not receive "any consideration, directly or indirectly, for playing"—turned out to be unenforceable.

In 1931, members of <u>Augusta Country Club</u> looked through the trees and over Rae's Creek at an extraordinary sight: scores of men, mules, and earthmovers building a course on the adjoining property. Some days they could see Bobby Jones hitting golf shots to help architect Alister MacKenzie gauge turning points and bunker placement. Through the years, ACC played the steady older brother to its flashy younger sibling, Augusta National. But with recent renovation, the course where Jones played so brilliantly in 1930 became quite notable itself, as one of the purest expressions of Donald Ross architecture in the country.

Far from being reprimanded for his actions at the U.S. Open, <u>Prescott Bush</u> was named USGA president in 1935. In 1953, he was elected to the U.S. Senate from Connecticut. Both his son and his grandson became presidents of the United States.

<u>Archie Compston</u>, the lovable Englishman who led the 1930 British Open after three rounds, left England for a club pro job in Bermuda.

<u>Leo Diegel</u>, the brilliant, erratic runner-up at Royal Liverpool, died at age fifty-two. He won the PGA championships of '28 and '29, but everyone who saw him play said he should have, could have won many more of the biggest events.

They charge only $15 (Monday through Thursday) to play <u>Forest Hills Country Club</u> (formerly known as Forrest Hills) in Augusta, where Jones played possibly his best rounds of 1930. Carts cost $10 extra. Rates are higher on weekends and holidays.

<u>Young Frank Freeman</u>, the man who brokered Bobby's movie deal, rose to the heights in Hollywood: He became head of the Paramount studio, got a star on the Walk of Fame, and received the first Jean Hersholt Humanitarian Award from the Academy of Motion Picture Arts and Sciences. "David, I never saw so many soldiers as were used in *Gone with the Wind*," drawled Freeman when presenting David O. Selznick with the 1939 Best Picture

Oscar. "Believe me, if the Confederate Army had had that many, we would have licked you damn Yankees."

The Grand Slam would never be won again. In a way, it ceased to exist, because without Jones, neither the British nor the American Amateurs could be considered majors. Professional golf ascended from 1931 on; the United States PGA Championship gained the status the Amateur events lost. Jones and his partner, Clifford Roberts, founded the fourth major in 1934, the Masters.

Placing the achievement of 1930 in context requires no great debate: No golfer and no athlete in any other sport ever had a better year. Rod Laver won the four tennis majors in 1969, but—not to disparage that magnificent achievement—tennis is an easier sport for a superior performer to dominate because it is a sport of matches, with no equivalent to the uncertainties of golf's stroke competitions. Woods won four consecutive majors in 2000 and 2001 but seemed miffed to discover that he was the only one to consider it a Grand Slam. The rest of the world perceives the magic in doing it all in one year, as Jones did: His was *sustained* excellence, as if he had won the Tour de France four times in five months. When you consider the constant pressure he felt from within and without, the Grand Slam is that much more amazing. And he did it with such style. Although he was suffering off the golf course, he didn't let it get to him on it. After the deal was done at Merion, *Time* magazine was moved to eloquence: It was "the completion of as perfect a gesture as ever was made in any game."

The only annoying thing about it was his knee-jerk humility afterwards. Jones wrote of his regret at his inability to slam the door on his opponents when he had the chance, to turn small advantages into insurmountable ones. He didn't approve of how he won many tournaments during his competitive career, and he didn't think he won enough. He hadn't been a complete golfer, Jones said.

Walter Hagen had nine more wins in him after 1930, none of them majors. Long after his prime, however, he kept his air of magnificence. "He used to look at the rest of us like we were trained seals," recalled Skee Riegel, the runner-up in the 1951 Masters. Golfers might raise a glass on October 6, in memory of Hagen's last cocktail hour. The most colorful great golfer in history died in 1969 at age seventy-six.

Hickory golf shafts fell out of use. Jones swung hickory for every shot he hit in the Slam, but steel had a handful of unbeatable advantages. It didn't warp or break as easily; and you didn't need pocketknives, sandpaper, and magic to make a good set. And when they invented steps—those whip-producing gradations in the shaft—steel became standard in almost every golfer's bag. Johnny Goodman won the U.S. Open with wood shafts in 1933, hickory's last hurrah.

After losing to Jones in the final of the U.S. Amateur at Merion, Gene Homans dedicated himself to the Homans Agency for the Equitable Life Assurance Society. He was a member at four great New York–area golf clubs and served as vice president of the Englewood, New Jersey, Republican Club. He died of a stroke in 1965, at age fifty-six.

How I Play Golf and How to Break Ninety were the titles of the series of ten-minute movies Jones made for Warner Brothers. Keeler, armed with his typewriter and dozens of bottles of corn liquor, accompanied Bobby to Hollywood and did voice-overs and collaborated on the instructional message. Jack Warner assigned an accomplished director, George Marshall. A number of golf- and Jones-smitten movie stars appeared, no charge. The plots setting up the lessons from Jones were corny and faintly humorous; most of the dialogue from the actors was ad-libbed. But Jones's scripted speeches—to W. C. Fields, for example, advising him how to get his legs into the shot— were jarringly pedantic.

The instruction itself was odd. Although it was a treat just to see the Grand Slammer swing, and the results of his shots (with a little editing) were unerring, Jones's method was neither orthodox nor suited to the new equipment. He stood with his feet so close together and so casually upright that most people trying to duplicate it would fall flat. His butt-tucked stance contrasted sharply with the athletic, rear-end-out posture that the emerging corps of great steel-shaft players would adopt. He loosened his grip at the top of his backswing, then grabbed the club again as it started down. He moved his head—a lot—when he putted. As much as possible, he began his backswing by throwing his hands back, creating a lag that he thought helped build power. "No one ever swung the club back too slowly," he said, which simply isn't true, but his own long, ornate backswing gave his stroke its music. All this showed that making consistent, solid contact with a set of hickories was as much art as science. A lot of what Jones advocated didn't work for ordinary mortals or with steel shafts.

There's a legend at Interlachen that, many years after Jones hit it there, a diver found a ball that could have been Jones's in the pond on the seventeenth hole. The jewel-like club near Minneapolis will host the 2008 U.S. Women's Open, continuing its policy of entertaining big events like the Walker Cup, Solheim Cup, and USGA Men's Senior Amateur from time to time.

Big Bob, Robert Purmedus Jones, Bobby's father, handed out the first-place check at the first Masters in 1934. He was a lively, popular member of Augusta National, and his son's dearest friend, but he never tried to make it appear that he was the brains behind Bobby's success. He died shortly before the 1960 publication of *Golf Is My Game*. Jones dedicated the book to him: "To my father, to whom I owe all this—and a lot more."

R.T., Robert Tyre Jones, got old. Bobby's grandfather liked to sit on his favorite bench near the door inside Jones Mercantile, a three-story red brick building across the street from his big, white house. Buckets of chickpeas, Ferry's seeds, and several kinds of beans squatted on its wood floors. Metal signs advertised Big Star Soap, Ivory Soap It Floats, Post Toasties, and Welch's Tomato Catsup. Employees wore aprons and a helpful look.

R.T. couldn't see the other things he owned from his bench—two cotton mills, two mill villages—but he could see the Depression. Somehow, though, R.T. never laid anyone off. He died in 1937 at age eighty-eight.

"He was a man who could be rigid in the application of principles to others," E. A. McCanless wrote of R.T., "but was even more rigid in their application to himself"—a sentiment that also applied to his grandson.

Liver disease claimed the life of Oscar Bane "O.B." Keeler on October 15, 1950. He was sixty-eight. "I get a little bit sentimental," Jones said in a speech in 1955. "Nobody ever had a better press agent than Keela was for me. Keela would fight the boys in the press tent about me and anybody else who wanted to say anything."

"Keeler made Jones," eulogized Ralph Trost of the *Brooklyn Eagle*. "He WAS Jones. He told us what Jones said, what he hoped, his aims . . . many of us got to know Bobby through O.B."

On the last Sunday in September, Merion remembers the final day of the Grand Slam. After a Scotch Foursome golf tournament, the participants put on tuxedoes and follow a bagpiper down to the eleventh hole. Waiters circulate with trays holding glasses of champagne. The course is lovely in the twilight; some years, the leaves have started to turn. "To Bobby Jones," the toastmaster says, and they all raise a glass and drink.

Nothing much changed at The Old Course at St. Andrews. It continued to be almost an easy course on the rare calm day and brutal when the wind blew, and it continued to host the Open or the Amateur every few years.

Jones's departure gave the tournament part of professional golf an obvious boost, and the Depression lifted it a bit, too: With country clubs closing their doors right and left and no jobs available anyway, a lot of good young golfers decided to join the tour and at least take a shot at a couple of bucks. One such man from rural Texas was asked in 2004 if the Grand Slam inspired him: "Once or twice I went in the theatre and saw him hitting shots in the news-reel," replied the old man, who was a teenager then. "But I never thought that much about it. I can't say that I was inspired by Jones." But getting laid off from his job as a railroad clerk did provide inspiration and an opportunity to try some new high-tech steel-shafted clubs, which he shanked for a solid week before he started to get the hang of them. But diligence and talent paid off for Byron Nelson, the first master of the steel shaft.

With Jones gone, the best golfers in the world were American professionals: Sarazen, then Nelson, Snead, Guldahl, and Hogan. Henry Cotton, the best player in Europe, had his backers, too.

Howard Rexford, Jones's caddie in the final event of the Grand Slam, kept his Jones stories alive for years. One of his favorite yarns concerned the shock he felt when Bobby handed him a thick wad of folded money, and he went off by himself and counted fifteen ten-dollar bills, a fortune. Rexford made a success of the ink business he inherited from his father. He became a good golfer himself and won the club championship at Bala Country Club a couple of times.

Royal Liverpool, a.k.a. Hoylake, will host the 2006 Open. It's still tougher than a truck-stop steak.

Ben Curtis of Kent, Ohio, won a memorable Open at Royal St. George's in 2003. Jones played superbly there in the Walker Cup in '30.

It couldn't have been a coincidence that Gene Sarazen enjoyed a renaissance after Jones retired. He won his own double in 1932, when he took the U.S. and British Opens, his first major victories in ten years. In 1935, by holing a full four-wood shot on the fifteenth hole of the final round, he put himself and Bobby's new tournament indelibly on the map. In that second

Masters, Sarazen's Shot Heard round the World tied Craig Wood for first; he won a playoff the next day. With golf's majors permanently changed by Jones, Sarazen proudly billed himself as the First Winner of the Modern (or professional) Grand Slam; he even had the accomplishment made into a logo and sewed onto his hat. Gene and Bobby became very close in later years. Their lengthy and entertaining correspondence is preserved at Golf House, the USGA headquarters in Far Hills, New Jersey.

Savannah Golf Club, the last place in his career as a serious competitor that Jones did not win, built three new holes after it sold part of its property to the local independent school district. But it retained a wonderful playability and a Spanish moss–hung beauty.

"I really wanted to play Bobby," said Charlie Seaver, recalling his U.S. Amateur semifinal match with Gene Homans. "I had an opportunity to play him many times, but that one time I wanted it the most, I didn't make it." Jones invited Seaver to play in the first and second Masters tournaments, in 1934 and 1935, but the Crash and Depression had eroded the Seaver family fortune so much that he couldn't afford to make the trip from California.

Horton Smith won the first Masters, and the third, and married Barbara Bourne, the daughter of the wealthiest member at Augusta National. His impulse to organize and to set a good example led him to leadership roles in the PGA of America, probably at the expense of his playing career. He became president of the PGA in 1952. In 1957 he was diagnosed with Hodgkin's disease, a type of cancer of the lymph system. He fought it; in 1961, he won the Ben Hogan Award for carrying on despite his physical handicap. He died in 1963, at age fifty-five.

Macdonald Smith, twice the runner-up to Jones during the Slam, contended in one more big event before he was through, finishing a poor second to Sarazen in the 1932 Open at Prince's. The Silent Scot swung the club as well as Jones but didn't have his will or his brain, or his luck. He never took a divot and never won a major. He died in 1949. He was fifty-seven.

Wallasey Golf Club, where a member invented the points-based Stableford scoring system and which Jones didn't play very well in Open qualifying, remains one of the most varied and enjoyable courses in England.

Between a radio show sponsored by Listerine Shaving Cream, the movies, newspaper columns, magazine articles, and a new line of (steel-shafted!) Spalding golf clubs with his name on them, Bobby Jones kept his name and face out there after retiring as a competitor. Even as all this was going on, he lent his name and his considerable intellect to the creation of a golf course. Augusta National revealed quite distinctly the things that were important to him: privacy and his own expression of golf perfection. The Masters seemed to be mostly his partner's—Cliff Roberts—idea. He played in it reluctantly and not well.

After World War II, Jones became ill with a rare, slow-growing neurological disease, as is well known. He almost never complained about his cruel fate, which burnished his legend, but when they had a ceremony on the eleventh hole at Merion commemorating the twenty-fifth anniversary of the Slam, he was a little man with a sunken body, sitting in the wheelchair he would never leave, weeping.

He wiped the tears away. A whippersnapper of a radio reporter approached to ask what club he had used for his final shot, perhaps a nine-iron or a wedge? In his reply, Jones showed who he was more than trophies or wheelchairs ever would. He was genial despite everything, ironic, clever—and one up on you. "Well," he said. "The last club I hit was a putta."

The "wise innocent," Alistair Cooke had called him, but Jones was always more the former than the latter.

Bibliography

Allen, Frederick Lewis. *Only Yesterday: An Informal History of the 1920s*. New York: Harper & Brothers, 1931.

Aylesworth, Thomas G. *The Best of Warner Brothers*. Greenwich, CT: Brompton Books, 1993.

Bryant, James C. *Druid Hills Golf Club in Atlanta: The Story and the People*. Atlanta, 1998.

Darwin, Bernard. *Golf Between Two Wars*. London: Chatto & Windus, 1944.

Davis, Martin. *The Greatest of Them All: The Legend of Bobby Jones*. Greenwich, CT: The American Golfer, 1996.

Gabler, Neal. *An Empire of Their Own: How the Jews Invented Hollywood*. New York: Anchor Books/Doubleday, 1989.

Hagen, Walter, and Margaret Seaton Heck. *The Walter Hagen Story: By The Haig, Himself*. New York: Simon & Schuster, 1956.

Jones, Robert T., Jr. *The Basic Golf Swing*. New York: Ailsa Inc., 1990.

Jones, Robert T., Jr., and O. B. Keeler. *Down the Fairway: The Golf Life and Play of Robert T. Jones, Jr*. New York: Minton, Balch & Company, 1927.

Jones, Robert Tyre (Bobby), Jr. *Golf Is My Game*. New York: Doubleday, 1960.

Keeler, O. B. *The Boys' Life of Bobby Jones*. New York: Harper & Brothers, 1931.

Manchester, William. *The Last Lion: Winston Spencer Churchill: Visions of Glory*. New York: Little, Brown, and Company, 1983.

Matthew, Sidney L. *Life and Times of Bobby Jones*. Chelsea, MI: Sleeping Bear Press, 1995.

Mehlhorn, Bill, with Bobby Shave. *Golf Secrets Exposed*. Miami: M&S Publishing, 1984.

Mortimer, Charles G., and Fred Pignon. *The Story of the Open Golf Championship, 1860–1950*. London: Jarrolds Ltd., 1952.

Oates, Joyce Carol. *On Boxing*. London: Bloomsbury, 1987.

Sampson, Curt. *The Masters: Golf, Money, and Power in Augusta, Georgia*. New York: Villard, 1998.

Sarazen, Gene, with Herbert Warren Wind. *Thirty Years of Championship Golf: The Life and Times of Gene Sarazen*. New York: Prentice-Hall, 1950.

Variety. *The Variety History of Show Business*. New York: Harry N. Abrams, 1993.

And newspapers as cited in the text.

Photo Credits

Pages 2, 18, 42, 70, 111, 112, 142, 150: © Emory University Special Collections, Bobby Jones Collection

Page 29: Courtesy of the Savannah Golf Club

Page 64: Courtesy of Augusta Country Club

Page 67: Courtesy of Forest Hills Golf Club

Page 148: © AP Worldwide

Page 170: Courtesy of Interlachen Country Club

Pages 190, 226: From *Life and Times of Bobby Jones* by Sidney Matthew

Page 220: Courtesy of Merion Golf Club

Page 228: © Bettmann/CORBIS

Page 233: © Curt Sampson

Index

Boldface page references indicate photographs.

Traylor, Melvin, 166–67
Trevor, George, 146, 206
Triumphant Journey (Miller), 11, 72, 79
Trost, Ralph, 244
True Temper, 55
Turnesa, Joe, 185
Tweddell, William, 152–53
Twine, William Thomas, 130, 133

U

United States Golf Association
    (USGA), 126, 129, 157–58, 160,
    167, 173, 186–87, 234–35
    amateur status and, 81, 234–35
    class of people running, 73
    crowd control at U.S. Open (1930)
        and, 173
    headquarters of, 246
    Jones and
        financial gift and, 82–84
        golf films and, 160, 234–35
        relationship between, 57, 81,
            157–58, 167
        ruling controversy and, 81,
            175–76, 185–89, 193–96, 201–2
        sand wedge testing and, 124
    travel to Europe by executive
        committee, 80
    world championship match proposal
        and, 129
U.S. Amateur (1924), 210
U.S. Amateur (1927), 82
U.S. Amateur (1929), 44, 87
U.S. Amateur (1930)
    course of, 205, 210–11
    fifth day of, 219–22
    first day of, 215–16

fourth day of, 218–19
Jones's victory at, 226–27
practice rounds before, 211–14
second day of, 217
sixth day of, 222–27
third day of, 217–18
USGA fundraising match before,
    214–15
USGA. *See* United States Golf
    Association
U.S. Open (1899), 122
U.S. Open (1906), 122
U.S. Open (1910), 122
U.S. Open (1926), 24
U.S. Open (1927), 176
U.S. Open (1928), 28
U.S. Open (1929), 43
U.S. Open (1930)
    Bush's ruling during, 185–89,
        193–96, 201–2
    crowd control at, 173
    first day of, 177–78
    hot weather at, 176–77
    Jones and
        references to in his book, 193
        victory at, 188–89
    practice rounds before, 167–68,
        170–76
    pressure on Jones before, 169–76
    second day of, 178–82
    third day of, 182–89
U.S. Open Golf's Ultimate Challenge, The
    (Sommers), 186

V

Vagliano, Andre, 117
Van Gogh, Theodorus, 12–13